The Political Analysis of Postcommunism

Number Six
Eastern European Studies

Stjepan G. Meštrović, Series Editor

The Political Analysis of Postcommunism

Understanding Postcommunist Ukraine

EDITED BY VOLODYMYR POLOKHALO

Texas A&M University Press
College Station

First Texas A&M University Press edition, 1997

The paper used in this book meets the minimum requirements
of the American National Standard for Permanence
of Paper for Printed Library Materials, Z39.48-1984.
Binding materials have been chosen for durability.

This volume was originally published by the Editors of *Political Thought* with the financial assistance of the International Renaissance Foundation.

Library of Congress Catalng-in-Publication Data

Politolohiia͡ postkomunizmu. English.
The political analysis of postcommunism : understanding postcommunist Ukraine / edited by Volodymyr Polokhalo.
p. cm. — (Eastern European studies ; 6)
Originally published: Kyiv : Political Thought, 1995.
Includes bibliographical references (p.) and index.
ISBN 0-89096-783-0
1. Political culture—Ukraine. 2. Post-communism—Ukraine. 3. World politics—1989– I. Polokhalo, Volodymyr. II. Title. III. Series.
JN6639.A15P6513 1997
306.2'09477'09049—dc21 97-41505
CIP

Contents

PREFACE

Free political thought cannot be considered the exclusive prerogative of democratic societies with well-established traditions of unfettered political thought and independent scholarly inquiry. For the appearance of this publication in Ukraine, which was only recently an integral part of a totalitarian imperial state is no accident. The collapse of the communist system and of the USSR have become a fact of history. A postcommunist world has come into existence, and newly independent states have appeared on the political map. We are experiencing and trying to understand a unique experience. All this has laid the preconditions for overcoming our long intellectual isolation, where the ideologization of thinking prevailed, in order to expand our political horizon. We have taken initial steps to establish a full-fledged creative partnership and free exchange of ideas, insights, and information among scholars of various theoretical orientations, generations, and nations.

Open dialog, the interaction and cooperation of Ukrainian and foreign scholars in the comprehensive investigation of the social, political, geopolitical, and cultural transformations taking place in postcommunist societies, is precisely what the Editorial Board of the Ukrainian scholarly quarterly *Political Thought* has tried to establish, and on this basis the present volume has been compiled.

The publication of *Political Analysis of Postcommunism* has been made possible by the fact that in a relatively brief period of time our journal has been able to bring together and unite scholars primarily from the new generation of scholars, for whom intellectual doubt, scholarly objectivity, and, political independence constitute the highest standards. The journal is an open forum for scholars where the best insights of contemporary domestic political thought encounter those of the world scholarly community. This is greatly facilitated by the fact that *Political Thought* is published in Ukrainian, English, and Russian, distributed in more than thirty countries, and enjoys both a wide readership and circle of contributors both in Ukraine and abroad.

Editorial Board activities are not limited to publishing the journal. They also include regular seminars held by the *Political Thought* International Expert Club, scholarly discussions, and participation in internal Ukrainian and international conferences, television and radio panel discussions, *etc.* In essence, the journal has set out in a new scholarly direction, independent of postcommunist political authorities. This movement plays a unique role in helping to counter newly-minted political utopias and myths permanently produced and disseminated by tendentious scholarly structures and political forces.

The idea of compiling this book dates back to the summer of 1994. It was to be primarily based on works published in previous issues of the journal. Simultaneously, editorial policy took the shape of the future volume into account, and as a result many contributions to the subsequent issues of *Political Thought* were made more goal-oriented and focused on particular problems. Thus, in 1994 *Political Thought* laid a foundation for a new sub-discipline of political science — the political analysis of postcommunism.

An urgent problem of political science, which provokes much discussion, concerns what perspectives and alternatives of political development confront the various postcommunist states. In approaching the problem, many political scientists pose an either/or alternative: either an open democratic society or backsliding into the communist totalitarian past. But the real political changes in the former communist states witness the escalation of difficulties and contradictions in their development, which the authors explore. Quite plausible is a wide range of both traditional (democratic, communist, fascist, and nationalist) and innovative models of social development, sometimes chimerical, and eclectic but in their main features neototalitarian.

Aware that new approaches in political science and a fundamental revision of scholarly knowledge concerning politics and policy-making are indispensable, the authors do not claim to have invented some universal political science of postcommunist societies encompassing all aspects of studying the new, extraordinarily multifaceted political reality.

The volume offered, as one of the first attempts at interdisciplinary research in this area, is but an attempt at achieving an intellectual breakthrough in the social sciences. It is an endeavor to find the theoretical linchpin, without which it would be impossible to discern the trends of political thought and critically examine the political realities and contradictions in postcommunism. As such it is merely an introduction to a new branch of scholarly inquiry, the political analysis of postcommunism, the domain of which has only recently come under the eye of rigorous examination.

This branch of political science is still only in the process of formation.

The authors are confident that we are not late in publishing a timely book.

Of course, it is difficult to foresee the future awaiting journal *Political Thought.* At any rate, in the face of considerable obstacles and difficulties, the Editors have been able to regularly bring out new issues, while maintaining their intellectual freedom and financial independence from the object of their research, politicians and policy-makers.

The Editors are deeply grateful to all those who have supported our quarterly, have embraced its problems as their own, who assist in joining intellectual efforts from Ukraine and abroad, cooperate with us, and support research projects, which are called forth by the social and political realities of the postcommunism period.

Kyiv, June 25, 1995

Volodymyr POLOKHALO,
Editor-in-Chief,
Political Thought

The Political Analysis of Postcommunism

Introduction to the 1997 Edition

Two years have elapsed since the publication of the book *The Political Analysis of Postcommunism,* which we now offer the Western reader. The publication, prepared by the editorial board of the Ukrainian journal *Political Thought,* was widely acclaimed both in Ukraine and in other postcommunist countries, provoking numerous scholarly debates.

Some think the authors are too pessimistic concerning the perspectives of sociopolitical and economic transformations after the downfall of communism in the former socialist states. Others believe that the book is too Ukrainocentric and that for this reason its conceptual provisions and forecasts, particularly those about the tendencies and alternatives of postcommunist development, cannot be extrapolated to all countries of the former Soviet Union and East Central Europe. Is this right or wrong?

In my opinion the time that has passed since the publication in Ukraine of *The Political Analysis of Postcommunism* has confirmed the basic solidity of the authors' approaches (although they are open to discussion and refinement) as well as the fruitful results of international research into postcommunism as one of the most important phenomena of the late twentieth century.

At the same time, the "democratic temptation" in the countries of Central and Eastern Europe and the former USSR after the fall of communism was so great and social expectations so overblown that numerous intellectual traps appeared and still remain today on the road to assessment of the new postcommunist reality. This primarily reflects a desire to skip sociohistorical time in appraising and modeling complex political processes—a result of a penchant to the point of dogmatism for embracing methods and traditions of political research based mainly on West European and North American material.

These traps, unfortunately, give rise to numerous myths and pseudoscientific hypotheses. Although postcommunist societies are already historically mature (in terms of the scale and dynamics of sociopolitical transformations they are undergoing), a certain segment of political scientists, sociologists, philosophers, and others remain captive to their own and imported scholarly stereotypes and simply cannot overcome their own inertia in understanding the essence of postcommunist transformations, especially in understanding the possibilities and prospects of the democratic development of those societies.

Let us consider this in more detail.

Among other things, in the political thought of the postcommunist period most persistent and widespread is the idea that the general degradation and collapse of communist ideology was simultaneously accompanied by the degradation, delegitimation, then collapse and disintegration of communist totalitarian power, a power personified by the party/state *nomenklatura* and communist bureaucracy. At first glance it would seem logical and convincing to build the following quasi-theoretical model on the pyramid: antitotalitarian revolution (1989–91)—post-totalitarian power—post-totalitarian state—post-totalitarian society.

In other words, it is almost axiomatic that totalitarian power has exhausted its potential, that therefore the state and sociopolitical life have been "detotalitarianized," and that there have been or are being successfully implemented principles of organizing power along the democratic vector of political development: individual—society—state (power).

Meanwhile, the experience and practice of the postcommunist transformations testify to something entirely different: in the postcommunist states, or in most of them at any rate, nowhere has the nomenklatura's power been either abolished or taken away by anyone; the nomenklatura itself has never given up power voluntarily to anybody, and the communist nomenklatura system of power as such has never fully disappeared anywhere.

Paradoxically, the greater part of the former communist elite, especially in the former Soviet Union, profited from the collapse of communism much more than did the rest of society. Having removed from power the old leaders and partially renewed itself at the expense of other groups, that elite not only managed to preserve its own positions of authority but also to strengthen them greatly, retaining power and property in its hands. The skeleton of the nomenklatura remains essentially the same since the Brezhnev period. The postcommunist elites in the post-Soviet states that emerged on the surface of political life are clannish structures which had already formed under communism.

Today there are sufficient scholarly grounds to identify certain trends in the political development of Ukraine, Russia, Belarus, and many other postcommunist states.

I would single out two main trends in this introduction.

The first trend is the carrying out of a "revolution from above," the purposeful self-transformation and self-reforming of communist totalitarian power and, as a result, the emergence of new types and varieties of power relationships genetically, essentially, and historically connected to previous ones. The special feature of this unusual "revolution" is primarily the evolutionary transformation of political and state power into a new type of ownership by means of the illegitimate, shadow appropriation and distribution of the totalitarian nationalized "property of the whole people" by its actual possessor, the former party bureaucracy, on the initiative of its pragmatic "reformist" segment.

The second half of the 1980s saw the beginning of, first, the conversion of political and state power of the ex-communist nomenklatura into clan/corporativistic, nomenklatura economic power; second, the intensive concentration of this new/old power outside society's control; and third, the formation of a new postcommunist financial oligarchy. In this sense it becomes possible to state that a new merger of politics and economics occurred—the direct transformation of the appropriated property into political and state power and vice versa. In this respect during approximately the last ten years in the postcommunist states (with some exceptions) a self-sufficient, mutated system of power gradually evolved, a system commanding adequate resources, totalitarian in essence, and simultaneously alienated from the majority of society. Into this the old communist nomenklatura (both its pragmatic "reformist" and orthodox wings) and, accordingly, with the appearance of new so-called "opposition," including neocommunist parties, the greater part of the postcommunist nomenklatura were organically assimilated.

The second trend is the "mafiaization" of power. This includes the criminalization and corruption of power structures and the state bureaucracy, the growing role of the shadow economy and shadow group (clan) politics, and growing claims to power and influence upon "necessary" decisions by publicly unconstituted power centers.

Many postcommunist, especially post-Soviet, states are characterized today (and are being spoken of very critically in the West) not only by an unprecedented scale of venality among their civil servants but also by the transformation of corruption into a norm of sociopolitical existence. These countries are witnessing a symbiosis of state bureaucrats at various levels, leaders of semilegal and shadow economic enterprises, and criminal world bosses, and a cementing of these forces into a shadow nomenklatura. On this basis total control is exerted over the distribution and redistribution of state property and economic resources ("nomenklatura-run privatization"); over the spheres of production, market, and foreign trade; and over economic and social policy as a whole.

In essence, political power has become a universal commodity, which, depending on supply and demand, commands a certain price. However, this commodity, unlike political power in western democratic countries, has become an object bought and sold only on a black market, a political market closed to the majority. This is a monopolistic trade in which a greater or lesser portion of power becomes a universally liquid commodity traded among strong criminal (nomenklatura) corporativist clans.

It is not by accident that it has become normal and natural that many leaders of these clans (or their agents) gradually emerge from the "shadows" to political front stage, seeking social recognition and public legitimation. They have been actively drawn to politics and openly buy themselves key positions in executive and legislative bodies at both the national and local level. It is clear that under such circumstances the anticorruption campaigns announced in almost every post-Soviet state are nothing more than populist posturing. It is understood that such campaigns cannot have even the slightest measure of real success in the near future, for this would mean destroying not only the political and economic conditions but the very mode of existence of contemporary postcommunist power.

Thanks to the above trends, the crisis and, hence, the ruin and fall of the state's totalitarian communist ideology have not meant an irreversible destruction of the very essence of totalitarian power relationships. Nor have they created conditions for democratic transformation.

The real delegitimation and collapse of communist political doctrine did not lead to the delegitimation and ultimate collapse of communist totalitarianism in its various degrees, from moderate in the countries of Central and Eastern Europe to more rigid in the former USSR. Moreover, communist nomenklatura-based power in the former socialist states has displayed extreme permeability and adaptability to new conditions, having sensed the weakness of the Marxist-Leninist political ideology with respect to its main function, total control and legitimacy, long before the collapse of the communist system. It is in this sense that we should understand the emergence of the first alternative elements as compensatory surrogates of the old doctrine—"new thinking," "the priority of common human values," etc.—in the official lexicon of the 1980s. The collapse of communist ideology did not catch the communist nomenklatura unawares. The nomenklatura had prepared for it even before the deideologization of the masses took place.

Thus, the fall of communism and the official self-dissolution of communist parties and doctrine at the turn of the 1990s did not result in true liberation from totalitarian rule of most Ukraininans, Russians, and many other nations of the former socialist camp, although of course the forms of the individual's dependence on the authorities have changed greatly. When the former party and state nomenklatura reformed itself, it was able to get something of a second wind, reinforce its power resources, and find enormous opportunities to reproduce itself in the new postcommunist reality.

As is shown by the practical political changes underway in Ukraine, Belarus, and a number of other postcommunist countries in the past six to eight years, the world is witnessing the making of a new, unprecedented variety of totalitarianism, which I would call postcommunist or pseudo-democratic neototalitarianism. In the broadest sense it may be characterized as a type of political system under which an overall control over the individual and society is exercised, whether in rigid or relatively mild form, not through ideology as earlier, but through other, equally effective means (as a rule, using nominally democratic procedures such as elections) which exert total control over and act to deform both the objects of power and social processes in general. Here we are dealing with a multidimensional dependency, assuming both obvious and latent extra-economic (social, sociocultural, legal, etc.) and economic form, which determines the various forms of power relations associated with coercion and violence or the threat of its use.

Without doubt, this does not mean that the postcommunist nomenklatura ceased to value the legitimizing significance of political ideology as a mechanism for all-out control over society or at least as a formidable obstacle to the formation of truly democratic opposition parties and a full-fledged counter-elite. In essence, the nomenklatura treats political ideology as a certain meta-ideology within which are carried out the production and dissemination of a conglomeration of ideas, myths, and slogans based on a specific sociopolitical situation and certain sociocultural peculiarities.

Postcommunist meta-ideology is not a certain ideological condition but a process of filtering various ideational-political attitudes, of testing various views in terms of their ability to reproduce power relationships according to the totalitarian model of dependency: state (power)—society—individual. It can deftly combine in a broad repertoire both populism and the "pure" classical political doctrines (communism, nationalism, and fascism) and form hybrids by mixing these totalitarian elements with elements taken from other political doctrines, including democratic ones (liberalism, social democracy, etc.). But all the recombinations of postcommunist meta-ideology remain aimed at the preservation and cultivation of the social and political Utopias which constitute the ideological dominants of totalitarianism.

In the final analysis, the answer to the key question of comprehending the essence of postcommunist neototalitarianism and neototalitarian power—whether a person plays an active role in power relationships or is an object without rights (passive or active) in thrall to those who wield power—is neither simple nor unequivocal, especially within the context of the new, extraordinarily complex, and contradictory realities in the former socialist countries in the late twentieth century.

Without doubt, recent years have witnessed essential qualitative differences in the political life of, say, Poland, the Czech Republic, and Hungary on the one hand and Belarus, Ukraine, and Russia on the other. The former three, as well as some other postcommunist states of Central and Eastern Europe, have much greater chances for democratic transformation and entering the world family of civilized nations. However, the political reality now being formed in the latter three states and, I think, in most postcommunist countries remains, at best, contradictory and amorphous.

Further postcommunist development in these countries cannot be put today within the frame of a specific, especially democratic, scenario. It is certain that the preconditions for a true, and not decorative, democracy will arise sooner or later in, for example, Ukraine. But unfortunately there are more reasons to forecast the existence of a more pessimistic paradigm of political development. In any case, postcommunist neototalitarianism is a very serious and realistic prospect for the foreseeable future.

Certainly, the authors of this book—political scientists, historians, sociologists, and others—did intend to try to answer all the fundamental questions raised by the extraordinarily complex and at times chimerical practices of the postcommunist world. And they did attempt to abandon traditional ways of thinking and rely on original approaches to and research methods of political analysis. And while most materials presented here reflect the specific experience of Ukraine, they are quite useful for understanding the situation in other postcommunist states as well.

In other words, unusual and sometimes extraordinary and bold approaches and conclusions which are open to discussion (for example, I personally cannot fully share some postulates offered by the authors) are not only important for understanding the development of postcommunist societies in the countries of East Central Europe and the former Soviet Union. They also offer vivid testimony to fresh research in modern political science in general.

Now the book *The Political Analysis of Postcommunism* is in the hands of the Western reader. All the authors have to do is to anticipate that the reader will find what we have to offer provocative and useful in understanding the unprecedented situation brought about by the collapse of the so-called second world.

April, 1997
Volodymyr Polokhalo
Editor-in-Chief
Political Thought

Series Editor's Introduction

Professor Polokhalo and the contributors to this edited volume offer a sobering and important analysis of the realities of postcommunism, not only in Ukraine, but also in other nations freshly liberated from Communism. These realities, which are still relatively neglected by most Western analysts, include the following: widespread and deep corruption in postcommunist societies; fundamental ambiguity in Ukraine and other postcommunist nations as to whether they will move into the cultural orbit of the West or remain in a quasi-Eastern orbits exemplified by Russia and Serbia; and what the authors call "social insanity," by which they mean civil wars, violence, interethnic violence, and the rise of Mafialike groups that rival the legitimate, elected governments for control of various countries. How did this distressing situation come about, and what can be done about it?

The West shares some of the blame for the negative developments analyzed by these contributing authors. When the Cold War ended in 1990, Francis Fukuyama's dream of "the end of history" dominated most Western foreign affairs analyses. By end of history, Fukuyama (along with other postmodernists) meant that capitalism and democracy had triumphed over Communism and totalitarianism once and for all. Western consultants sold their services to formerly Communist governments at very high prices to teach them capitalism and democracy. Seven years later, it is evident that the West should have done its homework; it should have sent ethnographers, not consultants, to formerly Communist nations to perform fieldwork, not preach capitalist ideology. And it should have listened to social scientists already in place in formerly Communist nations who could tell them, the Westerners, what these newly freed nations needed and wanted. One wonders how many teams of investigators such as this one by Polokhalo and his associates have been ignored by Western analysts. It is certain that *most* books and analyses published in the West about former Communist nations have been by Western authors, not by authors who lived in, suffered under, and knew the Communist system intimately.

Polokhalo and his associates are probably right that it will take fifteen years or more for most formerly Communist countries to "catch up," in any meaningful sense, with the West. The problem is that during those fifteen years, conservative social forces are going to work against the forces pushing for free markets and democratization. For example, the authors are quite right to note that *no one can live on their official income* in most formerly Communist nations. From Poland to Croatia to Ukraine and Kazakhstan, it is simply impossible for an average family to live on less than the equivalent of $100 U.S. per month. How *do* people live in these new nations? Until this question is addressed seriously and answered completely, the notion of converting these peoples to free market economies will remain nothing but a pipe dream. One must first understand how they function now: with the underground economy, in terms of the hoarding and saving habits of the heart that are foreign to Western notions of infinite consumerism, and relative to the strong family and sense of community in which sharing and pooling of resources are normative.

Polokhalo and his associates are also right that the "civil societies" in Ukraine and most other formerly Communist nations are inherited from the previous, oppressive regimes and are eviscerated and deformed. This observation helps to explain why former Communists continue to be reelected in droves and continue to run the nations that ostensibly repudiated Communism. Nor should this tendency be surprising. Alexis de Tocqueville noted long ago, in his book *The Old Regime and the French Revolution,* that aristocracy in France was stronger as an institution *after* the French Revolution and after the guillotine than before. The sobering problem that Western analysts must face is the following: How will the genuine dissidents and opponents of Communism take control of these deformed civil societies and revive them into healthy, democratic institutions?

And how will these nations survive a host of "social insanities" (as they are called by the authors) in the coming years, including but not limited to increased crime, rule by local mafias, interethnic conflicts, and corruption? Polokhalo and his associates point rightly to the former Yugoslavia as an extreme case study of these tendencies, but more importantly, they link these ominous developments with similar tendencies in Russia. I agree with them that one must get used to thinking about the former Soviet Union as a Russian Empire and the former Yugoslavia as an internal Serbian Empire. The coming years will no doubt witness a tug-of-war between these two centers of gravity (Moscow and Belgrade) and the West. This is already evident in the tensions surrounding the expansion of NATO, but also in the ambivalence of Ukrainians and others as to whether they want to rejoin the old empire or join the West. Similarly, in the Balkans, Belgrade not only won the war in Bosnia, but it is also pushing toward leadership in proposed Balkan economic arrangements (such as the Southeast Europe Cooperation Initiative, or SECI) that will, in some ways, revive the old Yugoslavia. One should not assume uncritically that the West is more desirable to these ambivalent nations. As Polokhalo and others note correctly, the West has erected a new, economic Iron Curtain that is excluding formerly Communist nations from Western markets. The promise of NATO security has been tarnished by NATO's public failure to deter genocidal aggression in Bosnia.

In sum, this is a serious book that raises the sorts of issues that serious analysts ought to have considered long ago but certainly should start considering now and in the foreseeable future. It is time for Westerners to set aside their hubris and to look carefully at what trained social scientists from formerly Communist nations, such as Polokhalo and associates, have to teach us.

Stjepan G. Meštrović
Series Editor

Chapter 1.

The Political Philosophy of the Postcommunist Era

- Theoretical Foundations for Understanding Postcommunism
- Nationalism and the Legitimation of Postcommunist Regimes
- Political Discourse in Mass Communications

Periods of considerable social and political changes are always accompanied (preceded or crowned) by transformations in the political philosophy of society. By the latter one should understand not only such by-products of rationalization in the guise of numerous social theories and scholarly constructs but also those forms of mass experience and popular self-understanding on which are based the legitimacy of the whole bulk of collective existence, the recognition of social institutions, and expectations of certain social and political reforms and events. It is at first obvious that in the everyday practice of relationships and attitudes toward oneself, truly tectonic – latent, invisible – changes in the course of history are stored up and at certain historical junctures suddenly surface and erupt onto the political landscape as cataclysms – revolutionary transformations of society, which then have to be recorded, theoretically understood, and explained.

Initial steps toward attaining mass understanding and public discussion – attempts to create the social conditions for awakening the individual (Gorbachev-era glasnost against the background of the so-called Brezhnev "period of stagnation") – were no doubt, indicators of the social and economic crisis of the "communist project," which were only the first signs of coming profound and radical changes. The demolition of the Berlin Wall and the "wall of silence" around the little man of the "great" Soviet people resulted in the public articulation of all the latent individual and collective moods, desires, wills, and expectations which constituted the basis of the social legitimation of the previous political system, political order, and political institutions. This is why the changes that have occurred in this period in the language, public discourse, and mass media constitute a watershed and the institutional consolidation of essential transformations in society's political sphere as a whole.

People's awareness of their national/ethnic and cultural identity has assumed great significance in altering the system of political legitimation in the postcommunist period. Political philosophy and the practice of legitimizing postcommunist authority are indissolubly linked with unflagging attention to problems of ethnic identification, national culture, and nationalism.

Society's "idiosyncrasy" of Soviet Bolshevik ideology and, at the same time, to the political theory of classical Marxism freed up the intellectual sphere, which was then flooded by hasty and foolish revisions of the old political textbooks on scientific communism and historical materialism, by "theoretical" quests for a "particular" ethnospecific "third road" to the future, or by the unsystematic and superficial borrowing of terms from the vocabulary of Western political philosophy like "democracy", "parliamentary system", "rule of law", "law-governed state", "civil society", *etc.*). All this points to the need for a radically different approach to and understanding of the postcommunist experience.

The essence of this chapter resides in the analysis of the conceptual and theoretical foundations for understanding postcommunist political realities, the ethnic and cultural factors shaping the current regimes, and a critical assessment of the verbal modes of political discourse in the postcommunist period.

Theoretical Foundations for Understanding Postcommunism

§1. The Concept of Postcommunism

Beginning with the Modern period and that of the so-called bourgeois revolutions, the awareness of historically decisive discrepancies between the conscious, *i.e.*, rationally goal-oriented socially significant acts and actions of individuals (as "rational beings") and the unforeseen consequences of their common collective life (as "political animals") in time led to the formulation of the classical or the Modern type of socio-political theory and political philosophy in general. Its distinctive peculiarity (already laid down by the Modern period in the socio-political genesis of political science) lay in the fact that political theory, from its very inception, was designed to accomplish a dual task: first, to lay bare the rational structure, an essence or general law, of the motive forces of society and of its cataclysms and, second, to construct such a system of political knowledge and ideas (ideology), on the basis of which the collective forms of human life could acquire purposefulness and rational predictability. It is precisely in the political theory of the philosophers of that era that the motto, "knowledge is power," which dates from that time, reveals its true meaning as a total will to power in the form of a projected domination over reality based on rational control over the latter.

A system of universal, world-view certainties, of general assumptions, "foremeanings" or "prejudices" (H.G. Gadamer) arose, on the basis of which all further empirical judgments about the structure of the world as a whole and especially on the law-governed nature of social life, the factors affecting its development, and the possibility of comprehending it scientifically. We call such a system of assumptions (interpretative framework) the project of the Modern, which characterizes the possibilities of historical development in a dialectical spirit. The issue is primarily one of understanding history as progress in human self-understanding, of the idea of emancipation through progress of the Mind, science (or social action led by scientific knowledge as in Marxism), and also of the attainment by such means of maximal material and spiritual welfare.[1] This ideological foundation (beginning with Spinoza, Hobbs, the Enlightenment philosophers up to and including Hegel, Marx, Comte, Spencer, and so forth) makes up the basis of political thought, the political ontology of the project of the Modern. Its collapse is experienced by the postcommunist political being as the destruction, first of all, of the ideology and theory of a rationally understandable (scientifically-planned) organization of "politics" in the broadest sense.

The period following the break-up of the Soviet Union and Soviet bloc, following the collapse of the communist system as a whole, is linked by contemporary social and political thinkers to the termination of a certain historical epoch. Both its content and the plurality of new social, geopolitical, economic, cultural and existential realities which have emerged and are emerging before our eyes, replacing the simple bipolar macropolitical concept of confrontation between two world systems – "communism" and "capitalism" – are currently the focus of political studies, ideas, and projections. The global nature of these transformations, which touch the political life of virtually the whole world and entail tangible changes in peoples' ways of life in the former socialist countries and far beyond, gives every reason to view our time as the postcommunist era in world history.

Unlike those political scientists who treat postcommunism as a spontaneously coined and vague term applied for the sake of more convenient description of tumultuous current developments in the so-called postcommunist states, our journal endows the concepts of postcommunism and postcommunist era with universal theoretical content, promising methodological value, and great heuristic potential.

To begin with, its semantics reflect the feeling of a certain cultural epoch coming to an end, which is today universal. Beginning, if not with Nietzsche and Heidegger, then — more distinctly with Guardini, Lyotard, Derridas, Eco and other modern philosophers, this feeling was expressed in common images of the end of morality, metaphysics, ideology, of the end of new times, and in its generalized form it got fixed in the socio-humanitarian thought in the image of the universally known today "post-modern." In our opinion, historian and political scientist Francis Fukuyama resorted to a typically post-modern image of the end of history, indicating an intrinsic connection between the notions of the post-modern and postcommunism.

Unlike the post-modern, however, postcommunism has explicit enough sociopolitical content. Proceeding from the historical fact of the end of the communist system, it also points to the termination of a great all-European epoch marked by a certain political ideology and methodology of political thought, which evolved in the seventeenth and eighteenth centuries concurrently with Utopian and the Enlightenment belief in the possibility of a rationally organized society based on scientific planning and total control. With the collapse of communism, whose ideology and content were oriented toward a maximal imposition of these classical foundation of West European ontology on reality, albeit through police and state coercion, torture and violence, the inadequacy of classical political thought also comes to light. The postcommunist era calls for qualitatively new, non-classical attitudes for its scientific and theoretical substantiation and potential political prognostication and management.

In terms of political theory, alongside the notion of a postcommunist era we encounter a different type of political thinking which Mikhail Gorbachev, unwilling to part with the communist epoch, traditionally dubbed "new thinking." All the subsequent events of communism's overall debacle proved, however, that no renovation of the old political model and established patterns of political thought could bring us closer to a true picture of current political changes and transformations.

Thus, secondly, the concept of a postcommunist era does not reflect some "new" state of the "old" society, "modernized" or "renovated" according to various previously known types of scientific and political prescriptions. It reflects — and this is especially noteworthy — our time as a still obscure, theoretically unexplained epoch in world development as a whole and not just of "postcommunist" civilization. This means, for example, that the classical linear scheme of explaining the contemporary stage in postcommunist society in customary terms of historical "succession," "progress," or "regression," indicating forward or backward motion, is, to say the least, insufficient. Attempts to explain postcommunism through comparison to either the so-called period of primary capital accumulation, or to modernization similar to post-war reconstruction in Western states, always miss the target in real life. The postcommunist era requires new explanations, methodological approaches, and analytical tools. Here post-modern philosophy and post-classical social thought can be of great help. Today's political and geopolitical map of the world seems closer to a pluralistic discourse, an interaction between different cultures and civilizations with equally worthy historical gains, which is relied upon by present-day research in the humanities, than to the classical idea of rationally realized advance by all nations toward a single perfect society.

Likewise, it is hardly possible to account for the current upsurge of nationalism, and the formation of new nation-states by mere reference to Romanticism as the classical ideology of the nineteenth century national movements. In all these instances we have to deal not merely with novelty nor with what could be called "the everyday modern," but with historically unprecedented sociopolitical phenomena.

Hence, thirdly, the concept of postcommunism implies the accumulation of special political experience, whose historical analogues — if any — are hard to find. And the experience we are going through here, in the focus of postcommunist life, is the most vital and the most indicative for contemporary political thought. Four or five years of postcommunism have vividly demonstrated that there are certain trends and certain political practice inherent in it, which, in fact, cannot yet be scientifically and theoretically interpreted because of a lack of relevant forms and standards. The first step in this direction is understanding the basic methods for analyzing the postcommunist experience.

§2. The Starting Point for a Political Philosophy of Postcommunism

Today, it is common knowledge among political theorists that, along with the epoch-making changes of 1989 and 1991, an urgent need has arisen to examine anew the fundamental premises, notions, and theories of modern political science as well as the latter's attempts to define the nature and proper forms of political life.[2] Moreover, there is every reason to argue that the problem lies not only in changing a professionally delineated social idea, political science, but also in a global change in the ideational reference points and methods of organizing present-day philosophical thought in general, which, not by accident, coincide in time with the "postcommunist revolutions" in Central and Eastern Europe. Politics, law, the state, and ethics comprise the institutions of the shared life of those we now place under philosophical scrutiny.

These discernible shifts in defining the central subject-matter of philosophical thought are of the same fundamental importance as the orientation of philosophy, beginning with the Modern period, toward the norms and ideals of rigorous cognitive style, canons, and rules in the explanation of Nature, elaborated in mathematical experimental study of natural history as well as in the field of the social sciences (Francis Bacon, Descartes, Hobbs). Recall that Marx and Engels undertook to develop "scientific communism" and "the materialistic (scientific) understanding of history" precisely because, in their typically Modern approach, accounts of social phenomena had to have objective certainty equal to that of the explanations of Nature provided by the natural sciences. Based on quite different premises, this century's logical positivism cultivated this same approach in the scientific explanation of social phenomena.

The current attention to politics in the widest sense of the term (as a universal mode of organizing social life, dating as far back as the ancient polis) holds fundamental significance for philosophical thought. The transfer of politics to the center of attention in the social sciences is equal to the discovery of the volitional basis of various forms of human self-identification in the world, made by Schopenhauer and Nietzsche on the basis of the nineteenth century Romantic revolution in culture (the arts, music, and world view in general) and in direct relation to the national-liberation movements of the 1848 *Springtime of Peoples in Europe* and national awakenings. The turning of contemporary thought to political life is no less important than Husserl's discovery of the crucial significance of everyday experience, the world of life (*Lebenswelt*), for the human understanding of all – notably social – phenomena, which produced offshoots in phenomenological sociology (A. Schütz, and in the 1960s and 1970s also M. Silverman, D. Phillipson, and others). The current "discovery" of politics is methodologically no less important than the formulation of the principles of the hermeneutic understanding of cultural phenomena (Dilthey, Heidegger, Gadamer) that proceeded from the recognition of a peculiar humanitarian method of cognition in the field of historical and philological sciences or the so-called *Geisteswissenschaften* or moral sciences. The postcommunist transformations of society and natural process of a broad complex of political issues coming to the forefront of intellectual life vividly demonstrate that political philosophy assumes the role of a fundamental paradigm for defining the ideational reference points for theoretical thinking in general and of social cognition, in particular.[3] However, the postcommunist thematization of political life (and possibly today's focusing of philosophical thought on political matters in general) cannot be accounted for by a simple borrowing or application of explanatory patterns elaborated by the previously mentioned precursors, to say nothing of the inertia of old habits of the simplistic interpreting of political problems in terms of the old "class analysis." The very situation of postcommunism is a visible result of those invisible sociocultural changes in society which are difficult or practically impossible to describe using the formulae of classical sociopolitical theories.

For all the complexity of these problems, one thing remains rather obvious and beyond doubt. Postcommunist transformations point, first and foremost, to changes in the very foundation of identity and social coherence[4] of political agglomerations, communities, and the nature of the political interconnection of people. The place of the monistic system of identification, universal in its criteria of affiliation (with "a single socioeconomic formation" – "socialism, real socialism, the communist camp," "fraternal multinational family of the peoples," "socialist camp," *etc.*) of the system of identification and the political regime, totally leveling and egalitarian in its socio-economic and legal aspects ("socialist equality of people," so-called "free" medical care, education, housing, *etc.*, "socialist legality") has been appropriated by a new social aggregate. This can be adequately accounted for in terms of the non-Modern world view.

On the one hand, this was a collapse, the disintegration of a large system of political identification and cohesiveness (the Soviet Union, the socialist camp, the communist world view and ideology) or, in the words of Jean-François Lyotard, with the delegitimation of "great narratives of speculation and emancipation."[5] This ruining takes place side by side with the destruction of reality and, at the same time, the illusion of existence of a simple homogeneous social whole based on liberty, equality and fraternity, simplistically interpreted in Bolshevik practice. On the other hand, this was a manifestation of new political communities, which emerged on the territory of the former USSR; the newly-independent postcommunist states, whose integrity, cohesiveness, and identity, along with problems of self-identification and self-determination, also require essentially non-classical (*i.e.*, non-Modern) methods of description and cognition, as do the definitions of their political, geopolitical and world economic relations in the changing interaction of present-day nations, cultures, and civilizations.

§3. The Inadequacy of Traditional Philosophical and Methodological Approaches

The non-Modern character of the political analysis of postcommunism does not imply only some self-sufficient terminological revolution, radical change in the traditional logic of theoretical description, or turning to some hitherto unknown methods of political studies. The postcommunist situation indicates a single but dramatic alteration in the world political map and that only a new constellation of already extant philosophico-methodological approaches can adequately describe postcommunist political experience. Due to the very manner of its "pluralistic" accumulation and existence, it cannot be reduced to a monistic universal pattern of explanation.

But such a constant gravitation toward the peculiar "methodological solipsism" of a single approach can be frequently found in current political science literature in both the East and West. Thus, the term *postcommunism* is often used as a simple designation of the transition period from the previous Soviet communist society (political regime) to what is assumed to be the normal democratic way of organizing society. The concept is thereby denied independent, positive meaning. Postcommunism becomes, so to speak, only a transitional amorphous designation of the road from one definite social system (communism) to some other definite social system of contemporary developed societies.

On the other hand, it is thought that postcommunism is simply an accidental mutation of communist society, an unsuccessful, subjective, and thus accidental experience of the ruin of an in principle viable, if somewhat incomplete, socioeconomic system (Alexander Zinoviev). Such views are justifiable insofar as they make it possible to critically examine the postcommunist world as a whole, *i.e.*, to comprehend that, first, "communism" may lay claim to undoubted historical achievements and merits; second, that an ultraradical critique of its social heritage is, in many cases, of a pathological and self-destructive nature; and, third, that modern forms of the liberal-democratic social system in the so-called developed Western countries have their own rather basic social shortcomings, which render the uncritical idealization of that system dangerous both from a political and political science perspective.

In the final analysis, such an approach is not justified. The situation and understanding of postcommunism has to be accepted not simply as a designation of the transition period of post-Soviet societies. Postcommunism is the general situation (and understanding) of the transition from one epoch of political organization of social life to another, post-Modern time in the understanding of society and its political practice. Postcommunism can be understood only within the context of universal changes in political world view, which are accompanied by the delegitimation of classical political ideals and possibilities on the one hand and by the search for non-Modern explanations and cognitive methods on the other. Those, who see in the notion of postcommunism only an apt term to describe social deformations, merely attempt to critically assess the present transformations from the perspective of traditional ideas of a perfect – be it communist or (Western) democratic – society. They are guided by a characteristic Enlightenment bias: if reality fails to conform to the ideal, so much the worse for reality itself. Continuing this classical perspective of thinking in one form or another serves only to spiritually nourish resuscitated communists and a certain segment of the socialists in the postcommunist states.

The inertia of what might be called "the Modern project" is also seen in those newly minted upstart postcommunist politicians who orient themselves to the postcommunist political expediency and try to find an instant, ready-made substitute for a discredited and thus uncompetitive Marxism in some other political theory/ideology, which may differ in its content but remains typically totalitarian. Such a re-ideologization is already taking place in many postcommunist states, most notably exemplified by radical nationalist movements and parties.

The attraction of classical explanatory models has real basis. A major factor here, in addition to simple habit, is the retention of the old forms of political and economic life within the process of postcommunist social transformation. So long as whole series of ways of viewing economics, morality, law, and the world which characterized the old social forms of identification and popular self-understanding is preserved within society, a postcommunist self-determination of the new reality will continue to exist mainly because the manner in which "communism" is criticized is one which can be described as postcommunist nihilism.

Postcommunist freedom is freedom in the specific sense of being emancipated from the old in the absence of adequately defined new social ideals and regulative ideas. This is why attempts to maintain stability in the postcommunist period rely mainly on the stability of intermediary, transitory, and in general situationally accidental forms and norms of social life along with their characteristic complement of situational leaders, instant politicians, and self-consecrated political scientists as well as numerous myths, social simulacra and stereotypes, criminal business, and adventurist capital.

The so-called postcommunist revolution is essentially different from its precursors, the revolution of 1917 or the bourgeois revolutions of the more remote past. Its basic aimless drifting is usually hidden under scathing assessments of the communist past, served up by the political discourse, mass media, language, and literature of the glasnost period. But this postcommunist nihilism cannot in any sense be called radical. Meanwhile, behind the radical facade of words and slogans which constitute the backdrop of public political posturing and struggle, leaders well versed in the habits and devices of the old communist nomenklatura suddenly pop up. The taste of this postcommunist "old-new" nomenklatura for administrative and command methods of governance and management is merely augmented by the concentration of power and property in its hands, thus generating what could be called a "local quasi-totalitarianism," based on decrees and orders, the manipulation of huge amounts of state money, and on spontaneous political and economic reflexes, both domestically and in international affairs. All this creates preconditions for the reproduction under postcommunism of what seem to be time-worn methodological patterns, now at a theoretical level of understanding.

One such echo of the past has its origins in the classical voluntarism of the nineteenth and twentieth centuries. Under postcommunist ambivalence, changes in the basis of social identity result in quests for an ultimate grounding (*Letztbegründung*), the function of which is assumed by "ethnonational identity." To a greater or lesser extent, orientations toward various forms of ethnic or national unity can be observed in the postcommunist period throughout East Central Europe and the former Soviet Union, the symbol of which might be the figure of Yeltsin on a tank under the Russian tricolor. In Ukraine, quests for a new national identity and social cohesiveness sometimes reproduce the ideology of the classical Ukrainian integral nationalism created by Mykola Mikhnovsky and Dmytro Dontsov, which affirm its traditional ideas of power as the will of the whole nation for the clan (ethnoculturally) based self-realization of the state. A rather archaic portrait of postcommunist society is thus cast in the traditional notions of the integrity of the will of the nation, its clan (ethnic) identity, and the unity of its political action under the slogan of a single "national idea."

§4. The Postcommunist Experience: In Search of a Methodology

The current almost universal political use of the ideological store of classical voluntarism masks an extremely important transformation of nationalism under postcommunism. The self-evident peculiarity of postcommunist nationalism is that here nationalism, which has come to serve as a basis for the postcommunist identity of large human communities and a prime factor of their legitimation as independent nations on the territory of the former USSR, turned out to be "nonclassical." From the start, today's nationalism has failed to conform to its Modern philosophical origins and to the way radical nationalist movements and parties would like to interpret and have it. In the first place, national identity was perceived not from the perspective of total force on the part of the general clan will but as the free and common expression of will for self-affirmation by communities different in their ethnic or national aspirations.

The main trend of the postcommunist transformation of society, cast primarily in the idea of emancipation from totalitarianism, gave rise to a regional cultural pluralization of society. Postcommunist nationalism offered an ideological basis for the recognition of a plurality of communities identified on a cultural-regional and ethnocultural basis within the borders of one postcommunist country (in Ukraine, it is the West, the East, the South, and the Crimea), *i.e.*, offered ideological weapons for the confrontation of many political wills (identities) for self-affirmation.

Traditional interaction of various sociocultural worlds – "forms of life" (sometimes meaning different civilizations) – was accounted for by means of a methodology which was elaborated within the framework of the cognitive and ideological quests of philosophical hermeneutics (Dilthey, Heidegger, Gadamer, Ricoeur, *etc.*). In the final analysis, the theoretical problem of interpersonal unity and collective identity, or in specific philosophical terms, reaching intersubjective understanding, according to the hermeneutic approach, has a solution, though not an "absolute" one. Confrontations of language, symbols, and various systems of values and norms are in principle resolved by this approach even if only by means of, say, mental conflicts but in the process of interpretation of "alien" values from other cultures. A basis for their possible merger may lie in the field of the senses: a peculiar international conference in an ideal palace built up of various moral meanings, theoretical methods (translation and *Verstehen*, understanding), intuitive-emotive methods (empathy) of mutual confrontation, and the dialectical reconciliation of various interpretations.

However, postcommunist experiences of murderous interethnic and international wars and terrible ethnic massacres (suffice it to recall ex-Yugoslavia, Nagorno-Karabakh, and Chechnia) make it evident that it is no longer so much the matter of collision, or a "conflict of interpretations" (P. Ricoeur). Hidden behind the political decisions and military actions of the postcommunist period is, in the words of H.G. Wells, a real "war of the worlds" or a conflict of political ontologies. What methodological premises can be used to account for this theoretically? In what direction should one look for possible political solutions to these murderous confrontations, which find their blind inspiration in definitely non-classical nationalist concepts? They are non-classical and non-Modern because the question is one of "local narratives," local – ethnic and national – systems of identification and coherence, though even in this version, confined by the borders of one's own "historical territory," totalitarian patterns of political thought and action are constantly reproduced. Under the circumstances, rationally argumented communication and the elaboration of traditions of open political discourse become essential to the positive evolution of the political process.

Alongside a massive socio-psychological motive for postcommunist transformations, the desire to create a life patterned on that of the developed nations of Western Europe, there is also an important motive for quests in our own Ukrainian juridical, political, ethical, and nation-making traditions. Importantly, the search is now underway for possible models, offshoots, or correlates of West European democracy (civil society and law-governed state) and norms of civilized and well-regulated social existence. That is why the tradition of West European social philosophy (from Hobbs, Burke, Rousseau, Kant and Hegel to Apel, Habermas, Rawles, and others) is one significant ideological source in the situation of postcommunist ambivalence. Moreover, this tradition makes it possible to define more clearly the requisite regulative ideas of social transformations – desired perspectives of a possible way of development, and already at present to critically analyze the emergence of a postcommunist political discourse and a new communicative community with their specific features. Along with assimilation of this philosophical and ideological tradition (which formed during the historical practice of establishing the modern types of developed Western democratic societies), the political analysis of postcommunism acquires conceptual tools to research a wide range of juridical and ethical problems, such as (communicative) ethics of international and interethnic relations, interrelations of law, politics and morals, ethics of responsibility, new global ecological order, *etc.*

Even the first contrast of philosophico-sociological images produced by current communicative philosophy reveals, so to speak, an incomplete conformity between the political ontology it delineates (*i.e.*, the ultimate basis of people's political interaction – the universal rules, norms, and values on which political discourse rests) and the political reality of postcommunism. Postcommunist political discourse cannot be reduced, without seriously damaging theory, only to the surface layer of people's political interaction, *i.e.*, to their political relations, with their rather definite features of regularity, standardization, and communicative rationality, in general. The experience of the political game which has accompanied the process of the East European countries' gaining independence over the past several years and the struggle of various political parties for their place in society – all these and other postcommunist political realities point to this tentative conclusion.

The point is that it is quite insufficient to understand by political relations only those communicative acts which are subject to legal and ethical norms, the norms and values of so-called "political culture." Incidentally, the topic of political culture has become rather pathologically popular with postcommunist political scientists as the least dangerous range of sentimental considerations about how "authentically" ideal politicians and statesmen should act and what they should know. But they have remained the same as ever. It is precisely their political behavior, acts, and actions, as well as their mass recognition as the powers that be by voters, that point to the existence of extrarational cultural-historical feelings, existential attitudes, collective "silent" political wills and resolve of rallying mobs, which are not argued for in political discourse but have only the quality of presuppositions.

Postcommunist literature abounds in leitmotifs of quests for cultural-historical "archetypes" of political organization of this or that nationality, people, or community, when, for example, direct historical parallels are drawn between "Tsar Boris" Godunov and "incumbent Tsar Boris" Yeltsin, or when the "principles of democracy always inherent" in Ukrainians are sought in the heroic myth of the Zaporizhian Cossacks. These perhaps naive examples (simplified by the mass media) of perception of a certain extrarationality of political life testify to the urgency of taking into account and analyzing theoretically the existential-volitional aspects of political discourse and human communication in general. In this sense, it is not only the matter of rational "*a priori* of communication" (K.-O. Apel) or formation of norms of discursive practice but also a peculiar "*a priori* of will" which can be discerned, for example, in the nationalist movements in the postcommunist states. Therefore, combining the experience of theoretical political science and philosophical analyses of the rational organization of the present-day polis with the post-Modern experience of the existential-volitional making of a pluralistic society and its most up-to-date "assembly" on new principles, thus far very little known, is a promising line of research in the political analysis of postcommunism.

The prospects for institutionalizing argumentative discourse in the postcommunist world are dependent on the level of social rationality. First of all, the issue is one of rationality of political action in all the major directions of the postcommunist transformation of society. This is why it is very important for the scholarly political analysis of the postcommunist period to maximally lay bare the "secondary" ideological accretions, neo-Romantic reproductions of old socio-political myths, numerous new illusions, political daydreaming, primitive slogans, and ideas which just do not make sense. But it is precisely these that largely serve the postcommunist individual as substitutes for stable forms of life and world view in the critical conditions of social (and ideational) ambiguity. And this is precisely the reason that they are transformed into countless simulacra.

Postcommunist simulacra, *i.e.*, the artificial reality generated by a mass media emancipated from state censorship, have been widely circulated by television, the press, and literary publications since the time of perestroika and glasnost. This is the ideational and existential reality people live in and are nourished by. It is practically inaccessible because there are no objective criteria for discerning truth from falsehood in it and actual reality from its interpretations imposed by television, radio, and the press. Simulacra are even more actively structuring today's political discourse. These are charismas of apparently not the best (in both the political and human sense) first presidents of newly independent states. Among them one can also mention images of "democracy," "entrepreneurship," "privatization," "talented young economists" and "old experienced managers," "honest parliamentarians" (the list reaches practically to infinity), which create a new postcommunist political and semantic reality. The rate of their efficiency is directly dependent on the level of population's political naïveté (a legacy from the time of the Communist Party's *Diktat*), and simultaneously on the degree of popular alienation from the ruling elites. Their fanciful, fantastic nature and falsehood is demonstrated by time and the natural historical course of events. Given this, the political thought of postcommunism may be fruitful in a positive sense, provided it embraces critical analysis, is based on the recognized methodology of analytical philosophy (with its methods of clarification and explication of the language and discourse of postcommunism), and studies the new logic of myth concocted by postcommunist mass media and the mass consciousness molded by them.

Political developments in the postcommunist states and political experiences of postcommunist reforms cannot be adequately understood unless they are considered in a world context, from the broad perspective of radical socio-cultural changes, reflected in the combination of the notions of postcommunism and the postmodern. Moreover, any other approach will inevitably result in reproducing outdated theoretical concepts in a new socio-political situation, thereby giving rise to dogmatism and phantoms.

§5. *How Can We Construct a Political Theory of Postcommunism?*

Rejecting classical explanatory principles and schemata raises the question of the feasibility of constructing a system of political knowledge and elaborating a coherent political theory capable of generalizing the experience of postcommunist life. From this standpoint the concepts of post-classicism and the postmodern in general are called into question by considerations of systemicity, integrity, and homogeneity, and this renders dubious any attempt to resort to available methods of socio-political research and the very notion of method as a familiar way of acquiring certain knowledge, which is a fundamental principle of Modern thought.

The principal conclusion regarding the situation under postcommunism is that current political thought is intertwined with everyday social practice. And the issue here is not merely one of the extremely politicized character of mass consciousness. The point is that a theory of postcommunism can no longer, as classical socio-political thought attempted, remain separate from politics, from the practices of the struggle for and exercise of power, *i.e.*, as a discrete, ideal system of thoughts and political abstractions. Along with postcommunist ambivalence, we face a situation where political thought works to define possible norms and establish rules of what is still to be created but only as something already established, to use the words of Lyotard. Viewed in this way, the postcommunist practice of political theory is absolutely performative, *i.e.*, it is an exercise in the political discourse of instituting. Using all available methods, political thought analyzes possible models of social development – under the conditions of what we called postcommunist ambivalence – and by so doing it becomes enmeshed in the texture of political events.

In modern social science, the notions of performative sentence and performative act are widely used to analyze situations when speech acts perform social acts and institute certain social facts. To take an example, an utterance of a political leader about the indispensability of some social change may very often institute this change, which was observed in the Gorbachev period: his affirmation of "glasnost" was, at the same time, a sort of institutionalization of the freedom of speech and, hence, institutionalization of a different type of discourse. The idea of a performative as an act of legal and political institutionalization was developed by Derridas in his analysis of the American Declaration of Independence. By the very fact of its adoption by "representatives of the United States of America who convened at the General Congress," the Declaration "contains two simultaneous discursive modalities – description and injunction (to be guided by this document – *author's note*), fact and law."[6] Note that postcommunism, unlike the lasting institutionalized tradition of American democracy, is nothing other than a period of various types and forms of the institutionalization of social institutions and structures which differ in their forms and functions. But no one can be certain of their future durability.

Just as form and context, objective description and intention, positive information and the act of institutionalization are merged in performative sentences, so too does the political theory of postcommunism coincide with institutionalization – but with an institutionalization of civilized forms of socio-political life, rather than an institutionalization of "novelty" in the Modern sense, leaving a gray area for some freedom of the individual who has left behind the world of absolute political nonambiguity in the communist past.

We use the notion of institutionalization, not coming into being. Its traditional understanding as "emergence" or "coming into being" is fraught with the danger of interpreting it in the classical Hegelian-Marxist sense of a linear interconnected succession of events or as the idea of steady historical progress in the political situation of postcommunism.

The fact that discourse of institutionalization is gaining wide currency among present-day politicians determines by itself the intellectual attitude, the logic of direction or nontraditional methodology of postcommunist political thought. The latter is beginning to formulate and become aware of the specific problems stemming from the contradictions observed between what is proclaimed by postcommunist politicians (the new regime) on the one hand, and their political action and the actual results of postcommunist social transformation, on the other; between the meaning of slogans, declarations, speeches, programs, and normative documents, on the one hand, and their actual (conscious or unconscious) intent, their political will and their orientations (derived from the character of political actions), on the other.

From the total lack of understanding and failure to grasp this fact of a lack of correspondence between the laying of political plans and the real outcome of political events, and the failure to accomplish seemingly the best of ideas, flows the real hallmark of the postcommunist period as such. Thus, the involved political project to reform the USSR (the "New Union Treaty") constituted the axis of Gorbachev's final actions.[7] But beyond the tragedy of this *King Lear* of communism and those around him, one ought to see the birth of a new era in the mirror of which moral recriminations and value judgments in the place of real understanding bespeak, at best, political naïveté.

Characteristically, the postcommunist epoch manifests not only a striking gap between ideology and reality, social theory and practice, which can be observed in all totalitarian educational political programs of the past, especially under "communism." The political discourse of institutionalization is essentially different in that it is characteristic for this kind of discourse to display a constant practical gap between ideal political intentions and the forms (plus results) of their realization. "They wanted to the best thing possible, but it turned out just like always!" — this maxim, uttered by a well-known Russian politician, can be used as an epigraph to the postcommunist discourse of institutionalization. Its Ukrainian version, presented to the world by our former President, "We have what we have," reads like a direct statement of independence (even from those who act) from the political "logic of intentions" — concealed or unconscious political volitional motives and, respectively, outcomes of their realization unexpected by the political game players themselves – from "the logic of knowledge," allegedly well-thought out political programs, substantiated methods of Parliamentary discussions and decisions made as a result of heated debates, *etc.*

In all these cases of the realization of the postcommunist discourse of institutionalization, we are dealing with a permanent performative contradiction of failing to realize what is instituted by the political discourse itself in a political action. This everlasting political ambivalence and ambiguity at all levels of social life is indeed the most significant impetus to postcommunist political thought.

This is where the peculiar nature of the theoretical thrust of the political study of postcommunism takes its origin. First and foremost, it is the question of the need for continuous explanation and clarification of the political practice of postcommunist transformation.

* * *

In the transition period of postcommunist ambivalence, there are quite logical and natural ideological, philosophical, political science, sociological, socio-humanitarian quests in the social sciences for purpose and knowledge, quite like Taras Shevchenko's expectation of "an apostle of truth and science" to arise. If the task of political thought today is not understood as pandering to the nomenklatura's or neo-nomenklatura's need for a "scientific" explanation to impose a new ideology of total control over society, then quite reasonable is the intellectual cliché that there is nothing better than a good theory. Theoretical studies in the field of political science should be conducted from the perspective of understanding postcommunist experience as part of a greater whole, of world sociopolitical and cultural transformations. The political independence of postcommunist nations is not merely a tardy response or a delayed reflex of history, a sort of redemption for past injustices by way of creating independent nation-states. Their independence is a logical outcome of the most recent changes in the political philosophy of society and the world as a whole. This means that the postcommunist period should be viewed not only as a period of critical uncertainty but also as a time of instituting socio-cultural forms of life. History knows similar big precedents: the idea of popular sovereignty ("social contract"), division of powers, individual freedom ("natural rights"), "civil society," and others acquired earlier (directly or indirectly), their institutionalization in political practice (constitutions, *etc.*) of today's most developed nations. This is why political philosophy and other aspects of the political analysis of postcommunism make sense only as independent *hic et nunc,* as the comprehension of lessons of world sociopolitical thought on the basis of a nation's proper experience of its own national-cultural identity. He who does not demand more loses all.

And in this sense we may pretend to have a certain coherent theory and simultaneously do not at all pretend to have created a final theoretical schemata or project for building postcommunist society. The main thrust of the work we submit to the reader's attention is to theoretically examine our own experience, to build a model from it, at best to prognosticate, and in no sense to have constructed a universal theory, which always and with devilish speed (especially in the political sphere) transforms itself into a new totalitarian ideology.

§6. Special Features of the Postcommunist Period

It is claimed that the disintegration of the Soviet bloc and the Soviet Union, and the collapse of communist regimes in these countries has ushered in a new, postcommunist epoch in human history. Such a view appears somewhat comical in the sense that in the West there never was a communist epoch. However, one may regard the era as communist when the West trembled with fear over the spread of world communism. So being relieved from this fear may well be proclaimed the postcommunist epoch.

Well, let the epoch that has set in be called the "postcommunist era." The name is not what matters here. What is important are the traits that characterize this period. Thus it becomes necessary to focus on some of its features which are generally ignored or interpreted in a certain ideological way (namely, in the spirit of anticommunism) that is as far from the truth as the old communist propaganda.

One should differentiate between communism as a particular ideology (ideological communism) and communism as a certain way of organizing society ("real" communism). In dealing first with communist theory we must discern the way it was shaped and influenced by Marxism, and the way it was molded irrespective of Marxism.

Communist theory emerged long before Marxism. Its originators were Thomas More (1478-1535) and Tommaso Campanella (1568-1639). We can ascertain the downfall and even the bankruptcy of Marxism. But this does not mean the complete failure of communist theory in general.

Portions of communist ideas have been adopted by all kinds of political parties – including labor, popular, socialist, and the other parties, by mass movements (like the Greens and the Alternatives), by trade unions, and even by religious groups and sects (like those in the USA). Communist ideas have "dissolved" in the ideological swamp of the present. But they have not disappeared forever nor will they disappear so long as what gave them birth, that is, the negative aspects of capitalism, continue to exist. They are, in fact, anticapitalist ideas.

The collapse of communist ideology in its Marxist variant was brought about by a set of causes of great historical scale. Most prominent among them was the transformation of Marxism into the state ideology of the Soviet Union and other communist countries. This resulted in the decline of its intellectual level, making it an object of mockery, led to its getting out of touch with reality, and led to it turning into a coercively imposed apology for real communism.

The negative practice of real communism in the Soviet Union and other countries, became an object of negative attention by Western anticommunist propaganda. It also enabled the West to succeed in repelling many people from communism all over the world. Capitalism has not vanished from the world arena, as was foretold by Marx. Instead, it has consolidated its positions, and at this stage of history it might appear to have won the competition with communism.

As for the proletarians who were viewed by Marxists as the gravediggers of capitalism, they have decreased in number (relative to other social strata) and come to play a secondary role, degenerating and ceasing to be a reliable mainstay and bearer of communist ideas.

The defeat of the communist world in the Cold War has, for a very long time (if not forever), buried the possibility and even the idea of socialist revolution in the Marxist sense (that is, a proletarian revolution resulting in the total elimination of capitalism, private property, and the establishment of the dictatorship of the proletariat). One cannot categorically exclude the possibility of a non-capitalist ("socialist") social system in Western countries being established sometime in the future. Should this occur, it would most likely be the result of the West's defeat by external forces or decisions of dictators. Thus far, the probability of such a development seems very low. In this respect one might agree with those political theorists who suggest that we are witnessing the onset of the "post-revolutionary" period.

In sermons about the postcommunist period two arguments usually figure prominently: the negative results of real communism and the lack in Western countries of a sufficiently powerful social stratum that has an interest in changing of the Western socioeconomic system. To this three more could be added. *First,* the West has learned to avert the danger of mass revolutionary movements as well as to manipulate them in such a way that any attempt to recreate the communist movements of the recent past is *a priori* doomed to failure. *Second,* to organize a stable mass movement requires money, quite a bit at that. Thus, someone must subsidize them. But who? In the past, communist states could financially subsidize communist parties in the West and other countries. But now there are neither communist countries capable of such expenditures nor communist parties ready to fight for the overthrow of capitalism. *Third,* the West has stolen the initiative from communists with respect to social transformations. The idea of a convergence of social systems (communism and capitalism) was put forward by Western ideologists rather than by communists. In developing the idea they relied on the clear evolution of the West towards "Eastern" socioeconomic policies.

Under such conditions, communist ideology in its Marxist-Leninist form has no chance of mass success and becoming an effective force in "Western" former socialist states. But, whether a communist ideology could arise on the scale of the Marxism, corresponding to the needs of the moment and interests of a powerful social strata, is a question which one cannot answer with confidence.

The whole history of real communism has hitherto been presented in the form of ideological falsification (in one way or another) and a system of prejudices. There is no need to say what shape the teaching of the communist social system had in Soviet ideology. It was detested and with reason.

Critical and muckraking sociopolitical literature and publicistics claimed to provide the only true understanding. But even they did not overstep the limits of ideological thinking. Critical attitude posed as truth. The harsher the criticism of anything Soviet, the truer it seemed or was intentionally treated.

In the West, the situation was no better. While formally the work of Western authors appeared more scientific than those of Soviet authors, they were nonetheless no closer to the truth. While Soviet ideology feared indicating the inherence of the shortcomings of real communism, Western ideology was afraid to recognize its merits. An apologetically false image of communism was built on one side, while on the other was a hypercritical false image. For example, Soviet ideology claimed that Soviet society was built according to the grand designs of "scientific communism" composed by Marx, Engels, and Lenin. Western ideology claimed that the nonsensical Utopian ideal of foolish Marx and bloodthirsty Lenin underlay Soviet societal organization. Soviet ideology held that communist social relations began to be formed only after the socialist revolution, while Western ideology held that those relations were imposed on the Soviet population by force and by fraud after the revolution. This parallelism could be seen in virtually all the most important issues concerning the understanding of Soviet society and the real communism in general.

Communist society is the social organization of a great number of people into a unified whole, not an artificially invented political regime. In the former Soviet Union, it was formed as a result of effective and objective social laws rather than according to Marxist design or by the will of Marxist ideologists. The people who built it either did not have a clue about Marxism or knew its doctrines rather vaguely and interpreted it in their own peculiar way. What finally resulted hardly looked like the Marxist blueprint, only in some aspects and in a rather strained interpretation. In reality, true communism is no less a natural social organization than any other social system, including that of the West.

It is customary to assume that everything that happened over the past decade to the Soviet Union and to the countries of the Soviet bloc prove the bankruptcy of the communist social system (real communism) and the advantages of the capitalist system. This is subject to dispute. The defeat of the socialist states was determined by a complex interplay of causes, including a role played by the deficiencies of the communist system as well. But this does not prove the nonviability and bankruptcy of communism. Likewise, the victory of the capitalist West also has its own effective causes – among which a certain role was played by the merits of capitalism. But this does not prove the latter's superiority.

The victory of the West over the Soviet Union and its allies was not a victory of capitalism over communism. The Cold War was a war of specific nations and states rather than of abstract social systems. Any number of examples can be supplied which, if one wants, can be interpreted as a proof of the superiority of communism over capitalism, for example: the super-rapid industrialization of the Soviet Union in the 1930s, the restructuring of the industry during the war with Germany and the victory over it, unprecedented advances in culture and education, guarantees of basic vital needs (employment, education, health care, *etc.*) and so on. In fact, it was the merits of the Soviet social system that engendered anxiety in the West, since they provided an attractive example for many people of the world.

From a historical perspective, real communist society existed too briefly to draw categorical conclusions about its bankruptcy. It also existed in extremely inauspicious conditions. To draw a conclusion about who beat whom — capitalism or communism — it is necessary that the adversaries be at least roughly equal in everything except the social system. In reality nothing of the kind existed. The West excelled the Soviet Union in all respects, including historical experience, accumulated wealth, human abilities and human resources in general, economic strength, level of technology, *etc.* What is surprising is not the fact that the Soviet Union was eventually defeated by the West in the Cold War but that it managed to survive World War II and hold out so long in a cold war which was beyond the strength of its people. And it could have stood firm for some time if the leadership of its country had not committed treason on a scale unprecedented in human history.

Developments in the years after the end of the Cold War showed that understanding the essence of the previous period's historical process as a struggle between two social systems — capitalism and communism — was superficial and in the final analysis erroneous. Here a historical form was mistaken for the essence of the process. In fact, it was the struggle of the West for the world domination against an adversary that blocked its way and laid its own claims to world leadership. The communist system in the Soviet Union and other countries was not the source of global confrontation; it was only a means of self-defense from Western global ambitions. The socialist states themselves launched offensives too, and these countries were perceived by the West not only as a military threat but also as a competitor in organizing all basic aspects of social life and for influence over the rest of mankind. Communism became the major object for attacks by the West because the world resisting and even attacking it had assumed a communist form. This world could resist and even from time to time win only in such a form. In those years the West's struggle against communism enabled it to justify anything it did anywhere on earth. The defeat of the communist states in the Cold War, their disintegration and downfall, and the bankruptcy of the communist systems in them unmasked the West's true intentions and its ideological and psychological stimuli.

The communist world, represented by the Soviet Union and its satellites, suffered a severe historical defeat. But this does not mean that communism has been done away with forever. Communist China is still around. The West would have to make a titanic effort to do to it something similar to what has been done to Yugoslavia, Eastern Europe, and the Soviet Union; and in the former communist states history has neither stopped nor rendered its final verdict.

The postcommunist epoch began with a euphoria occasioned by the collapse of the Soviet Union, the Soviet bloc, and the communist regimes in these countries. It began everywhere, not just in the West, where this moment had been prepared and longed for nearly half a century, but also in the communist states themselves, where people had long envied the West's propagandized seeming abundance of material and cultural wealth and were ecstatic at the sight of their countries being turned into flea-markets of Western junk and Western-encouraged scenes of license. Now the euphoria is over. The former communist states have witnessed not concord and confidence in a better future, as was expected, but quite the opposite — despondency, confusion, fear of an even worse future. And in the West the situation is no better in this respect. There, too, troubled anxiety is still felt that something unplanned and undesirable has happened. Gone or at least reduced to wretchedness is something Western people considered the source of all the world's ills and which gave them grounds to think that they were living in something approaching paradise. A general decline in business activity, the growth of unemployment, higher cost of living and taxes, and other unpleasant things automatically give rise to the suspicion whether or not this is the cost of the victory over communism; and if this be so, whether it was it worth it.

Although communism, which had once longed for its imposition upon all mankind, has suffered a severe defeat, the verdict of history is still out. However much anticommunists attempted to identify communism with the national-socialism of Hitler's Germany, the world community has accepted the comparison rather unenthusiastically. Too brutal was the falsification of real history. Indicative in this respect is the situation in Germany, where anticommunist hysteria still persists. For it is zealously being reinforced by the punishment of not only odious figures but of ordinary citizens somehow connected with the old regime. This farce could not hide the hard consequences of the process of introducing East Germany to the blessings of Western civilization, hard not only for East Germans but also for their western compatriots.

The most important results of the communist world's defeat is the idea of a "new world order" after Western patterns and under the West's aegis. This quite openly ignores the fact that the Western social, economic, and political system is not a universal blessing for all mankind. The capitalist system has produced positive results for only a small segment of mankind – namely for the peoples of Western countries. For the overwhelming majority of nations in the world it was and is alien. The people of Russia are no exception to this. When the Gorbachev (and later Yeltsin) reforms were enacted, the prerequisites were lacking for the economic, social, and political transformation of society along the Western lines, *i.e.,* the premises of capitalism and democracy. A need for such transformation had not evolved in a broad strata of the population, nor were these strata prepared to adopt these changes as the way to achieve a normal mode of life. The ideas of such reforms originated with the top leadership, that is, in the top echelons of the Communist party apparatus and ideological elite. They also originated under the influence and even pressure from the West. In other words, the ideas of change came from above and outside rather than from below and within the society, as a reflection of the inner evolution of Soviet society. Furthermore, they began to be implemented as violent reforms from above, by orders of superiors which was alien to the nature and capabilities of Soviet society.

In Russia a situation arose which was directly opposite to the one which had arisen during the formation of the Western social and political system. Western bourgeois revolutions resulted in the creation of political institutions and in legislative codification of already existing social and economic relations. However, the Soviet revolution of 1985-1991 began on the initiative of the top few in the communist leadership, who used all the might of the state, communist administrative methods, and the modern media of ideological mass indoctrination to impose their will on the usually obedient society.

The results of this revolution were not long in coming. Russia's ruling circles witnessed the bankruptcy of everything they tried to create in this new social order. They succeeded only in demolishing everything that had been created through the efforts of many generations of Russian people under extremely difficult historical conditions.

Ordinary Russians felt that in rejecting communism they lost many of the good things in life; while on the way to Westernization they have found only the evils of capitalism and democracy. They are still not aware of their having run into a historical trap, voluntarily. But sooner or later they will be forced to realize it.

After the utter rout of the Soviet Union in the Cold War, the world witnessed a situation similar to that which had occurred in Europe after the defeat of Napoleonic France, namely, a state of world reaction. In the current case it has assumed the form of a malicious and vengeful anticommunist theme. So, then, the epoch that has been ushered in may well be called an "anticommunist" one.

The whole Cold War was fought under slogans of "struggle for human rights" and "democratic freedom." One of the most crucial results of the fall of the communist "regimes" was that these rights and freedoms lost their earlier significance. What is the point? That the former communist countries enjoyed relatively high living standards. People were not hungry; they had jobs. Their basic vital needs were met, with guarantees at that. It was thought that they did not enjoy human rights and democratic freedoms, which Western propaganda portrayed as the highest values of human existence. Initially, it seemed to the citizens of communist countries that they might keep all the benefits they had, while adding to them the benefits of Western democracy – like human rights and democratic freedoms. But with the collapse of the communist system they have lost everything they had earlier. They experienced economic dislocation, inflation, the falling apart of the educational and cultural system, ideological chaos, moral degradation, and rising crime. Major problems have become how to survive under human rights and democratic freedom. Under such conditions, these values of democracy have simply lost any practical sense.

In the West the idea of human rights and democratic freedoms have been pushed into the background as well. As instruments of ideology and propaganda they have become worthless. They have been replaced by economic deterioration, rising cost of living, rising unemployment, rising taxes, and so on. The mass media have tried to hush up everything related to violations of human rights and democratic freedoms. The demand for such an ideological commodity has declined sharply.

The epoch that has set in is postcommunist. But the main feature of a historical era is not what it has done away with, but what it has brought. From this standpoint, the present epoch might just as well be called "post-democratic."

§7. Nihilism as a Foundation of the Postcommunist Type of Social Experience

It is difficult to understand the intricate plots of postcommunism without understanding one very important circumstance: we live in a realm of radical nihilism. Even seventy years' rule of the Bolshevik religion could not annihilate the main historical sense of the October *coup-d'état* of 1917, which first of all manifested itself in the fact that the reappraisal of values proclaimed by Nietzsche at the end of the nineteenth century passed from the sphere of academic discussion into political practice, incarnated in the flesh and blood of the state called the USSR. It is sufficient here to remember the rhythmically recited rewritings of the history and the kaleidoscopic change of banners under which the political purges and mass repression were carried out. In the womb of social consciousness (at least beginning from the French Revolution) the ancient sense of what is criminal gradually became insipid. It was lost in the mass crimes which, to a great extent, characterized mass movements. Law was supplanted by mystically understood historical expediency. Anything that contradicted the historical progression personified by the mass movements was considered a crime. Anything that promoted mass movements was considered to be the highest political truth. Thus the notion of expediency was transformed into a notion of truth.

In a paradoxical way the fusion of the prophetism and positivist religion, which became the vulgarized theoretical base of the Marxist *coup-d'état* in the Russian Empire, made absurd even the very will to construct political life on the basis of truth.

Strictly speaking, expediency itself laid the foundation of the new radical nihilism. That is why we cannot but agree with Gianni Vattimo who says that nihilism today is the final transformation of the value paradigm of usage into the value paradigm of change. The paradigm of usage presupposes first of all defining a measure of value by way of correlating an ideal and real object with the "true" nature of things. This frame of reference can be traced back to the Platonic concept of primordial ideas or *eidos*. The value of usage is conditioned by one or another technology (either the technology of transforming stone into a statue or the social technology of cultivating a loyal citizen). In its turn, the technology gives birth to the habit and makes things necessary. The technology supplants *eidos*, assumes its own sacral force and thus sanctifies itself. But Plato's dialog as genre personification of his theory of primordial ideas had already contained in itself the destroying germ for whole metaphysical basis of truth and thus also for value relativism as well as the groundless rationality which were the foundation of the so-called paradigm of "change."

This paradigm meant that value is created only in the process, in the very act of communication. The communication leans upon what Nietzsche called *resentiment, i.e.*, the spirit of furious competition and revenge and thus constitutes the metaphysical background of the authentic world. In this respect, if we recall Plato's dialog, the procedure of obtaining knowledge is at the same time a procedure of power realization.

Among other things, the Platonic tradition of dialog creates the culturo-historical premises for the specific phenomena of social life. J. Baudrillard calls them simulacra or generalized prostitution. For example, "Ukraine is a founder of the UN" and so-called *détente*. The first simulacrum served for the military and political compromise between Stalin and his allies on the basis of the game-rules elaborated within the confines of international law. The second was aimed at access to Western technology in exchange for promises to liberalize Soviet regime.

The very tradition that came out of Plato's dialog and flourished in Hegel's dialectical scholasticism found its most vivid reflection in the ideological practice of the Bolshevik regime. To a great extent this may provide a key to understanding the nature of the social chimeras which were inherited by postcommunist structures from the old regime.

In Plato's Republic there is a wish to build an ideal model of social structure that could transform some of its activities or some types of human being into a stepping stone to absolute social expediency.

In Plato's imagination the types of human beings that dominate during the various periods of political development (the oligarchic, democratic, or tyrannical person) are only steps of social imperfection and incompleteness. The philosopher, described first and foremost as ruler is presented by Plato as a universal alternative to these types of human beings. He acts not only rationally but also on the basis of teleological projection.

Who is this Philosopher? Who is this Ruler? Any definition of modern philosophy would be sufficient to describe his essential characteristics. He is neither analyst, modest therapist of language in the positivistic sense, nor an authoritarian prophet of Being. He is rather a priest of the Idea, the central protagonist of the totalitarian regimes in the twentieth century.

Thus, one can conclude that rationality of the social order, with Plato's Philosopher as guarantor, has a genuinely repressive character. Its peculiarity is that, namely, the ideal objects, *i.e.*, the projected human figures and strata of the perfect state, appear to be among the first to become the objects of rational-repressive influence. Fear and force expose the incompleteness of the eidetic model of state structure, the necessity to technologically process, *i.e.*, to install it in order to support the artificial idea in the state of real existence. The social technology that engenders habit or "usage," plays the role of a nonfundamental, rootless rationality and lays the foundation for nihilism. Thus one can say that the "value" of "usage" contains in its germ the value of "change."

This, in particular, is also witnessed by Plato's dialog. The issue here is the introduction into the dialog's structure of a conditional interlocutor, who only plays coryphaeus in the development of Plato's thought. The conditional interlocutor also symbolizes one of the major features of social communication at large, the presence of a will to power in any communicative act and thus the will to raise an objection to another person, to level him and to make the "exchange" inequivalent.

The imitation of a partner in a Plato's dialog also creates a prototype of what can be called "the institutionalization of truth." The very notion of the truth is supposed to create certain ideation of reality and then to carry out *Weltanschaung*-based judgment.

The priestly state, the contours of which Plato outlined, required parajuridical procedures, which regulate such a ruling, leadership role of the idea. Simultaneously different social institutions arise to support the truth. Finally, the institutionalization of truth at its core is a method of transforming a human being into a genuine object of manipulation or, as Plato would have it, of preparation for war.

With the spread of the reign of priestly truth and the consolidation of the totalitarian state structure, the prototype of which is given in Plato's dialog, the zone of the sanctioned contradictions (which always govern everyday human life) is narrowed.

The institutionalization of truth in the Platonic-Marxist tradition embodies a distinct externally-directed nihilism which fosters the creation of a totalitarian-type social structure and simultaneously negates it while transforming it into simulacrum. It may be said that the whole state becomes a simulacrum, and backstage from it there is a strange society, a society of chimeras, inexpressive, viscous, ironic, and agnostic.

Thus it happened that precisely this externally directed nihilism destroyed the very possibility of a rational grounding of power, the type of legitimation that was connected with the institutionalization of truth. This also conditioned the crisis of paternalism as the only possible "model" which totalitarian states retain from the past and which it could not annihilate totally because of its own incompleteness and imperfection. This is precisely why the coryphaeus still remains in the driver's seat in social activity today. The pseudo-revolution of 1991 was marked by this label and created two simulacra, Yeltsin on the tank and Gorbachev "imprisoned" in front of the TV-camera.

The possibility for radical liberalization and for the introduction of full-value democratic institutions after the sudden crash of the communist system in August 1991 failed to materialize is because the paradigm "usage" still remained dominant in all spheres of social life. Democracy, which in its core presupposes a permanent reevaluation of values and is based on what must be called the rationality of ungroundedness was presented as a "glimpsed" ideal. Instead of destroying the cult of history, a new struggle for history resulted in a new restoration of the ghosts of the recent past and their heroization. The paradigm of "usage" in the process of strengthening the new post-Soviet states acquires the forms of the nationalist world-view and the ideology of nationalism.

Nationalism and the Legitimation of Postcommunist Regimes

§1. *Culture as a Political Phenomenon of Postcommunism*

Culture as a political problem is a true historical discovery of the period of perestroika and postcommunist social transformations.

In their time, Soviet ideologists often abused the notion of culture which still remained, in fact, completely alien to people and their everyday practice. The Marxist ideological paradigm accustomed them to understanding culture as a domain and a specific creative affair of the intellectual, artistic, and power elites, as a spiritual field of "lofty" models of the "dignified life" isolated from drab routine. This is also true of the supervised cultivation of models of Ukrainian ethno-national culture (poetry, *belles lettres,* arts, music, and language) and, of course, the national artistic and humanitarian elite.

Today the problem of culture is virtually everybody's at the level of the daily self-affirmation of the individual – from a Ukrainian in central Ukraine or a Russian-speaking native of eastern Ukraine who feel their difference from the western Ukrainian of Galicia who is most confident in his authenticity and in his right to be a national culture leader. Perhaps it is just these geo-cultural differences, this cultural regionalism, that are most often exploited to their own advantage in present-day politics by politicians.

During the first years of Ukraine's independence, national culture and ethnocultural differences have taken on a far greater socio-political significance than economic issues. The slogan of national culture policy-making in the postcommunist period is being chanted along with the slogans of democratizing society, liberalizing it, and introducing market economy structures.

This is no accident. The crux of the issue is that the main active factor lending legitimacy to the political power and the transformation of the political order as a whole in Ukraine today was and remains the cultural sphere.

§2. The National Cultural Idea and the Legitimation of the Contemporary Ukrainian State

The legitimacy of power means that most of the population accept a given political regime and system as right and lawful. Legitimacy is ultimately the public recognition of the structure and institutions of power.

As long as the current political system is oriented to democratic foundations and norms for managing social life (through free elections, referenda, freedom of speech, and an independent press), problems of legitimacy will always arise. Within the framework of our national-democratic oriented political system (at least, according to social transformations theory), the idea of the national rebirth and cultural identity of Ukrainian society provides an actual foundation for legitimacy in Ukraine. Thus, it was the constant championing of national-cultural self-determination of the Ukrainian nation that distinguished the program platform of one of the most active, popular, and influential political forces of the perestroika period – *Rukh.* It is no coincidence that practically all the provisions pertaining to nationalist issues and the necessity to develop Ukrainian culture (see section "Culture. Language. Science"), spelled out in *Rukh's* First Program, are in wide political circulation today, including the new authorities' political glossary.

As new political systems encounter more and more problems, however, the concept of culture as the basis of national-cultural revival eventually loses its original legitimizing force. The political weakening of ***Rukh,*** with its reputation staked upon nationalist issues, which were presented as "the foundation for the existence and progress of the Ukrainian nation," is indicative of the political limitations to the concept of culture solely in terms of conservative ideals of national-cultural revival and originality.

§3. The Conservative and Democratic Content of the Idea of National Cultural Revival

Postcommunist political power in Ukraine ideologically exploits only the conservative side of the idea of national cultural revival. In the form of its political action, this side shows itself as predominantly ideational (officials' ritualistic attendance of cultural festivities, concerts, and performances) and ideological (fixed in the power structure's rhetoric in programmatic documents) support of cultural movements and initiatives aimed at the renewal, elucidation, and interpretation of a mass of customary, traditional, and ethnographic/folkloric forms of cultural life. In this context the notion of conservatism does not mean the wholly positive conserving cultural traditions as a unique way of preserving a national treasure. It means the political conservatism in the authorities' attitude to the cultural sphere, that is, the strengthening of the primary legitimizing function of the idea of a revived national culture, which is still inadequately developed under the truly democratic conditions. This conservatism perpetually tends towards cultural self-isolation, followed by economic and political isolation.

During perestroika, the idea of returning to the historical foundations of Ukrainian life was perceived by many as the basis for national existence, as the ultimate underpinning of Ukraine's rights to independence (including economic independence), distinctiveness, development, and direct participation in the global affairs of humanity without intermediaries. The disintegration of the Soviet Union did not occur according to the formulae of economic determinism. The decomposition of its monolithic social structure did not follow the fault lines dividing economically self-sufficient regions. On the contrary, the division took into account national and territorial borders between cultural worlds which had arisen over the course of time. This means that the national cultural idea encompasses not simply the conservative meaning of recreating history. When developed, it is not only a basis for the geopolitical separation of a nation but holds within itself the meaning of a natural basis for the open, democratic competition of various systems of social and cultural values. If we take as an example the contemporary Western European democracies, cultural identity loses its conservative attitude with regard to reviving national cultural. National features of cultural life are viewed as something self-evident, something that exist without making special political efforts to conserve and reproduce them. As to the main basis for the legitimation of power, it is found in the political systems and power structure.

The single national democratic nature of social transformations in Ukraine, however, gives no reason to be guided by any one political interpretation of culture, be it conservative or democratic. The real contradiction in the contemporary political elite's attitude to culture may be described as either giving priority to the conservative content of culture at the expense of limiting the democratic transformation in society, or stressing the democratic meaning of cultural identity as a formal precondition for organizing modern society and, consequently, inevitably losing the public support which was generated during the perestroika period. This may be seen, for example, in Ukraine's legislative and executive branches. Higher echelons of legislative power tend to cultivate the conservative aspect of culture more often, whereas, in cases when executive power is confronted with the necessity to interpret the idea of national cultural independence in democratic terms (for example, because it is being treated by the prospect of losing needed economic links with the other regions of former Soviet Union), it is often disposed to stress the formal interpretation of cultural uniqueness.

§4. The Idea of "Scientific Nationalism" in Postcommunist Political Literature

In Autumn 1993 the Ministry of Education of Ukraine sent out a letter of instruction with a syllabus of a new course, scientific nationalism, to institutions of higher education. The syllabus began by expanding upon the urgent need to restore to Ukraine its scientifically understood political history — the study of Ukrainian political life, history, and political thought. But soon this indisputable thesis took a somewhat different turn. The authors of the letter maintain that "so-called general political science," which had been created "largely by the West," lacks a clearly defined research object. Rather, it was seen only as a series of "abstract theoretical claims which, at best, can be useful as a certain universal political vision thereby constituting a general part of national political science." This latter was named "scientific nationalism" as a recognized academic discipline.[8]

But this undoubtedly testifies to the fact that the authors of this new syllabus in Ukrainian political science did not confine themselves to a traditional approach to the study of politics, its history and present state, whereby political processes themselves become objects to be understood by the social sciences. In the syllabus introduced by the Ministry of Education, Ukrainian nationalism itself, as well as its outlook and ideology, are regarded as a science (*i.e.*, as a scientific theory).

In other words, the authors held that Ukrainian nationalism itself can serve as a theoretical basis of political science, that it can represent by itself a particular methodology of scholarly comprehension of all possible political processes. "The Ukrainian national bias as scientific objectivity" is how the authors worded it.[9]

Making the idea of "scientific nationalism" public among broad circles of the national academic community implied that behind it was the most alarming theoretical confusion and muddled political thinking among Ukraine's intellectual elite.

The crux of the issue is that "scientific nationalism" is opposed to the previously dominant ideology of "scientific communism," which was also taught doctrinally and universally in all Soviet institutions of higher education. But at the same time this new idea is equally opposed to the system of liberal-democratic values (and consequently to prevailing Western political conceptions of social development which are oriented towards universal human values) as was "scientific communism." In the context of the collapse of the communist empire, the theoretical distancing from Marxist ideology can be regarded as altogether reasonable, and the antidemocratic theme of "scientific nationalism" remained, of course, in the background. But its ideological sources can be clearly understood as turning to the classic texts of Ukrainian integral nationalism, developed in the 1920s-1930s within the general trend of militant, exclusivist nationalist authoritarianism popular in Europe at that time. The most lapidary of these sources charged in 1940 that "a nationalist fights all other false theories down to their extermination," including "Marxism, international socialism, (and)... liberalism" which were "invented by enemies in order to corrupt and weaken the nation, and then hand it over to the tender mercies of alien plunderers."[10]

Thus, intentionally or unintentionally, the concept of "scientific nationalism" is nothing more than a reflection of extant political efforts to define, pursue, and achieve a distinctively Ukrainian "third way" between the *Scylla* of Communism and the *Charybdis* of Western Liberalism, between the conservative values of Ukrainian life and the threat to traditional Ukrainianism from the nationally denigrating values of the modern civilization, between the lofty political objective of creating independent statehood and West European processes of the economic integration of nations on democratic principles. All these contradictions constitute real conflicts in Ukrainian political thought.

But in current political life, which is in a state of primary structuralization and incomplete ideological stratification, pursuits of an "individual" way exist, virtually, in the "creative potentiality" of the Ukrainian ruling and opposition elites. Likewise, the notion of "scientific nationalism" rashly suggested by some political scientists is, in fact, a sort of ideological mule wielded together from two antagonistic ideologies, communism and liberalism. Its theoretical fuzziness reflects the existing lack of clear vision characterizing of political movements in Ukraine today. That is why it makes sense to consider in greater detail the real meaning of the concept "scientific nationalism" in order to better understand the future.

The dissemination by state structures of a Ukrainian political science program containing the idea of "scientific nationalism" was no accident. The political basis of official propaganda of a national *Weltanschaung* in Ukraine — begins with a special emphasis on traditional values, a single common language and spiritual unity, and ends with the evaluation of all international developments and cultural phenomena in the world in light of the recognition and consolidation of the Ukrainian nation. Since the perestroika era the ideas and ideals of cultural separation and national self-determination have been viewed by many as identical to the general political slogan of national statehood, thereby serving as a prime factor in the wide recognition of national leaders. After the sweeping criticism of communist doctrine during the period of glasnost, that doctrine was replaced by a Ukrainian national idea that embraced all sorts of hopes for a better future, which could be built only on the basis of national and cultural unity. Its main elements were people's perception of the distinctiveness of their collective everyday life (in the marginal social situation of the collapse of the Soviet empire), their collective political experience of being different from other national communities of the former USSR (just as these other communities, in turn, differ from one another), and their understanding of the particular features of the interpersonal relations that existed on the territory of Ukraine, together with an act of political to national unity. It was only natural that in real politics, the accomplishment of such a general visions of the Ukrainian national idea by the new leaders gave prominence to certain features of classical Ukrainian integral nationalism of the interwar period.

In order to understand the objective factors leading to the merger of the ideals of national independence with integral nationalistic ideology in current political action, it must be noted that at a period of the ideological restructuring of political life, Ukraine was and continues to be very reluctant to discard the old dilapidated foundation of the command system of administration and management. Thus, overly rash efforts to implement national ideas and values for the sake of political legitimation assume the form of direct command, unofficial administrative interference, along with the total control characteristic of a totalitarian state.

There are many examples of this, beginning with the current economic policies towards the preservation of national self-isolation at the expense of profitability. But, most striking of them, given the lack of a clear political vision of how to restructure Ukraine economically (suffice it to recall how a former Prime-Minister, who is now President, once spoke about the need to decide what kind of social system Ukraine wants to build), can be found in cultural and artistic life.

Between 1991-1994 new "commissars" from Supreme Rada (Parliament) commissions on science and culture often attempted to impose their visions of society upon academics and other intellectuals, making use of typically Bolshevik methods of accusing those who think differently of ideological national sabotage and insufficient national loyalty. Current Ukrainian politics confirms an apt remark, based on experience, by the late Professor Ivan Lysiak-Rudnytzkyj, one of the leading thinkers of the postwar Ukrainian emigration, that "Ukrainian (integral) nationalism falls under the rubric of a totalitarian movement: it strives to subject the whole life of the Ukrainian people, in all its manifestations, to its influence... The nationalist movement does not confine itself to political objectives but also demands control over the cultural process."[11]

These attempts to directly shape societal life and control the cultural process in postcommunist Ukraine, proceeding from an ideological system not altogether different from the old communist, one provide prerequisites for understanding what this "scientific nationalism" was all about. The new proponents of integral nationalism wanted to preserve the same old policy of total interference in people's lives and use the same general methods which were employed by the adherents of scientific communism.

We use this latter notion without quotation marks deliberately because the Marxist vision of the historical process was oriented explicitly towards the norms and ideals of European scholarship and natural philosophy. Completing the so-called project of Enlightenment, Marxist ideology mandated total rational control over the organization of human life and a Utopia of perpetually managed social processes, which its authors believed was to rely on laws of human historical development discovered by reason. Today there are very few people who doubt that the historical experience of one-sixth of the world proved (by its own example) that it is impossible to organize a political regime on the basis of a classical theory of Enlightenment scienticism. Essentially, the concept of "scientific nationalism" is based on much the same ideals of subjecting the diversity of human life to ideological principles, "scientific" standardization, and overall control. But Marxism differs in certain basic ways from the integral nationalist notion of why it claims that its ideology is scientific.

One may be certain that the scholars who put forward the concept of "scientific nationalism" never read such authentic texts of Ukrainian integral nationalism as Dmytro Dontsov's. Likewise, the philosophical foundation of Ukrainian nationalism represented in well-known works of Schopenhauer, Nietzsche, Spengler, and Ortega-y-Gasset, has escaped their professional attention. The only thing clear is that the idea of "scientific nationalism" was made possible because of the striking coincidence of political style between old communist and new postcommunist power-holders favoring the active and violent molding of social and cultural life. But the latter are diametrically opposed to their predecessors in ideological and philosophical content.

This can be seen from a general definition of Ukrainian nationalism by any authoritative author of this ideology. In the concise work cited above, Tkachuk points out that "nationalistic ideology" is not "an artificially constructed theory (science)" but "a number of closely interrelated truths...on the basis of which develops life... and, hence, the nation's life."[12] In Dontsov, the general thesis of Ukrainian nationalism assumed central significance as the guiding idea which he propagated all his life, the idea of a basic difference of the nationalist outlook from the ideals of European Enlightenment in general and those of its successors – positivism, scientific socialism, and scientific materialism in particular. It was precisely for such scienticism that Dontsov subjects nearly all nineteenth century Ukrainophiles and Ukrainian democrats (beginning with Panteleimon Kulish and ending with Mykhailo Drahomanov and his numerous intellectual followers) to unsparing criticism, dubbing their efforts at popular education and pro-socialist orientation as "Ukrainian provincialism" (in that they lagged behind the European irrationalism fashionable during the flowering of the European fascist dictatorships). At nearly the same time, but proceeding from the opposite philosophical assumptions as E. Husserl in the first third of the twentieth century, Dontsov independently expounded upon the idea of crisis in European culture and European nations. (See: his *Natsionalizm*, Lviv, 1926; a more refined exposition of the idea can be found in *Where Should We Seek Our Historical Traditions*, Lviv, 1937, both in Ukrainian). Just like Husserl, he saw the cause of such a crisis in the European world-view in the ideals of Enlightenment and scientific Reason, *i.e.*, in its rationalism. But in contrast to the famous phenomenologist, the Ukrainian thinker came to opposite conclusions.

Dontsov argued that the crisis in Europe, which culminated in the outbreak of World War I in 1914, was a consequence of the maturation of national life worlds, that it was caused by the confrontation of national wills for self-affirmation, their struggle to win their own place in the world.

Basing himself exclusively on the latest modern philosophical tradition of his time, which called itself the philosophy of will, voluntarism, or irrationalism, Dontsov argued that the ultimate basis of human life, world view, and ideology is not rational consciousness but human will. For this reason he called his philosophy "voluntarist nationalism." Dontsov's idea of voluntarist nationalism is not fortuitous for the Ukrainian nationalistic movement as a whole. Under the rubric of this philosophical grounding, it constituted the central conclusion of classical Ukrainian integral nationalism.

Integral nationalism, in the sense in which it was historically established in the classics of Ukrainian nationalistic thought, is a system of "voluntaristic" truths as to the life of the nation. The philosophical concept of will or volition, is merely a general form of signifying a realistic attitude to the attainment of human wishes, desires, and aspirations. It may also be a reflection of the will to live, which is contained in all human feelings and experience and, which in its sources is not subject to rationality, but is motivated by all factors of human vital activity. Thus, for the Ukrainian nation, whose state of unrealized will for nationally existential self-affirmation is almost permanent, nationalism takes on real social sense as the will for its own culture and for independent statehood. But, just as volition and feeling cannot substitute for reason, so too nationalism is not in a position to carry out the functions of scientific knowledge and political theory.

Nationalism and nationalist ideology are not and cannot be a system of views that are based on the facts of consciousness and reason. Nationalism can be based only on an extra-scientific fact of volition, on the "national will" which is not related to any previous act of reason. "This will is the major feature of a nation and the crux of nationalist ideology."[13] Thus, nationalism cannot in any case be a science in its exact European sense. Our newly minted nationalists artificially invented or fantasized the concept of "scientific nationalism." Given their historical and philosophical primitivism, one might well refrain from arguing with them. But behind their idea of Ukrainian nationalist political science lurks the disorientation and real scholarly primitivism of the would-be politicians who would make (and are already making) use of such pseudo-scientific claims.

Martin Heidegger, reflecting on his own tragic experience under the domination of nationalist ideology and "German science," after the Second World War put forward the idea of the inherent "subjectivism of any nationalism" ("Letter on Humanism"). No one familiar with this great German's life and philosophical contribution would attempt to interpret this as a vulgar denial of the national idea or national existence. He meant genuine subjectivism, *i.e.*, the unwillingness or inability to face the realities of life which the nationally oriented consciousness acquires when it assumes the role of official ideology and scientific knowledge.

The point is that nationalism always falls prey to subjectivism, when, on the one hand it is unwilling and unable to address life as it really is, but rather rationalizes away the variegated nature of the actual national will and, on the other hand, when a certain group of people demand the imposition by force of their own nationalist world view in the guise of a rigidly rationalized "program," "methodology," or "ideology." This gives rise to a theoretical and political situation where private, partial, or one-party feelings, desires, wishes, and hopes, (*i.e.*, one-dimensional, inadequate, deficient, incomplete, and, thus, biased visions of social life) are presented as scientifically valid and indispensable "arguments," "proofs," "explanations," "explications," as a search for "laws of social development," *etc.* Historically, the direction and power of human will is changeable. Its codification in the guise of an official ideological discourse or pseudoscience of politics marks the triumph of political dogmatism, and this means that society is fated to political caprice and the demise of democracy in any form.

There is only one known way of being safe from the possible consequences of subjectivism that can be bound up with the transformation of national will into a pseudoscience of politics. In the context of our discussion this is to see the national idea or nationalist world view for what it is — the nation's will to national-cultural and national-political self-affirmation in all those regionally diversified and socially changeable forms, in which this will manifests itself in real life and political practice. This also suggests the ability to accept nationalism as an integral part of the Ukrainian political establishment, that is, as one of several established systems of views, thoughts, and slogans embraced by a certain group of people, movements, and parties, that is, within the context of democratic pluralism.

§5. The Idea of Democracy and Proto-Democracy

The sense of the culture and content of the democratic organization of society have many points in common, but they also differ greatly. While the postcommunist authorities and today's "instant" politicians make avid use of the former, they simply ignore or are in no hurry to notice the differences.

Aristotle gave the first general and simple definition of democracy. He understood democracy as the self-government of free and equal people,[14] *i.e.*, a social procedure whereby individuals freely and jointly determine what leaders they should elect and exactly what powers they are willing to give them. On what basis do they come to such an accord in selecting their rulers? For Aristotle, this problem is not one to be pondered over. For the "first democracies" such a consensus was ensured by common tradition and ethos, *i.e.*, generally accepted norms of life, the self-evident nature of cultural coexistence, *etc.*

However, for the modern forms of developed democratic systems the issue of social concord and the problem of civic consensus gain overriding importance. In other words, this is a question of on the basis of which program different, but politically equal, people can come to a social consensus. It is also a question of the legitimation of power, *i.e.*, the free recognition of the "leadership" by the majority of citizens.[15]

The sense and experience of most Ukrainian citizens that they differed existentially and culturally from other great communities of the former USSR led to them to opt for Ukrainian independence in a referendum. Not least important was the awareness of their own national-cultural differences (not to be confused with ethnocultural identity), which acquired legitimizing significance by their free recognition of their own Ukrainian state and the need for it to have an independent policy as expressed in the referendum of December 1, 1991. Ukraine's political independence, political order, and independent state can rise or fall according to whether or not it continues to recognize its own national-cultural solidarity and community. The awareness of national, cultural, or, if you like, geo-cultural community had assumed the quality of a proto-consensus necessary for Ukraine's proto-democratic self-determination as a full-fledged political entity on the map of the modern world.

The simplest and most general concept of culture is one of a phenomenon which unites us all into a single national — and beyond this, human — world. An ethno-national community is a network of relationships, social ties, and cultural consensus which are bequeathed to us by history and cultural tradition. Dontsov provides a more accurate term in this connection: the unity of the will of Ukrainian society, the unity of its volition for self-affirmation. But — and this is for us the most important point — an ethno-national community today, in the developed European world, with its present day economic ties, personal mobility, and great variety of information impacting upon it, etc. is far from ensured by tradition. At present, an ethno-national community cannot serve as the sole basis for the democratic consensus, for which many of our current politicians hope. The cultural regionalism of Ukraine bears conclusive witness to this undeniable fact. The current stage of Ukraine's social development gives every reason to define the situation as a proto-democratic one, as only the first step toward the realization of the idea of democracy.

In its origin, the idea of the democratic organization of society is inalienably linked with its prospects for overcoming national narrowness and interethnic conflict. The outstanding theoretician of civil society, secular ethics, and law, Immanuel Kant perceived "the general universal state as a prenatal chamber in which all elemental potentialities of the human race gradually become full-blown."[16] Indeed, the idea of democracy, just like the idea of justice, even with its appeal to the free accord of equal people cannot, in principle, be limited by the slogan "democracy only for one discrete community among other communities."

By arguing the universality of the democratic idea, Kant certainly did not foresee, for example, the specifics of the "denationalization" of, say, the Germans of East Prussia, but rather saw in civil society a necessary condition for achieving interethnic peace. Likewise, the goal of politically consolidating democracy today does not supplant other urgent issues of national-cultural revival. The issue is one of its modern contextual interpretation. A developed understanding of democracy goes much deeper than the simple inarticulate unity of a given ethnic stock.

"The inarticulate unity of ethnic stock," which at perestroika rallies seemed to give democratic consent to the expression of a common national will, can no longer suffice today, when it is necessary to go further in developing our model of political behavior. It can only serve, and now serves as a basis for the "new" nomenklatura, which came to power using slogans of "culture-making" to impose its partial, imperfect, narrow, and partisan vision of social and cultural phenomena. Thus, one part of the all-Ukrainian community, heterogeneous in its cultural and ethnocultural features, is placed in opposition to others.

All theories of developed democracy maintain that it is based not simply on natural ethnic unity. The basis of democracy lies in a developed public dialog (communication) of representatives of various political orientations. Such communicative acts can in no case be limited to a blind and dumb national-cultural identity. True national identity itself is merely a developed outcome of historical connections, a result of rational argumentative communication[17] among representatives of a single political nation which can be composed of various national and other subcultures.

The loudest appeals to the idea of democracy in post-communist Ukraine can often be heard from politicians who view the social significance of their parties and movements from the "national-democratic" perspective. However, both practical abidance by that self-designation and political understanding of social goals in the notion of "national democracy" are fraught with a real threat of an "eternal coming back to the same" (Nietzsche): an incessant admiration for proto-democratic features of Ukrainian community and, hence, political narcissism and constant repetition of outdated romantic slogans taken from the period of miraculous national liberation.

In this context the critical analysis of language and modes of understanding is of great importance, for they form the semantic culture of postcommunist discourse and are consciously or unconsciously utilized by the new regime as its primary public means of self-legitimation.

Political Discourse* in Mass Communications

§1. Special Features of Political Discourse in the Transition Period

The state's domination over all spheres of life, in other words, the substitution for the public sphere by the institutionally organized acting on the basis of different types of compulsion is expressed on various levels. But the impossibility of total control, typical of the old regime, makes possible the spontaneous creation of discursive practices of criminal character: "The agreement" is made according to the conventions of discourse formed by those of the criminal world and those of traditional, pre-civilized societies.

From this standpoint, the self-structuralization of discursive practices represented by the mass media takes place. Traditionally mass media in democratic society (newspapers, radio, and television) is a correlate of civil society. Mass information is easily identified with one or another of its sectors. But in the postcommunist states we are dealing with peculiar hermetic conventions which reflect the special zones of non-transparency which have appeared in society. This is precisely why the language of newspapers, its stereotypes

* The notion of *discourse* is used here in the broadest sense possible as the fundamental condition for the verbal structuralization of a communicative act (including a political one) based on the will to power. At the same time *discourse* lays the foundation for the practical establishment of a communicative reality (including a political one) according to the power intentions of this act.

and clichés, which have become so widespread in the so-called transition period, are the most expressive articulations of the non-structured (non-civil) postcommunist society with its strange agglomerations. A spontaneous manifestation of latent aggression and plethora of metaphors in political texts now call attention to themselves. Aggression points to the priority of coercion and intimidation, the heritage of the totalitarian state, while metaphor points to the lack of responsibility and "discursiveness" in the civil dialogue. Metaphor touches the unconsciousness mechanisms that function in the extra-linguistic realm and causes affects which undermine normal discursive practice.

In a paradoxical sense the press, the media of mass information, which create the infrastructure and thus the whole field of discursive practices, are thus transformed into their opposite. Instead of preventing conflicts by people in areas of total transparency with the help of social thought (Michel Foucault) they increase and preserve inexpressive paleo-symbolic speech simultaneously with the increase of various stereotypes and party jargons. Here we see the manipulative nature of the public word which is typical to the totalitarian regimes. The types of rationality which ruled the USSR and values orientation system of the old regime have transformed discourse into a "clinical" monologism. Political decisions and economic activities were turned into instrumentalities of propaganda. The postcommunist period has witnessed the simulation of democratic rule: without any direct relationship to real power, the individual has at the same time acquired total responsibility for the efficacy of state functions. The moral double standards characteristic of Soviet consciousness and its internal censorship complex have become pervasive. Only totems and taboo change.

Thus it is difficult to speak of political discourse as such in the so-called "transition" period. The path to discursive democracy as a source of legitimacy for the institutions of modern civilized society is complicated by the fact that the social dialog in postcommunist states is still greatly perverted by the traditions of totalitarian newspeak, which has produced a widespread type of verbal behavior whereby the articulation of meaning is substituted for the social dialog by aggregates of compulsion and special conventions. This is why the view that discourse as a medium, with the assistance of which individual and collective rationalities come together, simply does not work in the particular conditions which have come about after the collapse of communist ideology. The interests, needs, and dreams of postcommunist "wild man" cannot be understood and interpreted in the light of discursive practice. They are endowed with meaning in the sphere of nonpolitical reality.

The methodology used by Michel Foucault in his doctoral dissertation, "The History of Madness in the Classical Age," can be quite effective in analyzing discursive practice under postcommunism. A key term in his work is "delirium," and here language constitutes the initial and final structure of folly. If we understand democratic discourse as an ethic of dialog, then delirium always indicates the violation of this ethic and the potential for falling into a state of affect. This may be expressed on a verbal level by irony, silence, the reign of stereotypes, metaphoric talks, or hidden and open threats. In the postcommunist socium, mutual understanding and dialog are substituted by the affects of tyranny. From this point of view it becomes difficult to even speak of democratic discourse because its very basis is rendered unstable, mobile, and vulnerable. It was after the Bolshevik *coup d'état* of 1917 and consequent sociocide that the institutions of civil society were ultimately destroyed and the basis for an ethic of dialog disappeared, pushed out by everyday rituals of loyalty.

The renewal of political discourse came about mainly as the result of *perestroika* and was not of any organic development of the institutions of civil society and thus of language. This was a direct consequence of how the repressive and manipulative character of the whole system by which man was drawn into social life, the result of his having long existed in a realm of *propaganda,* pervaded by compulsion. The collapse of this realm creates a chain of contradictions on the level of political dialog. Today many employ political rhetoric but they are unable to adequately use specialized economic, political, and philosophical terminology due to their occupation, life experience, and, above all, their economic unfreedom. To some extent such verbal activity is a result of the ideology of equality, decrepit illusions about social classes, and thus the idea of the superiority of manual laborers. It is also the product of the attainment of universal literacy in a broad sense.

But, of course, we mean here not only professional responsibilities. Any type of society has its, so to speak, gnosiological ardor. The each of consciously realized ultimate aim on the individuality level, the communist ideology supertask orientation destroyed normal political discourse and brought into it almost unalterable units. A sort of closed circle appeared such that the lack of institutional tradition of civil society prevented the formation of democratic discourse and the democratic institutions of a normal civil society. Thus faith in saving competition or market pricing looks illusive. Competition without rules of institutional ethics and culture degenerates into the competition of criminal structures and the mass dissemination of falsehoods.

The factors of political language, speech, communication, and discourse are becoming cornerstones of politics in the postcommunist period. The future Ukraine is maturing through communication. "What kind of society do we want to build?" was persistently asked by the former Prime Minister and now newly elected President Leonid Kuchma. This strategic question cannot be answered *a priori,* in advance. Such an important choice of a political future, the choice of Aristotle's "good life," must be legitimized in political discourse and all its real social manifestations.

There is a certain psychological complacency in being aware of participating in something much more progressive (*i.e.*, market economy, democracy, reform of the political system) than it was before. But this gives no reason for complacency, for dreams of the future do not guarantee automatic progress. Western experience proves that the future depends on the degree of our handling of today's situation on the level of political discourse. For we have witnessed a fundamental shift in the terms of reference in political strategy — *i.e.*, a transition from the silent manifestation of power to political discourse, by and through which politics is actually conducted.

Hence, political values are not just reappraised in the head of a political scientist or a practical politician. The reappraisal of basic values is something we all experience. That the common people are actively involved in political discourse is evidenced, for example, by the rather heavy voter turnout in Ukraine's most recent parliamentary elections. The overwhelming majority of us have assumed the qualities of a *political animal,* that is, of an individual who (one way or another) feels that his everyday life is dependent on political developments at various echelons of power, on the course of economic reforms, and who understands the long-term connection of his own future with that of the state as a whole. This involvement in a real political process leads to the formation of communicative competence or civic maturity, when "mass man" begins to bear a conscious responsibility for his own political choice and, hence, actions of social significance. Those who are still silent, "unconscious," in "the period of political discourse" provoke a new wave of social infantilism, which favor certain charismatic authoritarian-type leaders. Therefore, for us, the uneasy task of learning to speak has become indispensable.

Present-day political life in Ukraine has given urgency to the meaning of the political word. It essentially changes the system of requirements for a politician, each member of society and the whole situation. A politician has to know how to express in easy-to-understand terms his ideas and, hence, the political will of the community he leads; an enigmatic politician has no chance at all. This becomes the norm in a situation of political discourse, which requires revelation of hitherto hidden realms of thought thanks to the spoken word. Since the forced limitation of the horizons of thinking was based on ideology, glasnost politicized the whole of life. The word became a ray of light illuminating the darker sides of our existence. It is here that the enlightening role of political discourse lies. Immanuel Kant long ago defined the "state" as a condition of "resonating public consciousness".

This role of the word in politics has become historically obvious. However, the word cannot be merely reduced to a method to be mastered, for political discourse determines not only the boundaries of political thought but also the feasibility for political action. The deeper meaning of political discourse reveals itself only when it becomes clear that the word is not merely the bearer of a simple sum of facts and propositions. For linguistic discourse comprises various human volitions, desires, aspirations, *i.e.,* different "facts" of life, multi-directional practical prescriptions, as well as juxtaposing the various forms of human existence.

Everything we accept as fact is already our interpretation of the environment. Our language, especially political language, always contains an interpretation of the world, as well as covert and overt assessments of real and potential political phenomena. Political ideas and relationships of power find their expression in language. This is why political discourse predetermines the possible forms of political practice.

The degradation of political regimes and collapse of ideologies take place through degradation of the language. Ideological concepts influence our life by way of discourse. We still feel the influence of Soviet "newspeak."

Language defines the pretenses of politicians and simultaneously marks the boundaries of the will they represent through their own participation in the discourse. However, the old language cannot be done away with mechanistically. It should be narrowed in terms of discourse. Ideological patterns of Soviet "newspeak" must die in postcommunist discourse as unfit for an open society.

§2. The Monologism of the Will to Power as Political Legacy

To what extent does political discourse depend on a type of politics or an acquired political legacy? *Zoon politicon* falls into a public type of political life defined long ago by Aristotle, who believed that politics was constituted in discourse, and political life took place in the market place

— at the *agora.* Following the tradition of the ancient Greek *polis,* the modern notion of discourse means openness to public criticism and conceding to others the right to have a liberal attitude toward political life. It is only in this kind of public society that a human being can form himself and become an individual.

Our "agora" laid out only prefabricated ideas and ideologemes, while political will itself (*i.e.,* the will to power and the conflicting expressions of this will) took place in the quiet corridors of power — under both the imperial bureaucracy of tsarism and the communist bureaucracy of the command-administrative system. In the bygone days of our discourse, political action always took place away from publicity. The Aristotelian type of politics can be said to have been replaced here by the Machiavellian type, hidden and manipulative. Even the general definition of politics as "the relationship between people and power" represents precisely this political tradition. The notion of power is a necessary but not sufficient key to understanding this ideal type of politics and "pure" idea of the state. The ultimate goal of politics, in this view, consists in imposing one's own will upon all members of the socium by any and all means. Thus, it can be characterized as a voluntaristic type of politics.

Such a concept of politics has deep metaphysical roots, namely, the domination of what Martin Heidegger called "subjectivism" in a broad sense. Orientation toward the Enlightenment ideal of the lucid understanding of reality and history becomes primary. A statesman's greatness lies in his ability to understand and change the course of history. This conviction, for example, inspired Lenin to state without any doubt that "politics has its own objective logic, independent of how it is defined by any person or party." In other words, a subjectivist orientation to understanding the phenomenon of power leads to a complete leveling of political discourse and elimination of the institutions of civil society. To reduce the political role of the latter to a minimum was a deliberate educational and ideological objective of the communist regime. And this is why the development of conditions for political discourse can surely serve as a criterion for the approach of postcommunism.

What limits this type of voluntarist politics? It may be discerned by the boundary of its enhancement, that is, when the factor of will in politics runs into radical restrictions or stops functioning altogether. Will is limited by political discourse only when a politician begins to squeeze out of himself, not a silent slave but, a general, a revolutionary, a political commissar, or a leader as an immediate agent of political action. Moreover, this squeezing-out occurs, not only in real politics but also, in the reinterpretation of politically significant history and culture (*i.e.*, in terms of politics). Political discourse becomes actualized only when the skill at negotiation is more highly valued than a violent will.

§3. The Domination of Sacral Political Discourse

The forms of political discourse in Ukraine are essentially influenced by a traditional political type characterized by us as voluntarism *par excellence* and made sacred. Will as a manifestation of authority – its manipulative, behind-the-scenes, hidden nature – manifests itself primarily in the ability to negotiate, arrange, or somehow come to agreement with members of the ruling elite, party in power, "our people," *etc.* This political discourse of agreement, hidden from the public, may be considered dominant in certain types of society. It is a form of intra-political discourse. As to the forced expansion of political ideas into the outside world, it was carried out through a system of totalitarian ideological institutions merged with governmental bodies.

This type of political discourse is ostensibly oriented to reason and argument. However, the main indication of a politician's skill became his ability to come to an agreement, to conduct a kind of negotiations. Suffice it to recall the history of the former Soviet Union. After lifting ideological restrictions, a negotiating discourse emerged which has proved to be the most interesting in all political history. The pre-war negotiations (agreements) with Nazi Germany, the Yalta conference (also aimed at a certain redivision of Europe into spheres of influence), and particularly the debates and behind-the-scenes struggle in the leading echelons of the Communist Party – still attract the attention of experts and laymen to the secrets of its hidden influence on the destinies of millions of people. This kind of public exposure has become possible only in recent years, after such political discourse lost its sacral nature. However, this desacralization within the dominating discourse of agreement has had the greatest effect on political history. The discourse of modern politicians and bodies of authority largely remains closed and sanctified. This is a discourse of a sacral community still patterned on the Politburo. Despite proclamations of glasnost and omnipresent political talk, truly influential discourse remains an "internal" affair of politicians.

This negotiation type of political discourse prevails in the CIS countries; little wonder, if one bears in mind the "mysterious Russian soul" and the Byzantine-court traditions of Russia. Meanwhile, Ukraine, in the well-known words of Dmytro Dontsov, is still "of two minds" about East and West. The essence of the "European" (Western) orientation toward the negotiation type political discourse still dominant in Ukraine is its treatment of politics as a "procedure." By this we mean the bureaucratic regimentation of the negotiating process, multi-layered nature of negotiations, and the tremendous painstaking work of groups of experts who prepare agreements for signing at the summit level. The length and complexity of this process is vividly demonstrated by negotiating efforts in the former Yugoslavia.

A different picture is painted by the negotiation discourse between Ukraine and Russia. Suffice to consider the Massandra Summit between former Ukrainian President Kravchuk and Russian President Yeltsin on the Black Sea Fleet. Those negotiations showed that there was little need for institutional experts, for their work did not promote agreement. Only the summit meeting agreement between the highest officials made it possible to solve the problem. But this harmony was mere illusion. It turned out that it was technically impossible to implement the agreement because the experts had been ignored. This became apparent only *post factum.* In other words, there were many objective reasons why this negotiated settlement could not work. The point is that all such agreements, owing to their voluntaristic irrationality, are interpreted differently by the contracting parties. From the very outset, this creates great problems for the advisers, the "hermeneutists" of politics, and for the future consequences of unresolved political problems to the common people.

Political discourse evolves in this case like a mystical and sacralizing show. It brings a pervasive element of irrationality into politics. The above example is typical of Ukrainian politics. This is very dangerous when personal relationship, friendship or hostility, becomes the ultimate argument in politics, or when intimate sentiments decide the destinies of the state and citizen.

In this connection, political life itself serves as teacher. Recent elections have taught us many things. They showed that faith in political parties (institutions) and their leaders who sought to embrace a wide political spectrum was clearly insufficient. The idea that the electorate's interests were expressed by parties and party leaders has been undermined. The political struggle is now evolving into a political discourse which loses a great deal without duly taking into consideration the specifics of the political listener and without understanding his interests.

The ideal of an open society brings the problem of political discourse to the fore. Power no longer acts as a machine of repression. The very existence of a community and its institutions (above all, the state) largely depends on the way in which political communication evolves. In an open society this is characterized by the political significance acquired by the language of the Other. A realistic policy can not be confined solely to the implementation of even a seemingly ideal political project drawn up by monologue. No political and strategic (not to mention tactical) decision can be made forever and in advance. The choice of the best type of politics depends on the "yes" or "no" of other participants in political action. Politics is not limited to goal-oriented activity. As for the ideal type of politics, it becomes legitimized through communication and cannot be regulated outside political discourse, while the discursive form of politics, in its turn, determines its respective political content.

Open discourse makes it possible to join and enter into political dialog, while an open society fundamentally differs from a traditional one in the latter's communicatively limited quality. Under totalitarianism, civil society has no autonomy from the state. The state has only subjects, not citizens who can manifest their will in terms of discourse (*i.e.*, who could have the ability to freely express their ideas).

In an open society discourse stands at the center of politics. Concerning the reasonable lucidity of argumentation, we are not carried away with optimism. Different peoples choose different paths. The poet's words, "we do for ourselves," is a constant in politics. They have an ontological sense, illustrating the localness of cultural worlds. The significance of doxic views, beliefs, and guesses in political discourse is no less than in addressing universal Reason. But all the various institutions which safeguard political discourse cannot be extrarational because their sense and social role consists in the rationalization of the will to power.

The revival of the nation and making of a civil society are what determine our political life. Our political future depends on the degree of "cultural resonating publicity" (Jürgen Habermas) established in our country rather than on exploiting mythologemes, the "silent ground." Our national and cultural survival depends on the extent to which political power becomes the power of discourse.

To sum up, let us note that politics in modern society cannot be effected according to traditional formulae that only too often serve as classical models. Politics cannot be reduced to a manifestation of what is thought up, prepared, and calculated single-handedly. Politics has ceased to be the prerogative of prophets. It cannot be reduced to the realization of a political ideal, created monologically by either rational or extravagant means. Politics objectively exists externally – in the world and in political discourse – which is the means of its being.

Thus, as a means by which real subjects, fixed in time and space, act, politics cannot be completely liberated from the legacy of the past, which is fixed in the schematics and stereotypes of how the world, electorate, and politicians are depicted. It is tempting to formulate the requirements of contemporary political discourse by paying heed to the experience of the developed democracies. However, it must be recognized that it will continue to have many anachronistic characteristics and differ only externally from the political discourse of communist societies. Such is the case, as the following will serve to illustrate.

§4. The Sociopolitical Characteristics of Postcommunist Mass Media

The media of mass information is that social institution through which the political discourse of postcommunism first acquires real legitimating force. This is merely the slogan of glasnost with stimulated widespread use of the term *democracy* to denote post-Soviet phenomena which could hardly be considered democratic. However, in determining the level of democracy in a society, mass media is actually a prime indicator, criterion, or scale of measurement.

The point is that mass media by its essence is the best indicator of a democratically organized society. Under certain ideal conditions mass media in its methods of operation is merely the concentrated expression of the idea of open public discourse, a social institution organizing interpersonal dialog, and civil consensus. Naturally, we must also bear in mind its destructive potential (possible ideological brainwashing of the population, indoctrination of ideas and views in the regime's interest, *etc.*). Thus, in order to verify the idea of democracy in Ukraine and to better understand its prospects for the immediate and medium-term future, it is worth looking more closely into how the Ukrainian mass media operates.

To return to the essence of what is nowadays called the media of mass information, one can see from this designation itself that the point at issue is the modes of information distribution which serve as mediators of human communication in modern society. Traditionally, they are defined as means of conveying information flow from one person to another or from one group to another. In this case mass media are said to give information, *i.e.*, to "form internally" our consciousness. This is only half true.

The problem is that mass media itself mediates between people and actually forms the reality in which they live. Since the sociopolitical fabric of life is woven from human relationships, mass media touches the context of life with a certain additional awareness and fashionability, *i.e.*, it impacts upon the organization and modes of human relationships. The very fact of mass media news coverage, its choice of themes and interpretations, makes mass media a reality to be reckoned with.

Moreover, information has another important quality: it is never neutral or inert with respect to people, no matter how eloquently the opposite might be argued. In the mass media, information is always language, a speech act, even if in written form. When one speaks and fixes attention on an event or a person, by so doing, this seemingly innocent act of the mass dissemination of information generally affirms the speaker's understanding, vision, and will to power. This is precisely what mass media is: simultaneously a means to mass affirmation of a will to power, desires, expectations, and will. Thus, mass media is perceived as a power in its own right, as the Fifth Estate. Having information at one's disposal and controlling its dissemination is very close to having power and coercively molding other people's consciousness and existence. This was unmentioned during the total domination of communist ideology and the Communist Party press. There was only one power, one ideology, and one self-affirming will. Such homogeneity and reductionism in informing and interpreting information produced an impression that the mass media played an educating role. It seemed to fulfill an enlightening or informational function and thus seemed not to be an instrument of total control.

The present-day changes in the former socialist countries, including Ukraine, are called *postcommunist*. Here we should differentiate between two meanings of the term "postcommunist mass media." First, postcommunism is perceived, quite naturally, if somewhat inaccurately, as something "after communism." But, second, to be more exact, "after communism" comes first the ruin of the communist regime and totalitarianism, *i.e.*, the first thing which emerges is its criticism, negation, the ideological banishment of old forms of consciousness and psychology; and here mass media helps "deconstruct the model." Under so-called glasnost there was much ado about freedom of information, pluralism, *etc.* But, in fact, only one thing was meant – an opportunity to deconstruct the "communist model." Still, along with this laudable goal, the half-born, "new" old mass media came to be deformed by the same agency.

Martin Heidegger once aptly remarked that he who runs after will follow after. Or, to paraphrase, he who only ruins will himself be ruined. Lashing out at the "communist" or "nationalist" mind-sets as a way of institutionalizing the new mass media as a precondition of their "postcommunist" existence indicates only the persistence of totalitarian thinking, understanding, and information manipulation. It is precisely for this reason that in Ukraine numerous newspapers, magazines, radio and TV programs appeared and attempted to transform mass informing into an instrument to mentally impregnate people with new political and ideological stereotypes and, hence, to impose a framework of human relations which one or another political regime finds desirable.

Undoubtedly, this is not yet a real democratization of the mass media. All this is but a primitive ruination of the recent past and, unfortunately, ourselves, because by "postcommunism" one should understand not only a destruction of the old "model," not just a deformation of the information space and old forms of human relationships, but above all the dissemination of different views directed above all at the creation of radically new social interconnections and relationships rather than toward destroying or forming anew, violently, *i.e.*, in a neototalitarian way, some "new model."

A new positive role of mass media, according to which it can be considered a true mass mediator among people, is quite clearly reflected by the notion of a developed community. This can be defined as the openness of civil society, *i.e.*, as the opportunity to make public all actions of the power structures and all acts of will directed against others. In this case theoreticians of open communication (Jürgen Habermas) mention a brilliant expression of Kant who designated such a state of civil society's openness by the term "resonant publicity." In this sense the social function of mass media is not to form some new human being, say, a "real Ukrainian" in place of the late but not lamented *homo soveticus*. Under such conditions the mass media remains only an instrumentality of power, a means of communication for the ruling elite; it must be transformed into real mass mediators, *i.e.*, mediators in society, into mass media as such. Only then can it "form," *i.e.*, create such conditions, such a common reality of life that could claim significance for all: "reds" and "pinks," "greens" and "blacks," nationalists and communists, etc. Only on this basis can a real pluralism of ideas, views, speech, and texts be established and, hence, make possible relatively equal and just conditions for the multiplicity of individual wills to power.

Under such a system of open communication a new type of discourse can also be instituted – non-partisan, civic, and civil. This is why the situation under postcommunism is really a situation of not only and not so much one of multi-party politics and, thus, of a supposedly pluralistic press. It is only one of the inception of a non-partisan and, hence, pluralist mass media. It is the beginning of the exuberant growth of the prospects for forming civil society.

§5. The Cultural Paradigms and Prospects of the Ukrainian Mass Media

Two paradigms dominate contemporary approaches to the study of mass communications. The so-called *post-modernist* perspective constitutes the first; the communicative perspective – the second.

In the first case, social demands on the mass media center on the notions of a new kind of social control, the so-called "control through the temptation" of the public by means of creating a special, sensual, symbol-laden reality. In the second, such social consequences are linked with the possibility and hope of bringing about a certain true social integrity based on essentially intersubjective human actions. And the very feasibility of being oriented toward these paradigms is reassuring because it enables Ukraine to fit in (so far, theoretically) with movement of world culture although, to be frank, the peculiarities and prospects of our communicative situation are rather unattractive.

Still, the Ukrainian reality constituted by the mass media contains attributes of what we today call "post-Modern culture" and a certain proto-rational discourse. This is, in particular, the duplication of images of the world, social structure, political life, etc. All this exists together with a constant inter-textual quotation (*i.e.*, the construction of dialogs by means of quoting different texts) coupled with a stylistic multitude and all kinds of simulacra which pander to the readers' wishes or appear as a result of the journalists' intentions to fulfill the will of sponsors who interpret these wishes in their own way. True, it can hardly be said that we have now fallen into the "ecstasy of communication" promised by the media theoreticians (Baudrillard). Ukrainian mass media works in a follow-up mode, as if trying to catch up to a lost tradition or cling to certain hastily assimilated Western clichés. In this movement of interpretation, symbols are sure to largely precede meanings, thus engendering myth-making. True, there is not enough money, and hence paper and screen time, for even a detailed mythological, let alone rational, interpretation.

From this flows a situation that gives rise to opinions, which are not subject to argument, which are abrupt and primitive, but which all the same seem to assume the equivalent of content. The mass media is transformed into a helpful maker of hastily concocted names and symbols. These symbols lose any integrated content, they seem to shake off their meanings. Although in this case our language constantly brings out certain primary meanings, it is not easy to hear them. For example, the symbolic word "democratization" has quickly become part of mass-media rhetoric and successfully replaces the more precise "movement toward democracy." Therefore, the long movement toward an ideal and the complex process of reaching the latter may be either arbitrarily shortened by the word "democratization" or, on the contrary, stretched to infinity (shifting there the ideal itself), sometimes even without articulating at all the complexity of democratic movement ("we favor democracy" may mean that "we are already hard-core democrats" or that "we also favor democracy in principle," *etc.*).

Other features of this mass-media reality should also be mentioned. For example, an element – like game. This does not at all mean the participation of the mass communication media in political games. What I mean by game is the creation of a special reality which is not the battlefield of lie and truth and cannot be mastered by rules of rational discourse. It is important for us to understand that the mass media does not merely mirror something correctly or incorrectly, true or false: it creates a special reality and itself constitutes a game-like reality, which it makes no sense to evaluate in terms of truth or falsehood.

Still, it would be an oversimplification to say that now our behavior is so pre-determined by the disruption and stratification of symbol areas in mass communication. In any case this predetermination is not so dramatic as is the case in the monetary (also symbol-laden) field which, quite in the spirit of post-Modernism, has literally disintegrated before our eyes into the two non-interchangeable worlds of Ukrainian *kupons* and US dollars. Suffice it to recall our presidential elections. Of course, the result would have probably been entirely different if you went by our mass media alone. Moreover, our contact with the mass media is reduced to a minimum due to our lack of money and free time.

As to rational discourse and its capabilities in our communication network, here too, there is not much to count on in the foreseeable future. The point is that rational discourse, as understood by, say, Jürgen Habermas, is achieved in the line of a special communicative action of people who come into contact for the sole purpose of mutual understanding. But it requires several factors for such a communicative interaction to occur. The communicators somehow have to substantiate their claims as to the truth of the knowledge they offer, to the correctness of their linguistic (here, journalistic) behavior and, finally, to the sincerity of the reasons they advance. All this is not so easy to achieve under the current conditions of the political process in Ukraine.

This kind of a fully "accomplished" communicative act is a rare thing in mass communications. It occurs, as a rule, according to other canons and rules of strategic action. It is carried out as a means of achieving a specific purpose, *i.e.*, to change, form, or reformulate something as an object of nature. It is still difficult to overcome our heritage of the former totalitarian understanding of the mass communication media as an instrument of agitation and propaganda, an instrumentality for reshaping people into something like objects of nature.

All the same, today's mass media remains capable of fostering and creating rational discourse in Ukraine. For even now it marks out the space of public discourse, *i.e.*, its public sphere. This means it must create conditions for a more ample implementation and rationalization of the abovementioned mythology.

In this respect the Ukrainian mass media carries certain important attributes of contemporary culture, the culture of discourse and, say post-Modern culture. Certainly, such attributes are still very weak. In addition, unfortunately, the old "extraordinary" function of the mass media to exercise ideological control still persists, though not in such a total sense as before.

§6. Mass Media in Ukraine

The Ukrainian press has, by and large, passed through the period of civic choice or self-expression and entered a business mode. This business does not yet bring super-profits but there is no question of a mass dying off of newspapers, radio or TV stations. Isolated instances of failure are part of any business.

Analyzing the ability of the Ukrainian mass media to influence public opinion, we see a number of signs of the "no-longer-communist-but-not-yet-anything-else" period in which we live.

First, a geographical constraint: not one Ukrainian newspaper, radio or TV program can boast of influence over a very large part of Ukraine.

Second, a structural constraint: the social groups (from business people and politicians to homosexuals or artists) in different regions or even within one city are drawn, if at all, to qualitatively different publications. The reason for this resides in Ukraine's lack of a political nation, national mentality, and linguistic unity.

There is no single information arena in Ukraine, and Ukraine is not integrated into the world information system. It is no less difficult to read a newspaper from a different region than one from a different country, except for the Russian mass media which exerts influence on a very large part of Ukraine for various historical reasons. Simultaneously, the Ukrainian mass media encounters such obstacles as the non-structuralized nature of society, regional differences, scarcity of information, and an absolutely unequal competition with Russian media.

These obstacles will disappear as Ukraine forms a political nation encompassing its whole territory, enters the international arena, and moves toward democratic statehood. Our chance lies in the fact that the tempo of these processes is directly connected with mass media activity. Our post-communist world will not evolve into "something else" without the media's contribution, that is, without tactical and strategic steps to promote information flow among various regions, from Ukraine to the world and vice versa. It must foster the formation of a civil society — an indispensable prerequisite for creating a united nation. By the same token, it must either overpower the Russian mass media or make use of its capabilities in our interests.

§7. *Current Metamorphoses of Soviet Newspeak*

On the eve of the twenty-first century, perhaps the most essential problems of modern thinking in the postcommunist world are the problems of language and the problem of power. The catastrophic consequences of mass scale bewilderment caused by the long-term domination of the official ideological jargon still make themselves felt. Suffice it to hear the rhetoric in sessions of the Ukrainian Supreme Rada, where even now one encounters the same verbal hodgepodge used by the old nomenklatura. The Orwellian Soviet newspeak, not without reason, called the linguistic plague of the twentieth century, has poisoned all varieties of speech. For a very long time its verbal defenses have insulated the individual from his justifiable wrath at the totalitarian communist regime, while its value-laden norms of verbal casuistry carve the stereotypes of social hierarchy and set the ritual of verbal behavior. Newspeak cemented power relations more strongly and tightly than direct coercion.

The disintegration of the communist ideocratic system has created a unique vacuum. Recall that during the brief and fast-paced period of perestroika, it was philological critique that destroyed such sacred notions in the bowels of a language as class, Politburo, Central Committee, *etc.* But even now many speeches and articles still preserve the old Marxist-Hegelian clichés such as "working class", "peasantry" and "intelligentsia." This, despite the fact that even during the period of the self-construction of totalitarianism and creation of the ruling corporativistic community that the original class content of these pillors of "scientific communism" were already eliminated.

Word utilization, the orientation towards sacred notions under these conditions, has been, more often than not, a method of simulation and "controlled schizophrenia" (Arthur Koestler), of confirming double standards. However, these sacred notions in a society devoid of the intermediate centers of democratic civilization establish a basis for communications and legitimacy needed by the political elite.

The uncertainty, which pervades today's tireless search for an acceptable form of address corresponding to the spirit of the times ("Comrade"? "Mr."? "Sir"? "Friends"?), is also a sign of a crisis in communications as a whole and in the mutual understanding of the political elite and everyday people. "Comrade" was a form of address used in the semiotic arena of society to simulate communal equality of both parties in a dialog, to introduce into communication an element of intimacy and an impression that all were bound together in the supposedly common cause. This form of address, together with a system of sacral notions, helped disguise the ruling political elite and attributed to it characteristics it did not possess. A war of symbols has gone on since perestroika, a war which also, in an essential fashion, complicates the communicative links within society and prevents the formation of a new discourse of power capable of avoiding social conflicts. Let us examine this more carefully.

§8. Old Metaphors And New Paradigms

The dramatic events in Eastern Europe, which involved the most dramatic shift from totalitarianism to democracy, were expected to cause a complete, but no less dramatic transformation in discourse — be it literary, musical, political, or scientific. This transformation was bound to create a new paradigm as well. Indeed, the trivial clichés, such as "servant of the state," "builder of communism," "hero of the people," and "sincere communist" have disappeared from the pages of the new, so-called uncensored newspapers, giving way to new stereotypes — "market economy," "freedom," "democracy," "prosperity," "prosperous West," "poor and mismanaged socialist economy," "united land," "independence," and "self-determination."

The crucial issue here is that this new, allegedly "uncensored" discourse in the former USSR and Eastern Europe in general, and Ukraine in particular, is not necessarily new nor uncensored (*i.e.*, free). It tends towards remarks similar to the nineteenth century romantic paradigm and the twentieth century Marxist discourse. Moreover, it is still under heavy censorship. However, the censor is no longer an appointed official of the communist-Marxist state but a natural outgrowth of collective mythology from a source or group.[18]

Let us first recall what was the romantic paradigm of the nineteenth century – the age of hero worship, heroic battles, and inception of future tragic utopian theories. It was an age marked by romanticizing the archetypal hero and heroic renaissance. It was a century when the pendulum of philosophical values turned away from the Christian heroic code and ultimate hero, the Christian's God, and towards Marxist Atheism, with its pagan polytheism and denunciation of Christian values.

During the romantic period, the interest toward the primitive heroic self was revived. Themes of universal folkloristic heroism once again became popular. The key concepts of the romantic period had deep roots in the traditional philosophical categories – such as Good and Evil, Hero and Villain, Heroic Deed and Reward, Hero-Man and Nature. The archetypal icons which permeated the romantic discourse included:

Night/Day	Good/Evil
Victory	Destiny
Immortality	Remembrance
Liberty	Equality
Democracy	Freedom
War	Struggle

Maurice Pecham defined the romantic period as the "period of the establishment of the Self."[19] The romantic Self tried to redefine itself through heroic performance amidst the struggle for democracy (the French and American Revolutions); the struggle for scientific reinterpretation of the natural world (Charles Darwin's *Origin of Species*); and the struggle for economic "utopia" (Adam Smith, David Ricardo, and Karl Marx). Ultimately, the most radical expression of the romantic "Self" was to be in the October Revolution, with its struggle for the utopian dream of a new, proletarian "paradise" and the ultimate denunciation of Christian ideology (which Lenin considered the "opiate of the masses").

Christianity, with its specific agenda of struggle for morality and good, was theoretically shattered. Its ecclesiastical heroes, saints, and martyrs were pushed into the background, making place for the new "heroes" – Marxist-Leninist revolutionaries and ideologists, atheists, social reformers, and seekers of the new romantic "Self." As Pecham put it, "it was a revolution in the human mind," and so it was.[20]

But it was not only a revolution in the belief system of the sociopolitical order, it was also a radical change in cultural expression. The popular romantic motifs – such as struggle, love, hate, evil, underworld, paradise, and conquest – found their best expression in music, poetry, drama, journalism and scientific discourse.

The neo-pagan romantic renaissance coincided with a global shift from a primitive agriculturally-based society to an urban society with technology-oriented organizational structure. But the urban industrial realities failed to bring happiness to the millions of romantic "revolutionaries". Consequently, their anguish in the post-industrial urban "hell" was immortalized in the volumes of European romantic literature, which gave birth to the new "hero," a "thinking rebel," who suffered and felt deep nostalgia for the past.

The romantic renaissance also transformed the archetypal folkloristic hero into a national "hero-poet" and national "spokesman" for the collective interests of the group. If the eighteenth century was the "Age of Enlightenment" and deep belief in reason, the nineteenth century was the "Age of Feeling" and filled with anger, rebellion and collective omnipotence.[21] The romantic hero was not a thinker but a doer – an active "rebel" against industry, science, capital, and Christian philosophy. He acted upon impulse while denying, rejecting, and debunking so-called "reality." The ancient Greek mythical heroes once again became the seductive heroic matrices for the collective mimesis. The Judeo-Christian philosophy could no longer satisfy the heroic appetite of nineteenth century romantics. Return to the ancient heroes – such as Apollo, Prometheus, Zeus, and Agamemnon to replace Moses and Christ – was inevitable.

The romantic hero was anti-Christian in his basic essence; and a particular "national" hero of a particular nation had once again prevailed over the universal one. The Romanticism of the nineteenth century went parallel with the so-called "national liberation movements," which symbolically represented a violent romantic competition for the heroic title of "nation-hero." Thus romanticism and nationalism went hand in hand. Darwin's *Origin of the Species* inspired global competition for the strongest, wisest, and "chosen" nation. The concept of "folk/*Volk*" hero was central to the romantics, and the idea of nationhood shaped itself around this "folk/*Volk*" archetypal heroic paradigm.[22] It became a blend of all the heroic concepts of the past, a fusion of all familiar myths as well as their conflicts.

Thus the age was one of particularity versus universality; one single God for all nations versus individual gods and national heroes for each separate nation; the cult of a particular language or folklore versus the cult of a collective universal Marxist hero – the proletariat or "working man." Paganism, Christianity, Judaism, Atheism, Nationalism, and Marxism all put forward their own "heroic" doctrines, while the romantic ethos of the nineteenth century nourished all of them through the cult of a poet, writer, or spokesman for a particular group.

This brief digression into the romantic era was necessary in order to understand and account for today's collective mythology, which was created by the romantic renaissance of the nineteenth century. The break-up of the first utopian Marxist state (the former USSR) demolished the belief in the utopian philosophy and set the preconditions for the current collective philosophical "truth" and its new censorship. Furthermore, the strictest censors and propagators of current myth are its philosophical "truth" producers – the group. In the case of Ukraine, the romantic lifeline is rooted particularly in its restoration through the formation of an independent state. However, the pattern of discourse in this newly emerged and theoretically different state is remarkably similar to that of the not so recent past, as well as to the romantic past of the nineteenth century with its icons.[23]

To begin, consider some of the following characteristic themes from various periodicals. Similar examples may be found in any other Eastern European journalistic discourse, but since the present work is dedicated to Ukraine we shall limit our analysis to the most popular and most recent utterance in the Ukrainian press:

Our daily bread
Autumn of our anxiety
The first and last commandment
We cannot return to prison
Struggled, To struggle
We shall struggle
Your children, Ukraine
State of one's soul
If there is God in one's soul
The island of hope
Land and freedom[24]

There are several running motifs in these examples. First and foremost, the rehabilitated and resurrected Christian ideology. Previously a taboo in the Soviet Marxist-atheistic state, Christian ideology is now striking today's Ukrainian readers with such familiar and yet unfamiliar verbal icons as "God" and "Commandment."

There is also a secular archetypal theme of "Struggle," inherited from the nineteenth-century romantics, but never abandoned by Marxist dreamers of the romantic "socialist" paradise. After all, struggle for Marxists could equally apply to the "struggle for the victory of communism," the "struggle for the fulfillment of a five-year-plan," or "the struggle against capitalism." In each case the language possessed a kind of elasticity which enabled its users to stretch the meaning of the verbal icon in all possible directions. Thus, the archetypal *struggle* has changed its goals:

In the USSR:
Liberation of proletariat
Socialism
Downfall of capitalism
Communist paradise

Current political correctness:
Market economy
New paradise
Independent Ukraine
Condemnation of the past

Similarly, "to struggle against" has come to mean struggle "against" the pre-perestroika period of "socialist stagnation" with the same verbal icons displaying the vicissitudes of trust and mistrust, and vagaries of collective desire and collective mythical consciousness. Ironically, the powerful platform – "*land* and *freedom*" – one of the themes enunciated during the October 1917 Russian Revolution, was used again in the post-perestroika era with some substantial changes in the meaning of the old verbal icons.

Pre-perestroika:
Land for all peasants
Freedom for the downtrodden

Phrases for Today:
Land for a particular ethnic group
Independent Ukrainian land
Freedom for independent Ukraine

The trite metaphor "motherland" (forgotten in the Western hemisphere) was revived, echoing nineteenth-century romantic slogans. The Ukrainian nation state, which was not allowed to exist in the romantic past, emerged at a time when the passionate "Children of Ukraine" were being perceived in the West as rather naïve. This may be explained by the fact that the romantic anthropomorphism and the metaphorical pathos to the icon "*motherland*" have virtually disappeared from the contemporary Anglo-American press. One would be hard pressed to hear an American President ask American soldiers, when sending them on a military mission, to defend their "Motherland." Instead, they are usually called upon to defend "*freedom*" or "*democracy.*"

"Motherland" usually appeals to the sense of kinship and natural biological connection, and since most Americans are America's "adopted children" from various "motherlands," the familiar romantic icon "motherland" has been replaced by the ideals of their adoptive country, America. It reflects the historic reality of New World countries as well as the post-romantic and post-nationalist mentality of the newly conquered land which has yet to be discovered by the new Ukrainian and the other young, independent European nation states. At a time when the New World and Western Europe have painfully but finally abandoned the myth of a monoethnic state, and are trying to accept the reality of human existential dynamics with its mostly ethnic face, Ukraine and other newly formed East European nations are still vulnerable, it seems, to an unchanged romantic paradigm.

In the phrase "Your children, Ukraine," the speakers return to the past, to an old nineteenth century theme when "children" stood for the members of the same ethnic, racial, and religious group. But for those who are not "children of Ukraine," where is their "Motherland"? The verbal icon "children" is used interchangeably with the more current "indigenous population."[25] Despite the fact that among those romantic appeals to the past one may also hear in the phrase "Autumn of our anxiety,"[26] the disjointed postcommunist chorus is also dominated by the melodies of Gobineau, Hitler, and Stalin's racist rhetoric, neatly packaged.[27]

Analyzing the above examples, it is possible to detect the direction of the new philosophy. The themes of God, Soul, and Commandments suggest the restoration of the old, previously discarded and condemned, Christian philosophy. Marxism, which had not brought economic prosperity and Western standards of living to Ukraine, has been replaced by the resurrection of Christian ideology and iconography. Christ, previously a taboo, is revered and worshipped again; while saints and Christian martyrs have replaced the heroes of the Marxist state — the "servants of the people."

Following the same strategy of Christian teachings, Stalin (the embodiment of evil) is condemned as much as the archetypal Satan. In relation to this, the theme of lament and mourning over tortured political prisoners of the Stalinist era has become the predominant theme of the new postcommunist discourse. Ukrainian periodicals have dedicated special sections in their publication to the condemnation of the Stalinist past. Meanwhile, previously forgotten or unknown poets and artists are honored in the new press. Readers are now able to learn about an entire generation of forgotten artists, which were an integral part of Soviet heritage. Ukrainian readers now hear new names and are introduced to new potential cultural icons.

Other prominent philosophical themes (myths) include "the people," "nation-hero" and "folk/folklore." Echoing the romantic nineteenth century, the postcommunist East European societies have sought to escape from reality in the revival of theoretically genuine, but truly specific and particular folkloristic tradition. If past romanticism was defined as the rediscovery of the particular "self," then the contemporary search for "self" leads to the cult of folk and folklore as a unique and distinct origin and expression of the collective ego of a particular nation.

Sentimental accounts about the return of prayer and revival of the church are intermingled with the nostalgic escape into folklore, as well as folkloristic art and design. Panegyrics to folklore and popularly approved art— such as Ukrainian embroidery — fill the back pages of every popular Ukrainian journal. For example: "Embroidery is the beautiful and bounteous soul of our people. Each design is as a talisman, a symbol of the enchanted wisdom. I believe. I envy. Our art of embroidery is being reborn."[28] Black and red colors are used as romantic interpretations for the symbols of blood, sacrifice, struggle, and martyrdom.

Even the Soviet establishment had a strong ideological interest in the cult of art by the people. But the Soviet people in the past had also been encouraged to have a sense of the folkloristic "self." By cultivating folk song and dance ensembles, promoting the particular collective self, and keeping a good record of the folkloristic heritage, the leaders of the former Soviet Union substantially relied upon the cultural roots and cultural expression in their construction of the Marxist Empire.

The Soviet *demos* ("people") and *narod* ("proletariat")

never left the romantic paradigm of Johann Herder's *Volk*. Suffice it to recall that such Ukrainian poets as Tychyna, Bazhan, and Rylsky contributed substantially to this cultural policy. Being worshipped in what used to be Soviet Ukraine and having received numerous honors, these Ukrainian Soviet poets were not merely regarded as spokesmen for the Soviet establishment, they were also symbols of archetypal legitimate folklore as well as the romanticized and idealized art of the people. Surprisingly, the familiar Soviet archetype "poet of the people" has acquired new applicability in the changed circumstances of independent Ukraine. It has been slightly rephrased from "poet of the people" – to "poet of the reborn nation."

The nonviolent shift from Marxism toward democratic mythology that we witnessed during the perestroika era in Eastern Europe bears strong resemblance with the (mythical) pattern of the romantic past. On a daily basis new poets and new heroes are rediscovered, published, displayed, and offered up as new objects for intense public worship by the entire *dęmos*. The general trend of the new romantic narratives is to replace the incompetent, immoral, inept, and dishonest politicians by new talented, able, and allegedly sincere Hero-poets, artists, and new politicians. It is symptomatic of the new romanticism, that not only Vaclav Havel could lead a post-Marxist state in Czechoslovakia, but such Ukrainian poets and writers as Dmytro Pavlychko, Ivan Drach, and Pavlo Movchan take a most active part in the political life of the new Ukraine. The popular collective myth repeats its familiar cycle when the poet-artist becomes the new divinity. The pages of *Ukraina, Dnipro,* and *Literaturna Ukraina* are full of obituaries to the hero-poets, while political and social commentaries are written by poets, writers and artists. The traditional Carlylean hero-poet is adorned with contemporary mythical layers, such as "poet-victim of Stalinism," "poet-martyr," and "poet crucified by the brutal socio-political system." Disenchanted and disillusioned masses seek guidance and return to the familiar archetypal symbols. However, much like their romantic predecessors, the creators of the popular cultural text have dual mythical loyalties to both the resurrected Christian "mythology" and the rejuvenated myth of the poet-divinity or other divinity. Even those poets who were god-like figures in the old Soviet Ukraine are now rehabilitated to heroic status and their names have been added to the "heroic pantheon" in the new independent Ukraine.

The myth of "genius" and "national genius" is another preoccupation of the popular culture. Numerous articles have been devoted to the concept of the extraordinary human being, and many of them even include the term, "genius" in the titles. For instance, in 1991 *Literaturna Ukraina,* published an article by Lina Kostenko titled "Genius in the Circumstances of a Blocked Culture." The article had been dedicated to the memory of Lesya Ukrainka, the famous Ukrainian poet and evokes not only the romantic Carlylean myth of the poet as a divinity figure but also deals with "genius" as a cultural necessity, philosophical entity, and national property. A famous poet in her own right, Kostenko passionately asks: "Why is there no word "genius" in all the available Ukrainian encyclopedias?" She uncovers an interesting paradox – there is no Ukrainian word for "genius" – it happens to be a Latin word, but Ukrainian does not come from Latin. In one of her digressions from the main topic, Kostenko also speaks about the Ukrainian historian Mikhaylo Hrushevsky, presenting him to the reader in the following heroic manner: "He was an ordinary son of Prometheus; from the same family as Saint Volodymyr, Mazepa, Bohdan, and Taras."

By so writing, Kostenko uses the following heroic metaphors: (1) family – the Ukrainian nation, and (2) Prometheus – oppressed Ukraine tied to the rock (*i.e.*, the Russian-Soviet empire).

The vicissitudes in mythical thinking distort the process of history in the form of "icons" and thus, in turn, establish the discursive ground for the mythical plots and for the system of heroic values like "Free Europe," "liberators," or "a nation with a special mission." Eventually, it is the prevailing group that censors the names of its chosen heroes as well as its own creations and popular myths, be they romantic or neo-romantic, nationalist or racist, American or European, religious or secular. Thus can the meaning of the sign (symbol) be collectively created and sustained by the old metaphors in the new paradigms.

Chapter 2.

Political Transformations of Postcommunist Societies

- The Stages of Postcommunist Transformations
- Alternative Models of Social Development in Ukraine
- The Political System and Political Parties
- Political Power and the Political Elite
- Corruption as a Political Phenomenon Under Postcommunism

In practice, postcommunist societies have not yet displayed any lasting features of political development which, if properly defined, could enable researchers to more or less clearly identify and describe tendencies and trends in the transformation of postcommunist political structures, processes, and influences. Hence, such concepts as "political system," "political elite," "political power," "political influence," *etc.*, which together constitute the system of customary coordinates for traditional "pre-postcommunist" political analysis in Western societies, are often of little utility (both in terms of subject matter and methodology) in studying current political life and phenomena in the former communist states.

The reason is not only in the amorphous and arbitrary interpretation of well-known terms as instruments of political analysis transferred to a different political setting with a vastly different context of sociopolitical experiences. The very political reality of these countries, where the present is intricately intertwined with the past and there are still no clear indication of something new arising, reduces to the minimum the relevance of accumulated political science knowledge (in which the past clearly prevailed) and thus the very possibility of finding exact definitions of ideas and concepts with which we may understand the postcommunist transformations.

Conversely, trivial attempts at intellectual borrowing from other social science disciplines in hopes of instantly filling the conceptual vacuum in today's political science discourse have failed to create a new scholarly "instrumentality," that is, an ideational critical space outside of which any intellectual breakthrough is impossible.

Yet, the very fact of the "mysterious" and "sudden" (for political science but not for history) collapse of communism as the decisive event of the late twentieth century calls for an enrichment of various currents and patterns of political analysis dedicated to the explanation and assessment of the alternatives facing postcommunist societies and the highly contradictory and controversial political transformations taking place in the postcommunist world.

The authors in this chapter focus primarily on specific political changes, stages of the transformations taking place, the making of new political systems on the basis of old elites, how such systems differ from one another, how political power and elites are being transformed, and omnipresent corruption as a universal hallmark of the postcommunist world.

The Stages of Postcommunist Transformation

Time has now passed since the implosion of the communist state in Poland set in train a process that led to the collapse of the other Central European communist states. A bit less time has now passed since the implosion of the Soviet system itself, following five years of agonizing perestroika. It is, therefore, not too early to try to draw some lessons from the subsequent attempts to create, on the ruins of the communist systems, politically viable and economically successful democracies.

That on-going transformation poses intellectually challenging questions. When it began, there was no model, no guiding concept, with which to approach the task. Economic theory at least claimed some understanding of the allegedly inevitable transformation of capitalism into socialism. But there was no theoretical body of knowledge pertaining to the transformation of the etatist systems into pluralistic democracies based on the free market. In addition to being daunting intellectually, the issue was and remains taxing politically, because the West, surprised by the rapid disintegration of communism, was not properly prepared for participation in the complex task of transforming the former Soviet-type systems. Consequently, it has had to improvise very hastily over the last several years.

It is in this context that certain important questions have to be addressed. First, what should we have learned by now regarding the processes of postcommunist political and economic transformation? Second, what should we have learned regarding Western policies meant to aid and promote that transformation? Third, and in the light of the preceding two, what results can we expect to flow in the foreseeable future — over the next decade or so — from the ongoing efforts at the transformation?

§1. The Transformation Process

Regarding the broad lessons of the transformation process, the first is that expectations on both sides — in the old communist states and in the West — were much too high and rather naïve. The liberated peoples of the former communist countries had truly exaggerated and simplistic notions of the kind of help that they would receive from the West. There was a generalized anticipation of manna from heaven, of some new "Marshall plan" being applied on a vast scale, notwithstanding the actual historical and intellectual irrelevance of the Marshall Plan experience to the former communist countries. While in the West, there was a general underestimation of the systemic complexity of the changes required, of the resistance by the established and still-pervasive nomenklaturas, and of the duration of the process itself.

A striking example of the above is that the American aid programs, which were initiated immediately after 1989-1990 for Poland and then for the other Central European countries, were based on the assumption that the transition process would last for about five years.[1] We now know that it will be much longer than that — ten years at a minimum for the Central European countries and probably in the range of fifteen to twenty years for the other countries — before it will be possible to say that the transformation has been completed. (One may also add, parenthetically, that the West was also rather overoptimistic as well as simplistic in its assessment of Gorbachev — of his intentions, as well as of his program — and that to some extent we currently display a similar tendency in our reactions to Yeltsin.)

A second and more complicated lesson is that the transformation process itself is not a continuum, but a sequence of distinct phases. Moreover, not all of the former communist states are in the same phase of the process of transformation, nor are they traversing the respective stages at the same pace. It is also noteworthy that the rapidity of the shift from phase to phase is heavily conditioned by what transpired politically and economically during the final (preimplosion but also gestating) stage of the former communist systems.

The above requires some elaboration. The first critical phase, following immediately upon the fall of the communist system, involves a combined effort to achieve both the political transformation of the top structures of political power and the initial stabilization of the economy. The former typically means the imposition of top-down democracy; the latter typically requires stabilization of the currency while undertaking the initial unfreezing of economic controls. This initial stage is extremely difficult because it involves a fundamental change in established political and economic processes. It calls for boldness and toughness, being essentially a plunge into the unknown.

The first phase is also the critical one because its success is the necessary launch pad for the second stage, one in which the quest for broader political stabilization has to be combined with efforts at more pervasive economic transformation. The adoption of a new constitution, a new electoral system, and the penetration of society by democratic processes are designed to institutionalize a functioning democracy. At the same time a broader economic transformation has to be launched, involving, for example, the establishment of a banking sector, demonopolization, as well as small and middle-scale privatization based on legally defined property rights.

Only when and if that phase has been successfully completed can the next — the third-phase be undertaken, in which comprehensive democratic institutions and processes truly begin to take hold in an enduring fashion, while economic growth becomes sustained as a consequence of the comprehensive unleashing of private initiative. A democratic political culture and an entrepreneurial tradition gradually

Phases of Postcommunist Transformations

Phase One: 1–5 Years

Political Goal: Transformation
Economic Goal: Stabilization

Political	Legal/ Regulatory	Economic	Western Aid
Basic democracy; Free press; End of one-party state & police system; Initial democratic coalition for change.	Elimination of arbitrary state controls.	Elimination of price controls and subsides; End of collectivization; Haphazard privatization.	Currency stabilization; Emergency credits & aid.

Phase Two: 3–10 Years

Political Goal: From Transformation to Stabilization
Economic Goal: From Stabilization to Transformation

Political	Legal/ Regulatory	Economic	Western Aid
New constitution & electoral law; Elections; Decentralized regional self-government; Stable democratic coalition – new political elite.	Legal/regulatory framework for property & business.	Banking system; Small & middle scale privatization; Demonopolization; New economic class appear.	Infrastructural credits; Technical & managerial assistance; Trade preferences & access; Initial foreign investment.

Phase Three: 5–15 (+) Years

Political Goal: Consolidation
Economic Goal: Sustained Take-Off

Political	Legal/ Regulatory	Economic	Western Aid
Formation of stable democratic parties; Democratic political culture takes.	Independent judiciary & legal culture emerges.	Large-scale privatization; Capitalist lobbies; Entrepreneurial culture emerges.	Major foreign investment; Inclusion in key Western organs (*e.g.* EC, NATO, *etc.*).

become reality. This third phase can be described as involving political consolidation and sustained economic take-off. To make all this more concrete, one might hazard the judgment that Poland, the Czech Republic, and Hungary are now on the brink of entering that third phase. (See the enclosed table for a schematic representation of these phases on page 106[2]).

It is also important to note that the ability to embark on, and to traverse, particularly the first critical phase – the most important stage of decision – is heavily conditioned by the degree to which a particular fallen communist regime permitted both political relaxation and economic liberalization in its last years. The important fact to note is that, in effect, the agony of communism also served simultaneously (at least, in several cases) as a period of political and economic gestation for the emergence of postcommunism. The consequences of that gestation in the cases of Hungary (the Kadar regime in the 1970s and 1980s) and of Poland (the Gierek regime of the 1970s and the last five years of Jaruzelski in the second half of the 1980s) are self-evident.

The third lesson to be deduced from what we have seen of the transformation process involves the primacy of political reform as the basis for effective economic reform. A democratic political consensus and effective political processes are essential for the successful initiation and consummation of the first critical stage of change. One could theoretically postulate the need for an authoritarian system of discipline at this stage, because a great deal of social sacrifice is required (and generated) during its implementation. China obviously comes to mind here. However, in the wake of the collapse of the communist regimes in Central Europe and in the Soviet Union, an authoritarian approach does not seem feasible or desirable.

On the contrary, democratic consensus is imperative. But it must be organized and institutionalized. Initially, that typically calls for the presence of an effective, indeed of a charismatic popular leader – a Havel or Walesa – who can command popular support. It also requires the presence or rapid organization of a political movement that supports the leader in an institutionalized fashion, and is capable of sustaining popular support in the face of the social dislocations and deprivations that typically occur in this phase. But, above all, the initial phase, with its often euphoric postcommunist enthusiasm, must be exploited promptly to build the foundations for legitimate and formal democratic procedures within which longer-term economic reforms are pursued. By the time the second phase is reached, public euphoria tends to have waned, while disappointment with the transformation tends to escalate. Thus, much depends on the resilience and viability of the new democratic processes. Much of Russia's difficulties stem from Gorbachev's (and later Yeltsin's) failure to focus on the need for comprehensive political reform as an urgent priority.

The foregoing leads to a fourth lesson, which flows from the previous three: the rapid and comprehensive transformation – the shock therapy of the so-called "Big Bang" approach – is only possible if both the necessary subjective and objective conditions exist. The Polish case is a good example of the combination of the two. It involved the existence of a nation-wide counter-political elite, namely the Solidarity movement, which permeated society, was not crushed during the decade of the martial law, and could promptly serve as an effective counter-political elite on the national scale (rather than, as in some other cases, being confined to a few dissidents suddenly installed at the top of the national power hierarchy). That elite, moreover, was buttressed by the presence of a moral authority able to nourish the social will to sacrifice, namely the Catholic Church. In addition, a charismatic leader, who enjoyed special authority within the class likely to suffer the most from the social sacrifices, was able to personalize the political change. A free peasant class and a large underground economy provided economic responsiveness to the workings of the law of supply and demand, upon the lifting of price controls and the termination of subsidies. Finally, Poland benefited from the support given to its surfacing entrepreneurial culture by an engaged diaspora comprised of some ten million Poles who live abroad.

The listing of these factors suggests that while the Polish "Big Bang" approach may be exemplary, it may also be, in many respects, exceptional. In the absence of some combination of political cohesion, commitment, and consensus with economic receptivity and responsiveness, shock therapy is likely to produce political conflict and economic chaos, with well-positioned monopolies taking advantage of price liberalization simply to increase prices, thereby also stimulating inflation.

The fifth and last general lesson regarding postcommunist reconstruction follows from this last point: One should not rule out transformation strategies that involve slower motion and are also reliant on continued governmental guidance rather than purely on the unleashing of independent and dynamic market forces. Here, the warnings of the very prominent Japanese development economist, the late Suburo Okita, come to mind. He argued cogently in several papers that governmental intervention is needed in countries in which free market mechanisms lack tradition, experience, and appropriate social culture. He stressed that there are societies in which some combination of market mechanism and governmental planning is necessary for historical reasons, especially since the market mechanism is not always in and of itself infallible.

The examples of both Japan and Korea are very pertinent to the case made by Okita. In the summer of 1993, the World Bank was completing an exhaustive analysis of what transpired in the Far East in the last three decades and what lessons may be derived from that experience. According to a preview in the *Financial Times,* one of the Bank's conclusions regarding the Korean experience was that "...from the early 1960s, the government carefully planned and orchestrated the country's development.... [It] used the financial sector to steer credits to preferred sectors and promoted individual firms to achieve national objectives.... [It] socialized risk, created large conglomerates, created state enterprises when necessary, and molded a public-private partnership that rivaled Japan's."[3] Much the same could be said about Singapore as an example of successful directed growth. At the very least, such Asian experience should not be disregarded when contemplating the current political, economic and social dilemmas facing both Russia and Ukraine – countries without strong free market traditions and developed entrepreneurial cultures.[4]

§2. Lessons for the West

Let us now turn to the second of the four major questions posed at the outset: the lessons to be learned concerning Western policy designed to aid and promote postcommunist transformations.

First, Western aid is most critical during the first stage of transformation. In fact, significant Western aid is probably essential if that stage is to be traversed successfully. Later, after the first phase, Western aid ceases to be central, whereas access to Western markets and foreign investment become increasingly important. That access becomes the primary source of continued internal change and of export-driven economic dynamism. That is largely the case today in the relationship between postcommunist Central Europe and the European Community, with the result that the issue of "access" has become much more controversial than the scale of "aid." In contrast, the former Soviet Union is still in the first phase of the transformation process, when direct Western aid for stabilization and initial political transformation is essential.

Second, and perhaps more controversial, after the critical first phase, the inflow of external capital is not decisive. If Western capital was the key to success, former East Germany (GDR) should be flourishing, Hungary should have taken off economically some time ago, followed by the Czech Republic, with Poland trailing behind. Moreover, Russia should be doing much better than China.

Former East Germany has received monumental amounts of external capital over the last three years, at a rate of $100 billion per annum, for a population of a mere

16 million people. (Just calculate what anything comparable to such a per capita inflow would be required for Central Europe as a whole, or for Russia specifically!) But the crucial point is that the former GDR is still in a massive socioeconomic crisis. Similarly, Hungary and Czechoslovakia (prior to its division into two states in early 1993) have been the beneficiaries of much larger capital inflows than Poland. Yet today, Poland has a larger private sector and is the first former communist country to have attained a positive economic growth rate.

China has been the beneficiary of relatively small amounts in terms of grants, loans, credits, and until recently, investments. Over the first twelve years after the start of reforms in 1979, the total involved for China (a huge country with an enormous population) was less than $60 billion. This is much less than the Soviet Union/Russia has received since 1986 – some $86 billion. Yet China has done extremely well in terms of its economic development, growing over the last decade at a rate of 6 percent per annum, last year at 9 percent, and this year will probably reach 13 percent. Russia, in contrast, is still in an economic mess, with a negative growth rate.

In brief, after the conclusion of the first critical phase, during which external assistance is central, the nature of domestic polices, social discipline and motivation cumulatively become more important than the inflow of external capital in determining success or failure in the pursuit of economic transformations.

A third lesson with respect to the inflow of external capital is that explicit preconditions and strict supervision of its utilization are imperative. In fact, if a choice is to be made between quite limited but tightly monitored financial assistance and large inflows of external and largely integrated capital, the former is clearly more beneficial and, therefore, should be favored. This is especially true in the first phase, until trade and foreign investment replace the initial dependence on direct aid. Trade and investment almost automatically tend to be subject to more effective control by directly interested and personally concerned parties. In the absence of close external supervision, as experience sadly shows, massive diversion and extensive theft of foreign aid is to be expected.

The West should have learned this from its experience with Poland under Gierek. In the 1970s, Poland borrowed about $30 billion, yet it is very difficult to account for what happened to those funds. Today, there are even more serious questions to be raised regarding the $86 billion that has flowed into the former Soviet Union since the second half of the 1980s. Some estimates made in the United States conclude that as much as $17 billion of it has been diverted away from intended purposes and recycled to Western banks.

A recently concluded Japanese study, conducted on the eve of the July G7 Summit in Tokyo by a private think tank, Toray Corporate Business Research Inc., also addressed this issue. The study concluded that the Russian government has lost control over the capital flight phenomenon, with the consequence that large amounts of cash, gold and diamonds have been stashed in Swiss and Hong Kong banks. "The scale of the capital flight has already exceeded 40 billion dollars," the study asserted.[5] Though this estimate may be too high, it is nonetheless clear that the problem of illicit diversion is a very serious one.

Accordingly, precise targeting and close monitoring by donors should be explicitly asserted, even if it offends the national pride of the recipients. Specific conditionality is also essential regarding the fundamentals of reform. Stabilization in the monetary area, depoliticization of the banking system, demonopolization, at least initial small-scale privatization (including in agriculture) and the decentralization of economic decision making, are the minima that the West has the right to insist upon when granting aid, if the aid is to be helpful.

Fourth, the West ought to encourage the recipient countries to develop some longer-range mobilizing vision, one capable of sustaining domestic support for the needed painful reforms. Even with generous external aid, domestic sacrifices and a great deal of social pain are unavoidable.

Therefore, the articulation of a more positive, hopeful, constructive perspective on the future is politically necessary. The public must perceive a sense of direction which justifies their transitional pain and sacrifice.

For the Central Europeans such a vision largely exists already. It involves the notion of a united Europe, and of their eventual membership in it. That vision is very meaningful and tangible for the average Czech, Hungarian or Pole. It represents something to which they can relate personally. The issue becomes more difficult and elusive when one moves further east. What can provide such a constructive vision for the Ukrainian of today, who has found that independence has brought mainly socioeconomic deprivation? What is that vision for the Russian, who not only experiences similar socioeconomic deprivation, but feels acutely humiliated by Russia's loss of superpower status? It is not easy in these circumstances to generate a positive vision of the future.

For Ukrainians, perhaps it could be the notion of Ukraine eventually becoming and being accepted by its Western neighbors as a Central European state, and thus part of a community that is already moving closer to the West. That vision certainly would be more tangible to Western Ukrainians than to Eastern Ukrainians, but it might have wider appeal to Ukrainians who wish to define their nationhood in terms that differentiate Ukraine from Russia.

For Russians, perhaps, the appropriate vision might be one of becoming a partner of the United States, given the fascination with America that is so widespread in today's Russia. But if Russia is to be "a partner" of the United States, America will have to be explicit in insisting that such a Russia be truly a post-imperial Russia because only such a Russia can become genuinely democratic. The fact is that Russia has still a considerable distance to go in the painful process of adjusting to its new post-imperial reality, a process that was consummated in the case of Britain with the loss of India, in the case of France with the loss of Algeria, and in the case of Turkey under Atatürk, who defined the concept of a new, would-be modern/would-be European, Turkey. The process of post-imperial self-redefinition is a complicated and difficult one. One can understand why opposition and confusion surround this subject in today's tormented Russia: but the issue must be addressed.

§3. A Differentiated Future

In the light of the responses to the first two questions, what reasonable expectations regarding the postcommunist transformation might be entertained in terms of the foreseeable future — say, the next decade or so? It follows from the analysis already offered that the transformation will be differentiated — in kind and time — as well as difficult. But what is likely to be the overall pattern? Are all of the former communist states safely on the way to becoming pluralistic, free market democracies? Before hazarding some rather arbitrary judgments in response to this question, let me suggest the following fourfold predictive framework.

The first category includes countries with essentially positive futures, by which is meant countries in which it would take something altogether unforeseeable and, at the present time, rather improbable for them to be diverted from the process of becoming viable pluralistic democracies.

The second category includes countries whose prospects over the next ten years look somewhat better than even, but in which a reversal, indeed a political and/or economic failure, still cannot be excluded.

The third category involves countries whose political and economic futures, in my judgment, are likely to be unresolved beyond this decade and into the next century.

Finally a fourth category, essentially an extension of the third, comprises countries whose futures currently, and into the foreseeable future, look distinctly unpromising.

By this classification, as already indicated, Poland, the Czech Republic, and Hungary fall into the first category, as probably do Slovenia and Estonia. Of these, the first three are likely to become members of the European Community and NATO within a decade, and even perhaps within this century. Without minimizing their internal difficulties, their futures appear largely predetermined; although Hungary or Estonia could be affected adversely by some external complications (notably, ethnic problems). In any case, the first three can be seen as about to enter (or entering) Phase Three of the table enclosed on page 106, while the latter two are in Phase Two.

Even the likely success of the leading three, however, should not obscure the fact that it will take many years before the gap is significantly narrowed between the living standards of the richer West and even its most promising postcommunist neighbors. If one assumes, for example, that Germany and Austria will grow at 2 percent per annum, while Poland, Hungary, and the former Czechoslovakia will grow twice as fast, at 4 percent per annum, it would still take 30 years for Czechoslovakia, 46 years for Hungary, and 63 years for Poland to close the gap in their respective GNP per capita with their Western neighbors.[6] Even if the rates of growth were 2 percent and 8 percent respectively, the years required would still be 12, 17 and 23 for the respective Central European populations to catch up with Germany and Austria. Obviously the prospects are much dimmer for the countries listed below in the second, third and fourth categories.

The second category – countries whose futures are generally positive but which are politically and economically still vulnerable – includes Slovakia, Croatia (if it does not get entangled in a new war with Serbia), Bulgaria, perhaps Romania, Lithuania, Latvia, Kirgizistan, and Turkmenistan (the latter two because of indigenous economic potential). Some of them – *e.g.*, Latvia or Bulgaria – may be approaching Phase Two, but the others are still navigating through Phase One.

The countries which fall into the third category – those whose political and economic futures are likely to be still unresolved for a decade or more – are, first and foremost Russia, then Ukraine, Belarus, Georgia, Armenia, Azebaijan, Kazakhstan, and Uzbekistan. Finally, those in the fourth category, whose futures for a variety of reasons look rather grim, are: Serbia, Albania, Macedonia, Bosnia, Moldova, and Tajikistan. None of the above can be said to be very advanced (or successful) in traversing Phase One; some may not even have entered it. In fact, most of them are still governed by their former communist elites who masquerade under new labels, but whose commitment to a pluralist democracy and sensitivity to its nuances is still questionable.

Of those in the uncertain (third) category, Russia is, of course, the most important. One has to recognize some positive trends in ongoing Russian developments. There has certainly been general democratization, particularly of the upper-metropolitan levels of Russian society. In a number of the large cities, democracy is an operational reality, though it lacks genuinely pervasive institutionalization. There has also been some privatization of the economy and initial steps toward its stabilization.

But there are also contradictory trends. Economic chaos is a reality; there is no effective monetary policy, inflation is still extraordinarily high, unemployment is rising; the writ of the government is effectively limited to a few metropolitan centers and does not run throughout the country; there is a lack of policy cohesion and consistency; most of the privatized shops are still located in Moscow, St. Petersburg, and Nizhny Novgorod.[7] There is massive diversion of Western funds and aid by the remnants of the well-positioned nomenklatura and by a new class of middlemen; and many (probably most) of the new capitalists represent parasitic wealth, channeled mainly into consumption and not into productive investment.

Also complicating the economic picture is the evident renewal of imperial aspirations, which increases the likelihood of intensifying tensions with Ukraine and also generates problems with some of the other neighboring states. Most noteworthy here is the use of economic leverage and military pressure to informally preserve the essential elements of the Kremlin's former imperial status. Quite symptomatic of Moscow's continued reluctance to accept Kyiv's independence as an enduring fact.

All of this justifies – and generates – some uncertainties regarding the future. One can expect, most probably, continued democratization, but in a context of inconsistent reforms that run the risk of producing periodic phases of intensifying anarchy – and thus the temptation to eventually resort to more authoritarian solutions. As a result, Russia does not fit either category one or category two, but has to be placed – reluctantly and regrettably – in category three. The same is true of Ukraine, whose independence is still in jeopardy and whose internal transformation has been lagging even more badly.

The foregoing cumulatively suggests that history is still open-ended as far as the final outcome of the postcommunist transformation is concerned. As of now, politically and economically successful liberal democracy is not a foreordained outcome, except perhaps for five out of the twenty-seven postcommunist states.

Alternative Models of Social Development in Ukraine

The years of Ukrainian independence have produced a great quantity of political analyses and programs. Ukrainian specialists in all branches of the social sciences, starting with philosophers and ending with political scientists, publicists, political leaders, state functionaries, and leading state officeholders have offered their analyses of the socioeconomic and political situation along with models of development. Various philosophies of transformation have been put forth as have a number of foreign strategies. The basic course of domestic policy has altered repeatedly, and a certain measure of practical experience has already been gained in decision-making, ideological waffling, and nomenklatura maneuvering. But in all this, attention has been concentrated, as would be expected, on the role and capabilities of the top echelons, the state, *i.e.*, this present state with all its weaknesses, while the society for which transformations have to be carried out, continues to be treated, as in the times of "real socialism," like a passive object.

§1. State Policy and Social Development

Under conditions of normal societal development, with mechanisms of self-regulation in operation, even the most difficult periods cannot be called a setback or running in place. Crises are accompanied by adaptation to new conditions; and even minor political decisions serve to normalize economic processes. Ukraine, however, is now in a specific and especially difficult situation. First, we face a profound and all-encompassing economic crisis is compounded and exacerbated by the political ineptitude of the ruling elite, which is incapable of formulating a logical course of action. In other words, there is no self-regulation. Second, the economic crisis in many respects predates our independence, and the problems we face, which are by no means exclusively economic, significantly outruns the state's abilities to address them.

A certain spontaneity in the process of the USSR's collapse led Ukraine to be catapulted into independence. Along with this, in the economic sphere we inherited, along with crisis phenomena the economic system as such, and in the political sphere, a self-assured, self-serving, and semi-competent bureaucracy which only compounded the problem. Thus, the political sphere in Ukraine is far less developed than the economic.

A sufficient amount of evidence has been accumulated to state that our society, its socioeconomic sphere, and our very existence are generally out of control. They are so distorted, unstructured, and disorganized that they do not lend themselves to regulation. And here no program can do anything about it.

At the moment, Ukraine does not exist as a single organism. This implies not only problems of the relations among the various regions, but also an antagonistic relationship between society and the state. Our newly independent state treats society differently but in no way better than did the old Soviet empire. Society still exists under extremely adverse conditions created by the state. The constructive potential of the latter (if we do not take into consideration its self-construction) was and has been minimal. The main threat to independent Ukraine is the excessive dependence of society upon the state, that is, on an inefficient, irresponsible power structure, which continues to exploit society both economically and spiritually. It should be noted as just another example of this fleecing that the legislative and executive branches of power interact in complete agreement, while the judiciary branch fails to act consistently at all. Instead of a qualitative improvement of the state mechanism, we continue to observe its quantitative malignant growth.

The strategy of economic reforms offered by President Leonid Kuchma is the best of which the party of power is capable. Economically, this strategy is aimed in the right direction, a direction which has been long anticipated. The nearly unanimous conclusion is that the President displayed a *tour de force* and has demonstrated his political will to bring about change. But apart from this will and a classic and quite understandable intention to consolidate his power hierarchy, there is nothing political in his program. That is, the program is based on an activist role for the state, specifically, for the executive branch, because the present government has not as yet demonstrated its support of the ideas which make up the bulk of the Presidential program, and the executive branch officials will find it difficult to subject their own interests, for them the sacred thing, to the Chief Executive's new course.

How, then, do the political forces line up on economic issues after four years of independence and, specifically, on the President's strategy? The Parliamentary majority cannot really favor it while at the same time it does not want to risk unmasking itself by openly voting against the program, and for this reason it has to resort to sophisticated maneuvering in order to delay the adoption of crucial proposals. The managerial elite, including that in the regions and in some industries, will traditionally adapt any innovations to suit their own interests and thus will try to carry out their own program of transformations. To combat all this, guided only by the principle of an exceptional role for the state, will be very difficult. Support for the President's policy from below will not be sufficiently organized; the possibilities of gaining such support are, for the time being, rather limited, except perhaps for moral and psychological support from reform-oriented political parties. The President's team will have to make major efforts (if this happens to be part of their plan) to have the program agree with the immediate interests of the economically active segment of the population and draw into it the latter's energy. Otherwise, everything will again be decided within the power structure due to a lack of constructive participation by society at large. Thus, the most valuable thing in the program is its promise to decrease the dependence of society on the state rather than specific programs.

The present actions of those in power are impelled by various factors; they are not the result of either inner convictions or any profound understanding of mechanisms of social development. For some members of the ruling elite one more change of political course is a means of self-preservation, for others it is just another experiment, another option, the differences among which are not always sufficiently understood, and only for a few does it coincide with real convictions which do not rely on the vicissitudes of momentary economic or political advantage.

The etatists hold that, given the current socioeconomic situation, state bodies have to be entrusted with the most urgent and responsible tasks: handling the energy crisis, inflation, mass pauperization, combating rising crime, *etc.* But in fact, these and the other crises we face are caused by the state itself. Moreover, it causes them continuously and on an ever-widening scale while mitigating them only from time to time. Excuses and explanations offered by top leaders that the state is not in a position to do better and more for the people have become commonplace. As far as the state and power structure are concerned, this might well be true. But this simply dooms the people and the society to wait and see.

It is very symptomatic that all comprehensive programs of aid to the postcommunist countries presuppose precisely the opposite, *i.e.*, restricting the role of the state in society. This is seen as an essentially important prerequisite for efficiently utilizing the aid and acquiring self-sustaining viability.

The peculiarities of Ukraine's position in the world community and on the plane of historical development also stimulate the rapid as possible supplementing of state efforts by nongovernmental action. Geopolitical considerations cause Russia and our closest western neighbors to get priority attention from the developed countries. This is the reality of international politics. Much can be changed, if a "second front" of transformation is opened and Ukrainian society as a whole begins to assert itself internationally. Then the nation's entire potential, thus far little known, would be put to work.

In assessing possible alternatives and developmental models for Ukraine, the key notion is the purpose and goal of reform. Means must conform to ends. If we are to orient ourselves toward the experience of Western countries (which, in general, is coming to be ever more widely recognized), then it is important to realize that the corresponding model should be based on society's assuming the role of active subject. The state as such a mechanism is unable, in principle, to build a developed democratic society from the top down. Society as such must be capable of self-development and evolution, while the state must safeguard and foster the process.

Until the ruling elite is renewed in a real sense, so long as the system of management by an army of state officials (which is formed by the system itself as an anti-social force) is not displaced, the relationship between society and the state cannot be brought into harmony. To be carried away by and to limit oneself to "state-building" as the basis for a strategy of reform means to commit a tragic blunder.

Understandably, an amorphous society will not be able to find a proper strategy. The only thing we have had to rely on thus far was trial and error. Ukraine has been marking time in this way, without making any visible progress, for the past four years. This has been a period of procrastination, palliative measures, and political stagnation. Real problems have been ignored and put off rather than solved. And, most importantly, the constructive potential and the efficacy of our society as well as of the state itself have not been practically developed.

Today this process, if only in a semi-spontaneous version, can and must be accelerated. And what is important is that the outcomes of trial and error made should be politically recorded and made available to the public at large. A clear division of political responsibility among individual state officials and specific political forces for their political actions must become axiomatic. Only then can politics eventually perform a service to the economy, can the society become structured, and thus able to actively and purposefully transform itself.

§2. From State-Building to Building Civil Society

Ukraine's complex social problems can be solved only by building a civil society, not by state-building. Only in this way can two opposed energies be reconciled and harmonized: a destructive one aimed at destroying the old elitist set-up and a constructive one aimed at creating a new democratic order. However, it is essential to understand that the democratic nature of a new state (as well as its true internal and external stability) can only be achieved by forming a developed civil society, rather than forming it through any manipulations with the old elitist (oligarchic) state.

The main reason for the immaturity of civil society in the postcommunist (and particularly post-Soviet) world is the prolonged absence of political and economic freedoms. The formation of civil society in Ukraine is essentially complicated by its multiethnic or, actually, bi-ethnic character. Since democratic processes evolved here in close contact with those of national liberation (*i.e.*, the emancipation of civil society from the totalitarian state was largely identified in the popular mind with the emancipation of Ukrainian society from the empire) a large portion of the population, which is Russian or Russian-speaking, displayed a cautious wait-and-see attitude to these processes. And although this segment of the population did not support the imperial nomenklatura or the formation of pro-Moscow "interfronts," it also did not support the national democrats, keeping a kind of "neutrality" and displaying an unfortunate passivity toward the republic's political life.

The worst thing is that this part of the population,

while disliking the nomenklatura and mistrusting the national democrats, did not put up their own leaders and never constituted itself as an independent political force. Facing a choice between the "communists" and "national democrats," it naturally opted for a known evil over an unknown (hence suspicious) good.

This segment of the population was "lost," to some extent, by the advocates of an independent Ukrainian state who, as has already been noted, resorted to a fatal collaboration with the former communist nomenklatura. However, that same part of the population was "won," by the nomenklatura, which managed (using various propaganda ploys) to identify in mass awareness the notion of "democracy" with something purely "Ukrainian," hence "nationalistic," and thus "extremist," that is, "Banderite" (after Stepan Bandera, leader of the more radical splinter of the Organization of Ukrainian Nationalists in the 1940s and 1950s) or "Galician" ("West Ukrainian"). This same nomenklatura in Ukraine actually used against its rivals the same method as chauvinists use in Russia, the difference being that in Russia "democracy" was identified in the eyes of the ordinary man in the street with "Judeo-Masonic" plots, while Ukraine's Russified nomenklatura identifies democracy with a "Galician" or "West Ukrainian" conspiracy. In both cases, however, an "internal" enemy has been made an "external" one, and a large portion of the population has been persuaded that "democracy" is something "hostile," dropped on them from outside, the result of some scheme, plot, intrigue, a sinister import.

As a matter of fact, civil society in today's Ukraine mainly embraces Ukrainians not in an ethnic sense but in a political one (the nucleus of the still unformed civil society practically coincides with that of a still unformed political nation). Thus the problem becomes how to enlarge civil society so as to encompass the nationally indifferent segment of the population. And this applies not only to the Russian-speaking cities, but to the Ukrainian countryside, which still largely remains at a feudal, pre-national level of ethnic self-awareness.

It is clear that the structures of civil society in these two gigantic segments of the population have to be formed primarily from within. It is equally clear that this process can be catalyzed, speeded up, or retarded, and the latter is now being done quite successfully by the postcommunist nomenklatura. On the one hand, it restricts economic freedom in every way possible way, undermines the legal safeguards of that freedom, sabotages privatization, and prevents the appearance of a citizen, economically independent from it, that is, from this same nomenklatura.

§3. Cultural-Political Models of Social Development

Sociopolitical prognostication in present-day Ukraine is usually based on forecasts and considerations of an essentially economic or political nature. Economism in modeling possible paths of development naturally makes sense in the context of the practically hopeless economic collapse of the country. At the same time, the political struggle of small but numerous parties is marked today with juridical-legal accents. Therefore, the previous inter-party contests – the romanticism of the first years of national independence and cultural sovereignty – drifted to the juridical-legal side: a case in point is, first of all, the necessity of making and passing new rules of the political game under new circumstances (namely, adopting a new Constitution or the law on power proposed by President Kuchma, *etc.*). In other words, in the political projections – of both the present establishment and leaders of new political formations – primary attention is attached to matters of national, and particularly economic survival, and hence, to the preservation of their political status and the consolidation of their political influence. All this is in sharp contrast to the first years of independence, when the slogans chanted were of a primarily cultural and ideological nature.

However, a certain neglect of the cultural policy aspect in charting the future of Ukraine is far from an indicator of its unimportance for prognostication. Here one should not confuse a true cultural policy (we use the term to denote a true political analysis and understanding of the practical significance of national-cultural, ethno-cultural and civilization-related {general cultural} factors for a state's political guidance) given the previous period's slogans of national liberation, slogans which were easily transformed into authoritarian nationalistic dogmas. Such an assessment makes it possible to grasp the whole importance of culture-political thinking and practices in the postcommunist period. It is difficult to overestimate the field of cultural-political ideas, orientations, political motives, and actions for understanding the social basis of postcommunist transformations. This field is sometimes spoken of in everyday conversation as a common striving, and social upsurge (of will, volition) which is projected into the future for the purpose of creating the new and modernizing transformation of the presently available. Something similar to this can be seen from examples of the ambivalent period of Ukrainization in the 1920s, which was carried out parallel (and not by accident) to the violent process of industrialization and mass collectivization of farmers in Ukraine.

Recognition of the fundamental significance of the Protestant ethic for civilized forms of capitalist relations is now a commonplace in modern sociology and culture studies.[8] So what else can we hope for in Ukraine?

Modeling Ukraine's possible paths of development is directly dependent on answering the question of the preconditions of the all-Ukrainian cultural-political unification and the corresponding real culture policy of present or future authorities. At the same time, a choice between various political versions of such unification is also a selection of one or another model of economic modernization. Cultural choice and political and economic transformations are inseparable.

Based on the cultural-political attitude which is present in the political consciousness one can — to simplify greatly, of course — find such basic models of, if not development, then at least regular progress into the future.

The situation is quite likely to be recognized when a model of ethno-cultural political collectivity comes forward as a result of a socio-political choice, *i.e.*, a cultural-political model of state- and nation-building based on a radical nationalist understanding of the people's existential unity in Ukraine. If such a cultural-political orientation is chosen, its inadvertent result might well be a cultural, and hence, political distrust among various regions of Ukraine, its federalization, either official or unofficial but *de facto*; political conflicts, aggravation of political tensions, and confrontation. For there are essential differences in how Ukrainians from various regions of Ukraine experience their Ukrainian identity. If this does not result in civil conflict, then in a somewhat less grave version it will have to be dealt with as an unproductive situation which may persist for years. In this model, everything in Ukraine could wind up in a dead end.

In addition, this model of ethno-cultural political unity, consciously or unconsciously for its supporters, is genetically related to the traditionalist world view, *i.e.*, conservatism in respect to cultural-value orientations and political conservatism. That is why the disposition of mind toward modernization loses for this model any specific meaning along with all other urgent issues of possible economic modernization.

If in the situation of the rapid aggravation of the socio-economic crisis and utter impoverishment of the population people happen to incline toward the social model of political unity (and it is couched in "socialist-communist terms" of economic equality, as a matter of secondary importance of national-cultural ways of life), chances that the striving for independent state existence, Ukraine's own system of economic management, and national activism could fade away altogether.

The future of the "social" model is quite obvious. It is the establishment of a new form of Ukraine's dependence, primarily on Russia, of stagnation and cultural-political marginalization. In such a case modernization is possible only as a replication of what is produced by others. Starting with the formation of economic relationships based on Ukraine's own cultural specifics and ending with inventions of up-to-date industrial, social and commercial technologies – in all these extremely important domains of human activity the self-regulation of people's lives vanishes.

The contradictory cultural-political experience of the past four years makes it essential to prefer a model of state and societal organization which presupposes a socially and politically stratified society with developed democratic institutions. This, however, does not imply a dominant role for national-cultural cosmopolitanism.

Thus, the important point is to create on the basis of the proto-democratic core of ethno-national cultural networks – a common way of life, language, customs, and traditions – a modern state-organized civil community – a political nation. Only proceeding from such a cultural-political model is it possible to mold a maximally formalized, *i.e.*, a non-violent national political community in the judiciary openness of which all creative novelties, including economic modernization will find social legitimization.

* * *

Ukraine's path to the development of democracy and national culture can lie only in the state and politicians trying to do everything possible in order to construct a modern foundation for national political consensus. This foundation is civil society, the relations among people in which differ from the "national-ethnic, cultural" sphere proper by developed private interests, their rational grounding, and independence of people from political structures. This is a matter for the future – organization of the institutions of future democracy and the uniting of the political nation around the national nucleus of our protodemocratic community.

Ukrainian society needs a powerful wave of radical change which would bring about its liberation not only from foreign domination but also from its internal fetters of state-bureaucracy-corruption and thereby trigger its internal mechanisms of self-development and self-regulation. Regrettably, such a prospect is, in its turn, limited to a great extent by the feebleness of and lack of unity among the democratic forces, by their involvement in the power structures and their lack of readiness to implement their own strategy of reforms.

Progress toward solving societal problems in Ukraine should be measured first of all by the extent of the state's retreat on the domestic front, by how purposefully its functions in the economy, politics, and its presence in everyday life are reduced. Building civil society must be our top priority. To these ends the activities of all truly patriotic forces should be reoriented. For, without a civilized society, a Ukrainian state simply cannot be built.

The Political System and Political Parties

§1. *Special Features of the Political Systems in the Newly Independent States*

Today, there are various typologies for classifying political systems. Most, however, boil down to two major contexts. In the narrow sense, a political system is interpreted as an aggregate of certain political institutions (parties, power structures, social associations, trade unions, *etc.*), while in a wider sense it is an interdependent network of political institutions, relationships, political norms, and consciousness. Here we examine the political system in both contexts.

The postcommunist development of Central European states is characterized by an awareness of the importance of creating an open system of social relations and an adequate form of political system. Legal and political recognition of the value of each institution in the political system created certain preconditions for the development of real democracy. In this sphere a situation which differs in principle has characterized the countries of the former USSR.

The sociopolitical evolution of the newly independent states of the former Soviet Union from a political system based on the constitutional codification of the dominant role of the ruling Communist Party and the priority of labor collectives to a democratic system shares a number of common features. Leaders in various CIS states have faced the problem of defining key institutions of the political system which could enable them to supervise the evolution of sociopolitical relationships and make political decisions. The institution chosen to play this role is the presidency. The President has become the dominant element in the postcommunist political systems which have arisen in the wake of the USSR's collapse (except in the Baltic states). The President, who represents not any organizationally shaped political force but rather "the interests of the whole people," is able to act in an arena free from political commitments and election pledges. Moreover, the President is practically uncontrollable in his or her choice of appointments to posts in the executive branch since he does not have a stable political team of his own. This enables postcommunist presidents to act, putting it mildly, *very situationally.* Suffice it to recall former President Leonid Kravchuk who before his election had been the major opponent of the Popular Movement of Ukraine (*Rukh*) and once in office as elected President appropriated the national democrats' ideas and programs. A similar political metamorphosis can be seen with current Ukrainian President Leonid Kuchma. Candidate Kuchma presented himself as the bearer of moderate economic reforms and pro-Russian policies. President Kuchma has now become the representative of Western type radical economic reform. Thus, *replacing the dominant role of the Communist Party by the institution of the presidency as the main active subject of the political system has, in significant measure, solved the problem of legitimizing the renewed elite and laid the foundation of a "pseudo-new model" of political systems in the postcommunist states of the former USSR.*

However, a need has arisen for ideological consolidation of these changes in political strategy and the system of political relationships. After seeking possible candidates for the role of key elements in the realm of political consciousness, most postcommunist states have opted for religion or, more precisely, the church.

Turkmenistan provides the classic example of a postcommunist country, where the planned transition to a "new model" of the political system has been carried out 100%.

Under its constitution, the president is not only the highest state official but also controls both legislation and local government. The People's Council (Assembly) of Turkmenistan is composed of two parts: a popularly elected Mejlis with extremely restricted powers and a presidentially appointed upper house vested with greater powers. The president also appoints local authorities and consequently completely controls the situation.

The president himself and his policy have come to be seen as God-given and sacred for the people. This is evidenced both by Turkmenistan's national anthem and the numerous monuments to Saparmurad Niyazov (Turkmen-bashi) which have now replaced the sculptured figures of Lenin.

Close to this model are other countries of postcommunist Central Asia whose leaderships are apt in combining the institution of the presidency with popular religious traditions. Political developments in early 1995 in Kazakhstan made this clear once again. President Nursultan Nazarbayev dissolved the popularly elected Parliament under the pretext of a complaint by an unsuccessful female candidate, thus removing the problem of an institution which might have offered a measure of checks and balances to a strong presidency. A logical sequel, fully in line with the "pseudo-new model" of postcommunist political system being introduced, then took place when the President suggested a plebiscite on the need to extend his term until the year 2000. The majority chose to live through the transition period in peace and harmony with the reliable Nursultan Nazarbayev and accordingly voted to give their leader the power to act as "required" under the circumstances.

This is how the political systems of the Central Asian lands of the former Soviet Union are being transformed. For various reasons, this general rule has assumed special features in the Transcaucasus and Tadjikistan.

In Russia, despite its status as one of the pioneers of the Soviet-style democracy, the country's leadership has also managed to subject the democratic institutions of its political system to the above-mentioned element. The development of political parties and social organizations and the mixed character of the electoral system have failed to affect in an essential way the President's predominant status. A bicameral parliament and elected State Duma are counterbalanced by the Council of the Federation, controlled by the President and consisting of two representatives from each subject of the Russian Federation. This setup cannot in any substantial way prevent Boris Yeltsin from implementing his own program of actions and influencing the course of the political process. Moreover, the heart of the Russian political regime is the idea of a "Great Russia" sanctified by the Orthodox Church and religion, which in turn augments the legitimacy of the President and ruling elite.

An essentially different situation has developed in Belarus. After the collapse of the USSR, it sought to preserve the ideas of the communist model of political system. The communist elite and labor collectives were, until recently, dominant in the Belarus political process. At the same time, the ruling stratum's inflexibility and inability to legitimize itself by means of a certain idea or even an institution have led to its complete inability to pursue its own political strategy. Belarus' return into the orbit of a "new postcommunist Russia" testifies to its failure to form even the model of postcommunist, renewed political system analyzed above.

A less noticed but no less important phenomenon in the area of quests for a new political system in the postcommunist world is *the implanted political system syndrome.* A certain segment of democratic forces in postcommunist states, which have oriented themselves to the transplantation of the model of the Western world, either consciously or under pressure, propose to transplant the foundations of the political system of donor-countries in post-Soviet soil. A particular example of such an artificial transplantation is the attempt to introduce the Christian-Democratic model in Ukraine. The peculiarity of political donorship has resulted in the fact that the role of pioneer in this field is now claimed now by four political parties — the Ukrainian Christian-Democratic Party, the Christian-Democratic Party of Ukraine, the Christian-Democratic Union and the Christian-Social Union (although the latter two have not yet been officially registered). The "implantation syndrome" is also observed among political representatives of classical liberalism much criticized now even in that homeland of liberalism, the USA. The triumph of the political system of the nations of classical liberalism in Ukraine, Russia, and especially the states of Central Asia and the Transcaucasus would seem somewhat problematic. But still the influence of this trend persists.

§2. The Ukrainian Political System in Light of the Postcommunist Transformation

The model of Ukraine's postcommunist political system has formed spontaneously within the context of the general notion of state-building.

Etatism, which is at the basis of how the system of new socio-economic and political relations in Ukraine is being constructed, is characterized by the fact that the strategic objective was defined as state-building (or, more precisely, statehood) as a major determining factor in further reforms. But political leaders have not defined what Ukrainian state-building really means, how it can be accomplished, or how long it will last. In an interview on Russian Ostankino television former Ukrainian President Leonid Kravchuk indicated that, while the present generation was unlikely to live in a civilized country, the main thing was that it would live in its own state. This understanding of the state-building process (the mechanistic establishment of the institutions statehood, only after which generally recognized mechanisms and principles of reform could be approached) led society to inadequately understand a whole series of notions about the political system. Thus, opposition came to be seen, not as a mechanism of influence and control over state decision-making and the actions of the institutions of power, but as a mechanism that ruins the state. This in turn allowed the formulation of the principle that in the so-called "period of state-building," opposition *in* the Ukrainian state is opposition *to* the Ukrainian state.

A similar approach also characterized questions of state

structure and the mechanisms of economic reforms.

The self-sufficiency of state institutions, which supposedly brought closer the mythical statehood for Ukraine's leaders and aimed at expanding Ukraine's presence, above all, on the world stage, was covered by the mass media, not as one aspect of normal state activity, but as a great achievement. In this vein, the mass media created images of politicians who were building the state as a whole. But the question still remained of whether they had managed to do anything real in terms of carrying out their duties.

This state of affairs became a prerequisite for representatives of the old elite to join with a part of the new one, making it possible for them to build the state both in the center and the regions by the approbated methods but now without undue trepidation about being held accountable for any violations of the law. The attempt to influence the implementation of decisions at the local level and to set up a mechanism of influence on and control over local authorities by introducing a system of presidential prefects was *a priori* doomed to failure, for it was designed for "good people" who actually do what they are supposed to. In practice, the prefects, who lacked any real legal status and division of powers with other structures in the center and the regions, with time found appropriate niches in the state-building process in the regions they governed.

Along with etatism, *ochlocracy* (which for no apparent reason in Ukraine is stubbornly referred to as democracy) also found itself a place. Ukrainian ochlocracy displays the following characteristics: the incompetence of political power, disrespect for law, understanding law as whatever the state wants, and the manipulation of the attitudes of certain social groups in order to attain narrow corporative interests.

Ochlocracy, or Ukrainian democracy, together with etatism have become a convenient disguise for the dilettantism of those who wield power. By formally referring to the importance of global tasks of state-building (in the etatist sense) and democratic transformations (in the ochlocratic sense) state officials were able to disencumber themselves from responsibility and to satisfy their own narrow clan interests.

It was precisely under these conditions that the place of the institution of presidency as the key element of Ukraine's political system has come into ever sharper focus. All other institutions, and specifically political parties and social organizations, became mere satellites of the leading actor in political relations. In the course of pursuing the path of "state-building" there was even an attempt to form, on the basis of the Kyiv Patriarchate of the Ukrainian Orthodox Church, an official state church which would sanctify the actions of Ukrainian state-building. But let us return to the history of the formation of Ukraine's political parties, whose status has assumed that of social organizations of a satellite character.

The history of the emergence of the Ukrainian multi-party system has certain specifics of its own, and it is worthwhile to examine the contemporary party system in Ukraine in light of certain periods in its emergence.

The first period of Ukraine's multi-party system, which might tentatively be referred to as "pre-state/opposition," extends chronologically from the emergence of the first Ukrainian Parties (Fall 1989) until the juridical codification of Ukraine's independent status (December 1, 1991). Today the systems of ideological support of all parties and their ideological credos are, in large measure, uniform. The self-identification of party structures on the political spectrum took place only on the periphery. Different political forces turned out to be rather similar in their views on issues of state-building, socioeconomic system, religious, cultural, ecological, and other issues. The programs of these parties were full of general declarative slogans and appeals to the whole people of Ukraine in order not to restrict the zone of their ideological influence. Precisely this explains the presence in the documents of various political structures of a great quantity and general democratic dogmas. After an attempt to classify nationwide parties in the above period, one can conclude that of the twelve parties which existed as of December 1, 1991, all except the Communist Party of Ukraine (CPU) championed the ideas of parliamentary democracy and private property. As for Ukraine's political status, eleven parties, again except for the CPU, favored Ukrainian sovereignty either within a commonwealth system or as an independent state. Thus, the Democratic Party of Ukraine, Liberal-Democratic Party of Ukraine, People's Party of Ukraine, Unified Social-Democratic Party of Ukraine, Party of the Democratic Rebirth of Ukraine, Green Party, Social-Democratic Party of Ukraine, Ukrainian Republican Party, Peasant-Democratic Party of Ukraine, and the Christian-Democratic Party all stood shoulder to shoulder in the struggle for "sovereignty," "democracy," "the free market," "pluralism," and against communist ideology. Despite various negative trends, this became the principal prerequisite for their joint actions which led to the proclamation of independent and democratic Ukraine. The new parties were small, politically naïve, and were not drawn into the machinery of the state policy. Among them rifts, tensions, and confrontations soon reared their heads.

Since the proclamation of Ukrainian independence, a qualitatively new situation has arisen in society. From then on political parties, with only preliminary programs lacking any mechanism for attaining their goals, have become inferior subjects of the political system. Such was the status of political parties at the beginning of the next stage in the development of the Ukrainian multi-party system which can be tentatively called a "state-loyalist" one. Chronologically, this period spans from December 1991 to early 1993.

After the All-Ukrainian referendum on independence and Presidential election of December 1, 1991, all the major goals which had served as the basis of forming major political pre-election blocs, were in complete agreement with the President's own policy. A process began of "velvet" appropriation of the parties by the state. On the one hand, this split the opposition. Because of the socioeconomic situation, a considerable portion of the party structures and sociopolitical organizations came to support the President and either partially or wholly the government. The newly created Congress of National-Democratic Forces and, to some extent, the bloc of radical nationalists embraced (both in theory and practice) the thesis that "support for the President of

Ukraine elected by the whole people is support for building an independent state."

Accordingly, "opposition to the President means the ruin of our independent state." The political forces around *Rukh* and the *Nova Ukraina* association occupied the niche of a loyal opposition. Paradoxically, a *de facto* controlling interest in all realms of state power was retained by the so-called party of power," which is not a registered political structure at all. Thus, a new political elite was formed in Ukraine as a result of the compromise between a part of the old ruling party layer and a portion of the national-democratic opposition. Moreover, in this period *Rukh* and *Nova Ukraina* repeatedly switched back and forth from support to opposition vis-à-vis the President and government, thereby creating a problem of identifying the character of a Ukrainian counter-elite on the level of political parties.

Former President Kravchuk opted for the creation of a simplified mechanism to legally regulate the registration of political parties: The Ministry of Justice was authorized to register a political party when its program, statute, and founding documents were appended to a list of one thousand party members. This in turn created a legal situation stimulating the emergence of dwarfish quasi-political parties led by ambitious, pseudo-political leaders. Of course, in the developed democracies party registration is of no great significance. A political party's importance is determined by its participation in parliamentary and local elections. These Lilliputian party formations one by one joined the major parties, also without any real programs of action, and found a niche in the ranks of the loyal opposition. Their actual political participation was limited to periodic announcements about the nature of their opposition to or support for certain institutions of state power (parliament, the government, or the President) or their attitude toward what the Russian Federation did. The President knew how to take advantage of the situation of the political parties. For example, in order to strengthen his position, he initiated regular roundtable discussions of political parties on problems which were certain to be supported by the leaders of most parties.

Specifically, the round-table discussion on the CIS Charter forced the leaders of several parties of the loyal opposition to support the President's policy line, and this cast doubt on the depth of their opposition.

In this period, a type of party system was formed which displayed elements a of multi-party system: a significant number of parties and signs of polarization between Left (Socialists and Communists) and Right (radical nationalist organizations). This took shape in 1992-1993.

The next period, the "pre-election" one (1993-1994), was characterized by a shift of the center of attention to preparation for the Parliamentary election campaign. This determined the parties' main tasks: choosing acceptable slogans for their election programs and seeking to influence the passing of an optimal election law. As a result, a law was passed mandating parliamentary elections on a winner-take-all basis and stipulating the rights of political parties as subjects of the electoral system (but with a more complicated procedure of nominating candidates for parties than for groups of voters).

Lacking a developed organizational structure and enough sufficiently experienced candidates, political parties proved unprepared for elections on a winner-take-all basis. The election results (allowing for numerous violations of election laws) make it possible for us to draw some conclusions:

• Voters showed their trustful attitude to candidates to the deputies nominated by political parties or political groups and chose to vote for them rather than independent candidates.[9]

• On the other hand, regional differences in the influence of various political parties and lack of balance in the election programs of candidates made it impossible to form structured majority and opposition coalitions Ukraine's parliament.

In addition, there is not a single All-Ukrainian political party which would have demonstrated in the course of the elections its ideological, political and organizational influence in most of Ukraine's regions. Only the Inter-

Regional Bloc for Reform, which represents the interests of major regions of the country to some extent performs this role.

At present Ukraine is approaching the stage of a transformation of its parties, characterized by the process of unification of small political parties on the basis of proclaimed ideological, political, and economic affinity:

- Communists and Socialists;
- Social-Democrats;
- Liberals;
- Conservatives (represented largely by National Democrats, Christian Democrats, and various trends of Nationalists).

How real the influence of these orientations is in Ukraine will be shown only by the results of the next parliamentary elections very likely to be held on a mixed basis.

* * *

Thus, the period of political transformations in the states of the former USSR (except for the Baltic states) has certain common regularities. First of all, this is true for the nature of political system, codified in constitutional documents as democratic, pluralistic, and open. But actually the majority of the new political players, the parties, fail to influence the course of events. This is above all the case with political parties. Under the circumstances the main institution in the political system becomes the President or national leader who uses other political institutions only to secure and consolidate his own legitimacy. Political parties become transformed into formal declarative institutions of societies estranged from state policy-making. This situation is in turn conducive to the incompetence, irresponsibility, and corruption of the political elite, while the constant situational balancing of the ruling stratum between the principles of ochlocratic, democratic, and authoritarian forms of state organization is extremely dangerous and provokes calls for establishing something like a neototalitarian order. The political system at issue in the countries of the former USSR can be referred to as the transformative "pseudo-new" model of the postcommunist period.

At the same time, rather popular with democratic circles, still remains the model of the so-called "implanted political system" which would have to be based along the lines of the political structure of a certain Western state. Primarily, the principles dominating in a donor-country of postcommunist implantors underlie the basis of such "optimal" model of political system.

Obviously, we are dealing with two unacceptable approaches to developing an efficient and socially viable model of political system in the postcommunist theater. The basis for the optimal political organization of society must be:

- the functioning of generally recognized principles of democratic society;
- an appreciation of the national specificity of a given country;
- the mechanisms of political and legal guarantees against authoritarian, neototalitarian, or ochlocratic reflexes in the postcommunist world.

Political Power and the Political Elite

§1. *The Narcissism of the Postcommunist Elite*

In the postcommunist period the word "elite" can hardly be regarded as a neutral descriptive term of the social sciences. Its meaning is, undoubtedly, related to normative notions and is, to a great extent, narcissistic. The word is also a sort of social myth and, therefore, it must be approached with caution, if we do not wish to fall into a less than critical attitude toward reality. This danger can be very real. Today the postcommunist world witnesses much talk about the political elite and the intelligentsia quite in the spirit of Ortega-y-Gasset. *De facto,* all top state officials, members of parliament, and political leaders are assigned to the elite. It is referred to as a milieu that relegates leaders to the theater of social life. The elite is spoken of as a collective interpreter of the national interests and a center of competence for all spheres of human activities, *etc.* But, at the same time, few scholars have paid attention to the fact that "elitism" is not so much a quality as an ideological entourage, a desirable setting for the group of people in power who under postcommunist conditions pass for an elite.

Habitually, the elite is considered to be the chosen, the best (incidentally, its political sense is inherent in the Latin verb *eligare,* from which the French *élite* originated). What is more, this chosen nature is understood as self-evident in the context of the word "elite." It is no wonder that in the

West from the 1920s on, the concept of "elites" was put forward to counter Leftist rhetoric about the "ruling clique," "200 families," *etc.* The introduction of the catchword "elite" into mass consciousness (within the context of an ideology of life) can be considered a very successful ideological trick. The elite itself is the source of propaganda about its elitism: be it a political or intellectual establishment, acknowledged celebrities in the creative arts and mass media, the problem of elitism remains, nevertheless, narcissistic, *i.e.*, a problem of high self-esteem and positive self-identification of a group of people living in immediate contact in the immediate vicinity of power and taking (or wanting to take) part in the leadership of society and formulation of its ideological and political strategies.

All this is not to say that the word "elite" has no meaning. On the contrary, the problem of elite formation and renewal is a top priority task for a state – especially a postcommunist state, when the building of social edifice is just beginning and where much depends on how the top echelons of comport themselves.

But it is precisely in this respect that the situation in most postcommunist states is rather lamentable. In Ukraine under conditions of the primitive accumulation of capital by a narrow circle of people, often closely connected with the old communist nomenklatura, popular opinion associated the idea of power less with the word "elite" than with the word "mafia." The Ukrainian population's turnout (so strikingly high against the background of the depressing political passivity of the past few years) during the parliamentary elections held in March-April 1994 and the ensuing victory of the Left can be explained primarily by popular hopes pinned on those political groups whose political image does not correlate in the mass consciousness with an obviously non-elitarian image of today's *nouveaux riches.*

§2. The Political Elite and the Intellectuals

At first sight, the intellellectuals seem to be merely a part of the nation's elite or, say, its spiritual elite.

However, the words "elite" and "intelligentsia" have essentially different meanings, particularly, in their relation to the state. The difference can even be seen in their closely elated etymologies: elite from the Latin *eligo,* meaning "I pick up, pluck, select, *etc.*," while intelligentsia is also of Latin origin – from *lego,* "I pick up, gather, choose," with the prefix *intel,* "among, between," implying spiritual affinity. If, from the very beginning, the elite presupposes those who select it, the intelligentsia is such a "reasoning substance," which, so to speak, slips through the fingers of those who would create forms for it and seeks to autonomously regulate its being.

As a protest against the involvement of intellectuals in totalitarian political movements during the interwar period, Julien Benda in his book, *The Treason of the Intellectuals,* traced the intellectuial's calling to the medieval *clerc* (whence the word cleric also derives), who was concerned with the search for eternal spiritual truth and thus could not become involved in secular political affairs without betraying his calling as an intellectual. This distinction also makes sense in the postcommunist context. Under any circumstances, the elite is something that is selected or formed for some purpose. Its very existence is linked to the presence of a certain recognized establishment, a stable system of values, in accordance with which individuals are "enrolled" in the elite, and its possible evaluation is accomplished. For example, the activities of our current political elite might be assessed on the basis of the extent it works to affirm and develop Ukrainian statehood. Obviously, any elite needs a specific, carefully designed system of education and socialization – again, with some particular strategic objectives in view. Because the elite is composed of selected individuals, it is viewed less as an independent subject of power than an attribute of a larger entity. The intelligentsia is quite another matter. Embodying the very spirit of creativity, it cannot, in principle, be formed according to a set pattern or in accordance with some predetermined criteria. As a natural outgrowth of some corresponding community, it reflects all the idiosyncrasies of its specific historical manifestations and self-realization.

The elite as such seeks and is supposed to seek leadership and power; but this very craving would be impossible without recognition of super-power over it, one which grants power prerogatives and delineates the course which the leader has to follow, that is, the basic direction of contests among power-seekers. Intellectuals remain aloof from such contests and emerge, in their turn, as an agent which formulates responsible decisions relating to the spiritual destiny of the nation and its absolute values, not to the material acquisitions of political and state institutions, tactical and strategic decisions, and such. From this flows its inherent moral value. The basic attitude of the intellectuals toward power is not one of submission to or identification with it (which is typical of the elite) but a dialog (which is also crucial to those in power if they do not want to lose valuable insight about the situation in society) about the deep tendencies of the entity they represent. The unfortunate thing about intellectuals in a number of postcommunist states is not that they have abandoned all ambitions for power, but the opposite: it is the penchant of many intellectuals for superficial "elitarization," for being transformed into a quasi-elite that, without becoming a real elite, loses its sense of mission as intelligentsia. Suffice it to dangle before such an intellectual the external attributes and privileges today associated with the power elite, and he finds its easy to join, despite his lack of requisite qualifications and aptitudes. Perhaps not least because the very principles of forming the intelligentsia were until recently based on the specific Communist Party elitism embodied in the old "nomenklatura selection and placement of cadres" and such.

Postcommunist society is equally in need of both a qualified elite, which can feed the power structures and find appropriate solutions to strategic tasks of national development, and a true, spiritually mature intelligentsia. A crisis situation regarding the latter's formation and preparation is one of the most painful problems of postcommunist culture.

§3. The Dualistic Nature of the Cultural and Political Elite

There is sufficient reason to regard a political elite primarily as a political grouping or stratum of leaders; for the semantic core of the notion of an "elite" is power as such. Also of no exception is any extended interpretation of this notion as concretized against various spheres of human activities. For does not the very pretension to the status of being a spiritual elite imply some lost, unattained, unattainable power? And here *belles lettres* plays an exceptional role.

Rulers and poets seem to compete for the role of educator. Aristotle saw to Alexander the Great's intellectual health, while Louis XIV supervised the creative efforts of Moliere. Nicholas I corrected Pushkin's and Shevchenko's poetry, while Pushkin dreamt of Nicholas I's tyranny following but one step after the "majestic tyranny" of Peter I. Stalin kept an eye on the musing of Bulgakov and Rylsky, and Voltaire assumed the role of a lay confessor to Friedrich II. Still more examples can be cited from the postcommunist states, including Ukraine.

The very nature of verbal activity presupposes a certain coercion, volition, and will to power, but the former's specific coloring is almost always determined by the will for national self-determination and the etatist project as a guarantor of this self-determination in conjunction with a personal destiny. Moreover, the absence of a genuine Ukrainian state as a certain line-up of power relations, compels one to orient oneself towards destructive, anarchic types of power discourse, and towards compensating for the lack of legal and economic levers of influencing life by a literary and artistic syncretism. This situation actually describes the physiognomy of postcommunist cultural elite, especially in Ukraine. This may be defined as a catacomb type of elite. Its attitude to power (namely, an alien, hostile statehood) also shapes the type of discourse. It is, above all, prophetic speech raised on the background of Christian culture.

Paradoxically, it is the universal state with its functional idiocy and belief in the power of brute force that guarantees the emergence and strengthening of a catacomb elite as well as improvement of its subculture.

The catacomb elite is of a dualistic nature. On the one hand, it clashes with the authorities as a marginal intellectual, an outcast, and even as fool. On the other, it cherishes the ideal of statehood. Protesting against hierarchy, this elite is forced to address in itself what Nietzsche called *ressentiment* (the spirit of frantic competition, envy, and bitterness) and at the same time to play the role of "spiritual leader." This results in a certain diminishing and, eventually, loss of the symbolic force of this elite. Democratism gradually becomes its inevitable enemy. The catacomb elite is mainly oriented toward the cult of feeling and intuition. Like Jesus, it chooses God's fools, those bearers of the divine Logos, as its interlocutors, rather than the wise (remember "The Ex-Convict" and "The Idiot" by Shevchenko). "The Ex-Convict" is also the founder of mystic historiography expressed in "The Muscovite Soldier's Well." The representatives of this elite belong to charismatic leaders and divines who oppose themselves to bureaucratic structures and the system of rational repressive rules. Such a leader gains authority by relying on symbolic codes: these may be ruins, as in the case of Shevchenko, or, as in the case with Lesya Ukrainka, an authoritative cultural and historical analogy ("Orgy"). Such a symbolic code encourages the spirit of vengeance. Words arouse the energy of condemnation and program the ballistics of feelings.

The contradiction between, so to speak, the social disintegration of the catacomb elite and an inevitable struggle with the inner forms of power, immanent in the knowledge created by the intellectual, leads to its duality. It is the conflict between one's social role and culturo-historically articulated idea of his destiny in the world. In the final analysis, this process culminates in the emergence of a pseudo-elite, customary for totalitarian and neo-totalitarian political systems, including those in the postcommunist states. For servility and conformism becomes the main criterion for recruitment into the ruling stratum. Obsequious self-humiliation and obedience, a surrogate for Christian behavior, become the highest virtues in society. This relates, first of all, to cultural elites.

An essential moment in establishing an elite is legitimization. This presupposes popular recognition of a power hierarchy along with further mythologizing of the leaders' persons. Irrespective of value factors – intellect, brute force, or moral standards – its social basis remains the will to power.

In communist totalitarian conditions, legitimization was based on the so-called "Führer principle," *i.e.*, an essentially hierarchic fragmentation of the highest authority. This principle was reproduced in all fields of public life, above all in the ideological-spiritual industry. National artistic elites were legitimized in a dualistic system of loyalty: loyalty to the national idea and to the universal state with its communist totems. This very duality called forth a specific schizophrenic discourse with a depersonalized recipient-censor. This kind of schizophrenia is unnatural, for it causes an identity crisis in the individual. Hence the individual's desire to rid himself, at the first opportunity, of the burden of Other-directed discourse. And for this reason it is no accident that writers have found themselves among the staunchest supporters of the parties of power in many post-communist states. They seemed to receive the simplest way of overcoming this crisis of identity and self-assertion: they merely have to step up to the podium. Still, however, the schizophrenia of the statesmen/poets persists. For the democratic jargon used during the transition from a brief period of ideological "opposition" to that of defending the government was of a hypercritical nature. Integration into governmental structures has destroyed the old basis of legitimacy foundation grounded in this jargon, for the sake of defending those structures. Thus, any catacomb elite is the pluperfect of an elite which may be defined as a servile or conformist.

This is also witnessed by the process of changing the heroes of the power discourse. For example, in the days of the "communist archaics" the ideal hero was the communist fighter, who in the "totalitarian classical" period gave way to the communist secretary. Communal leader-worship transforms itself into the *Führerprincip.*

In the postcommunist period this kind of figure becomes the militant knight of national revival with some features of the bureaucratic hierarch, an angel with the bureaucrat's wings of paper. Noteworthy is a change of genre matrixes within which the power discourse is established. The languid lyricism of servile ritual hands over torch to a spokesman/preacher. A new type of parliamentary "homiletic" is born.

The catacomb and servile spiritual elites are different stages in the historical course of the will to power. The difference is that the catacomb elite creates its own subculture, a unique self-valued semiotic space. Orientation toward prophetic speech enables it to avoid the boring rituals of a lesson or service.

Clearly, typologies of national elites (especially in the postcommunist states) has, like all classifications, its flaws. First, it does not reflect the whole variety of leading social strata (groups) which may be called elitarian. Second, it fails to adequately embrace twentieth century sociopolitical experience. However, in contrast with Dmytro Dontsov, who considered self-sacrifice in the name of an idea and specific spiritual energy as the main feature of a leading stratum, one might well point to its will to power and the ambivalent nature of spiritual power. This will is materialized through a discourse which entails certain cultural and historical conventions. Nietzsche provided the most exact characterization of the rudimentary adherence to such conventions: "Trying to get power, the weak struggle for personal freedom, the strong for social restructuring, the strongest for happiness of all humankind."

§4. The Party of Power Between "Communism" and "Nationalism"

One of the most widespread images of Ukraine, now current in the West, has assumed a rather unattractive shape in the last few years since the West first took note of Ukraine's existence. Ukraine is thought to be ruled by a "crypto-communist" regime which has shown its total inefficiency and corruptness, bringing about political and economic collapse in a country hastily made independent.

However, there are significant essential and objective reasons for such an inadequate, primitive image of Ukraine. They follow from a specific, if not unique, situation in Ukraine which cannot be studied by mechanistically applying existing concepts because it differs essentially from those in East Central Europe, the Third World, and, in the long run, in Russia though it does have certain (sometimes rather deceptive) similarities with each of them.

To understand the true nature of the ruling regime in Ukraine, one should consider, above all, the phenomenon of the so-called "party of power," *i.e.*, an informal, non-institutionalized, but quite influential social force with certain political and economic interests as well as powerful means of defending the latter. At the very outset of Ukrainian independence, political scientists gave quite an accurate definition of the "party of power" as a political bloc composed of the pragmatically-oriented and deideologized upper strata of the old communist nomenklatura, representatives of the state apparatus, mass media, and managers in the traditional sectors of industry and agriculture.[10]

Since September 1991 when Ukraine proclaimed independence, its representatives continued to occupy key positions in the Cabinet of Ministers; dominate the local bodies in most regions; virtually monopolize the radio and television, control a considerable part of the national Ukrainian newspapers and an absolute majority of local newspapers; hold in their hands (as before) the courts, procuracy and police; form electoral commissions to their liking; and influence fundamentally the interpretation and application of national referendums, as well as others laws in this country.

This is, in fact, the party of the old communist establishment, *i.e.*, an "inner party" as it was aptly called by George Orwell in his novel *1984.* After the abortive coup of August 1991 this "inner party" accepted quite easily the dissolution of the "outer" one, *i.e.*, the multimillion-strong and largely show-piece party of the "workers, peasants, and the whole Soviet people." This occurred primarily because the years of so-called perestroika culminated the long process of deideologizing the "inner party," and its stratification into orthodox and pragmatic members. The latter ceased to regard the mass Communist Party as necessary and functional, and got rid of it at the first opportunity, and did likewise with the already ineffective (in terms of preserving its power) Marxist-Leninist ideology. Having discarded all things unnecessary, the "inner party" essentially increased its social maneuverability and adaptibility to new political conditions.

This "party" can truly be considered "crypto-communist," to a large extent, for its members habitually display political and economic conservatism, a penchant for authoritarianism and command-administrative methods of activity, along with a high degree of mutual protection and clannish association.[11] The nomenklatura is, in fact, the ruling oligarchy which used to be called the communist nomenklatura before 1991, and received the rather apt title, "party of power," thereafter, in spite of its social mimicry, change of slogans, and attempts to rule anonymously. Clearly, it was not a party in the true sense of the word, either before or after the coup. It was the state, *i.e.*, the state apparatus, the collective holder of political power and property; and it is this situation that it tries to freeze with its ostentatious "non-party status."

Even if we consider the activities of the "party of power" without any coordination, the very fact of its representatives' concerted actions testifies to their belonging to a certain community whose members have common ("correct" in Orwell's terms) instincts. These instincts help them survive in the postcommunist social environment. The only principle this "party" will never betray is preservation of its own power and property (in any ideological wrapping or under any political slogan), while all other "principles" are secondary, rudimentary, and dispensable.

The "party of power" seems to have formally "opted" for true political independence and democracy, a multi-party system and market economy, but only to the extent that it does not violate its main principle. This principle means, as stated above, preservation of power and property. This is why it "builds" a "market economy" in a rather specific way, peculiar to the mafia and oligarchy. This is why it holds in check and restricts in every way possible the evolution of real democracy and a multi-party system (and civil society in general) – from delaying the adoption of a new ("non-Soviet") constitution to the holding of real parliamentary elections.

Yet, the most complicated question is the "choice" of political independence by the nomenklatura. It is from this that most illusions about the "patriotism" of the "party of power" and, at the same time, most speculations about its alleged "nationalism" seem to have emerged. Not ruling out certain "patriotic" or even "nationalistic" intentions by some representatives of the old nomenklatura, one may still say that its "independence-seeking" is primarily of a clanish and corporativist, rather than ethnic or even state-building, nature. Any oligarchy "seeks independence" only insofar as independence from a "superior" sovereign expands its access to power and property without jeopardizing too much its previous privileged position. This "immanent" independence-seeking, given a certain weakening of the "suzerain" ("Godfather" or "General Secretary"), tends to manifest itself at all levels – from Union or autonomous republic through the region or district down to the individual collective farm.

The old Ukrainian communist nomenklatura "chose" democracy and the multi-party system only as a kind of counterweight to its own sovereignty. For it first had to overcome the resistance of more conservative, pro-imperial forces within its own ranks to achieve sovereign status; and to do so, required the bearers of the national idea as an ally. Second, still moving towards sovereign status, it also had to enlist the support or at least the sympathetic understanding of the liberal democratic West and, hence, accept ("choose"), if only in words, the current democratic rules of the game. And this is precisely what the "party of power" did: it borrowed almost all the national democratic slogans from the autumn of 1991, while preserving its old corporativist nature.

While fulfilling the national democratic program in a way corresponding to its own interests (independence, state building), the "party of power" also sought to fulfill the communist program: protecting "Soviet power," supporting the feudal collective-farm system, and preserving the so-called "property of the entire people" (*i.e.*, collective oligarchic property). In so doing, it consciously or unconsciously fulfills (at the level of "social instinct") its main function, namely, its own program aimed at the anonymous exercise of power and shadow privatization of property in the interests of the ruling elite.

Guided by "correct intuition" (Orwell) rather than "correct views," the "party of power" adjusts its slogans and ideology to the requirements of the moment, becoming a kind of mirror of social sentiments, their populist mediator and mouthpiece. This ideological eclecticism, in fact, reflects the ambivalent state of awareness. Orientation toward this awareness and exploitation of its inferiority can undoubtedly produce a short-term political effect. The "protean nature" and "ambivalence" of the "party of power" enables it to exert far-reaching influence on various social strata, gives it considerable room for maneuvering, and can really make it, for some time, a consolidating force in society. However, this strategy fixes, in the final analysis, an orientation to mutually exclusive values (a little capitalism, a little socialism; a little democracy, a little "strong hand"; a bit of the free market, a bit of administrative leveling, *etc.*) and thus deepens the social-psychological disorientation and social neurasthenia, leading to "inconsistent development of democratic processes" and objectively retarding the creation of a full-fledged civil society or even preventing it.[12]

Mixed attitudes to the "party of power" became, in fact, the problem which caused a fundamental split among the national democrats. This split actually began immediately after Ukraine gained independence, when a large number of national democrats decided that the main objective of the their movement had been achieved, and agreed unconditionally to cooperate with the "party of power," occupying important (though by no means pivotal) posts in the ministries, embassies, and the presidential apparat.

§5. *Neototalitarian Transformations of Postcommunist Power in Ukraine*

In any democratic state there is always a political elite (which consists of the ruling stratum or active and established political minority plus an opposed counter-elite consisting of another organized minority seeking power) and the majority of people. One of the main problems of democratic society is how to safeguard the majority's effective control of the elite in a way that most benefits the people. This is achieved by seeking and then establishing democratic institutions which provide for the large scale representation of society in the ruling stratum, ensure its qualitative renewal, and prevent it from transforming itself into an oligarchy, that is, a closed, ruling caste alienated from the people.

In Ukraine, which proclaimed national independence a few days after the abortive army/Communist Party *Putsch* in the former USSR in August 1991, political conditions remain almost the way they were when the monocratic power of the Communist Party still existed. Because these conditions remain basically unchanged, it is only natural that today Ukraine witnesses a plundering unprecedented in scope and violence of the majority by this organized minority. This is violence in the most literal sense, which inflicts colossal material losses on the majority, damaging their physical and emotional health. However, while the Stalin-Brezhnev variant of the political system legitimized violence by the elite with the aid of an ideological myth about the "radiant communist future," after 1991 leaders have actively used (and thereby discredited) the ideal of "building an independent democratic state."

In other words, in terms of its prospects of democratic transformations and the formation of civil society, Ukraine is today undoubtedly among the outsiders of the postcommunist world. The historical distance between Ukraine and Poland, the Czech Republic, Hungary, or certain other post-communist states is rapidly increasing and may already be decades apart. One of the main reasons determining the direction of the transformation of political power in Ukraine, which can be described as postcommunist, nomenklatura-dominated, and simultaneously neo-totalitarian, lies in its extreme uncertainty (when compared to the above-mentioned countries) as to where its interests lie and the weak political will of its socially active individuals.

It is also clear that societies are capable of assuring the large-scale representation of various social strata in the ruling political elite and the counter-elite interests and aspirations only under conditions of well-developed socially stratification. Ideally, such a society should be dominated by a large middle class (or "middle income group") which, in democratically developed nations, is the main element necessary for the socioeconomic development of a society as well as political stability in a nation. How, then, does Ukrainian society compare in this light?

Its social structure is a sort of amorphous mass, lacking any clear-cut social strata and social self-identification. This means that most of the population have not yet formed (nor become aware of) their real, concrete, well-defined social interests and social status. Under conditions of a drastic decline in living standards, the lumpenized stratum is growing rapidly, while the middle class remains numerically small.

Simultaneously, an increasing marginalization of a sizable portion of the population, particularly the young, is taking place. Uncertainty of social interests, along with the absence of civic values and civil consciousness have led to unprecedented aberrations in ethical behavior, especially among those who have been marginalized. These attitudes are characterized by vagueness and mobility of the distinctions between truth and lie, law and crime, *etc.* A widespread marginal self-awareness is oriented and conducive to social and political instability of society along with extremist actions in everyday sociopolitical life.

Ukrainian society as a whole is characterized above all by deep social disintegration. This is explained by the weakness of the interests and thus of social will on the part of the small strata of society which support economic and political modernization. The uncertainty of social interests and undefined quality of social self-identification in today's Ukrainian society prevents the formation of even the prerequisites for a transition to civil society and hence establishment of a democratic system for recruiting the ruling elite.

The majority of the population is unable to overcome in a relatively short time the stereotypes of authoritarian consciousness and communitarian way of life. In other words, Ukraine is not prepared to accept alternative values, in particular, those of civil society.

All this is connected with the socio-genetic legacy and genetic reserve, which Ukraine inherited after the collapse of the communist regime in the former USSR and disintegration of the latter. The politocide and sociocide (not only the 1933 famine, which wiped out almost all the peasantry, the backbone of the Ukrainian nation, but the complete elimination of its historically-developed natural social strata), countless victims of World War II, physical liquidation of the best representatives of the Ukrainian nation by the Stalinist regime, and Chernobyl casualties – all this has no analogy in world history (except perhaps for Cambodia under Pol Pot) and has produced catastrophic consequences for Ukrainian society, including its social, cultural, and political degeneration and disintegration, along with its still-prevailing paralysis of political will.

It should be borne in mind that the political independence gained by Ukraine depended on a lucky chance fortuitous opportunity related to the abortive August 1991 *Putsch* of the orthodox part of the old nomenklatura, and was not a result of such internal political processes as the national liberation struggle or democratic demands of the Ukrainian political counter-elite which began to form from 1988 to 1991. And this is only natural, for of all Soviet republics Ukraine was the most "law abiding," and the nomenklatura took root most deeply and retained the most favorable conditions for holding on to power in Ukraine. Thus, it was primarily the nomenklatura, and not the numerous social subjects of political life against which the nomenklatura discriminated, that received independence, along with social and political *carte blanche*.

Independent Ukraine also inherited the former communist totalitarian nomenklatura, which managed to preserve real power and property quite easily after August 1991 by means of a unique exercise in political horse-trading: recruiting to its ranks the most conformist leaders of the former counter-elite and by a timely change in its slogans for the sake of a new "legitimacy."

An analysis of the political behavior of the current ruling stratum in Ukraine gives ample grounds to conclude that during the period of decline and transformation from a Communist totalitarian regime, a considerable part of the ruling nomenklatura bureaucracy was able to change its political mentality and follow the path of social and political compromise, as long as they preserve their power and privileges. This elite often succeeds in winning the support of numerous other social groups, which lack both consciousness of their own real interests and political experience. Such a "consolidation" is maintained by a minimal level of cooperation between the ruling bureaucracy and its rivals from the opposition counter-elite camp.

The current postcommunist "market of power" in Ukraine began to take shape immediately after the abortive August *Putsch.* Its particular feature was that the former communist ruling elite, pressed by its most reactionary and most odious representatives, consciously opened the door of the power market to those democrats and leaders of new political parties most willing to conform. For with the collapse of the CPSU the Ukrainian nomenklatura faced a dilemma: self-renewal or death.

The strength of the ruling stratum, and the weakness of other social strata were shown when for several months in late 1991 and early 1992, the "party of power" managed to engulf most of the former opposition groups to the Communist Party, allowing them limited access to the market of power. This produced one main accomplishment: it drew a clear line of demarcation between the majority, who passively awaited change for the better, and the counter-elite which had only recently pretended to stand up for that majority.

This is witnessed by the spiritual and political metamorphosis of many opposition leaders, who had been in opposition to the CPU and had been cast by chance into the political arena in 1988-1991. By disarming and splitting the opposition, the nomenklatura strengthened itself greatly, because it was able to exchange a few small symbolic concessions and posts for the cloak of "national-democratic" legitimacy. In other words, there was a unique diffusion of power between the parasitic former communist elite and the conformist counter-elite, which rendered real political and market reforms impossible in 1992-1995. And the place which the former opposition counter-elite occupied in the political process before August 1991 has been left practically vacant.

Beginning in August 1991, the ruling elite was able to swallow up the former opposition by co-opting most of its leaders. It also gained the cooperation of those democratically-inclined intellectuals, who had not actively participated in the political developments of 1988-1991. It is for this reason that, for example, the state Duma of Ukraine and its collegia were established.

In this way the "party of power" gained in three ways. First, it gained legitimacy in the eyes of the segment of the Ukrainian intelligentsia which had avoided cooperation with the CPU during the last two or three years before its self-dissolution and ban. Second, it weakened the intellectual potential of its scarce political opponents. Third, the State Duma and other similar institutions created after the ban on the Communist Party of Ukraine, became a kind of "cadre reserve" for various political posts. This has resulted in the establishment of the intellectuals and intelligentsia's dependence on those who wield power. The elite is now in desperate need of intellectual "ideologists" and intellectual *clercs* capable of formulating and disseminating effective ideological and political myths to camouflage the real state of things and find new forms to legitimize its power.

Understandably, the old "new" postcommunist nomenklatura has not and cannot be objectively interested in the emergence of truly democratic institutions, which would ensure society's democratic progress, arouse and stimulate its political will, and assure substantive public control and influence over the political decision-making process. This would endanger the nomenklatura's dominant status, its ability to distribute and redistribute property. However, the low intellectual and cultural level of the current Ukrainian postcommunist nomenklatura (at all levels) along with its lack of professionalism and competence rapidly diminish its capability of social and political maneuvering, as well as its legitimacy. At the same time, it deepens the alienation of the current political power from the majority of the population. The latter's social discontent is gradually increasing and may in time develop into large-scale social unrest. This would make it all the more difficult for Ukraine's postcommunist nomenklatura to maintain the *status quo* by customary "peaceful" methods, tried and tested in the postcommunist period. It would also create objective prerequisites for using, in the long run, violence against the majority of the population, and enhances the probability of a permanent and long-term sociopolitical instability peculiar to the modern neo-totalitarian postcommunist regimes.

It is now obvious, not only to analysts but even the general public, that the changes now under way in the former communist states are of qualitatively different nature, different social content, and operate from a different system of social and political coordinates. From this we may find that unity and similarity among these countries which we have sought in their recent historical past, and perhaps we may also find it in the values and general slogans they declare, rather than in their reality of today and, even less so, in the reality of their near future.

As for Ukraine, as the preceding analysis bears witness, the essence of the transformation of political power after the collapse of the former USSR can be understood only within the context of a shadow political process of the ruling elite's painless, even organic transition from communist nomenklatura totalitarianism to postcommunist nomenklatura neo-totalitarianism.

Corruption as a Political Phenomenon Under Postcommunism

§1. Corruption in Postcommunist Societies

In the political lexicon, the term corruption is almost always used to mean bribery and the venality of public officials. Therefore, it embraces two interconnected aspects of one of the forms by which "public servants" are alienated from the people.

Corruption can be found in any political and economic system, and it constitutes a component of a mechanism by which bureaucratic structures may exploit society. Where democratic or authoritarian mechanisms function and guarantee the social organism normal life, corruption is localized such that it has little influence on the political situation as a whole or is kept more or less under control. Nevertheless, under both authoritarian and democratic regimes, corruption can be transformed into a structuralizing element of political and social life. This becomes possible when unrestrained self-interest prevails among broad segments of the population.

Practically all types of states announce their determination to combat corruption. Moreover, all states are forced to adopt in some form or another anti-corruption measures. In some cases, combating corruption may lead to the creation of a system of reliable legal and institutional safeguards of social and political control (democratic or autocratic) over the activities of state bodies, various organizations, and individuals. In others, it may be reduced to measures forced on the authorities by the need to restore basic order, or redistribute spheres of influence among various clans of the ruling oligarchy and Mafia-type entities, *etc.* A direct agent of corruption as a specific type of social relationships, *i.e.*, a person who out of his/her self-interest (and for a certain remuneration), engages in particular unlawful, immoral, or socially dangerous acts of commission or omission to benefit someone else, may be committed by a state official of any level, a politician, or an organizational functionary. The beneficiaries of such acts may be individuals, foreign or domestic companies, political or communal organizations, foreign intelligence agencies, *etc.*

As shown by the experience of postcommunist states, corruption creates a certain "distribution of authority" or, more precisely, a distribution of power among different types of politicians: pragmatists loyal to the national leader, members of the leader's clan, people whose mutual trust and alliance were formed through the joint shedding of other people's blood, various types of romantics whose political orientations may differ according to the cultural and historical features of a specific state or political expediency, and also mafia circles representing criminalized national capital and the comprador bourgeoisie.

Many states with such regimes have adopted legal normative acts on combating corruption. Usually such norm creation reflects an old bureaucratic tradition: legal normative acts permit the avoidance of real action capable of attaining the enunciated aim, appear energetic, and thus simulate socially important state functions. Very often "combating corruption" becomes a way of carrying out reprisals against representatives of rival political and economic clans or of legitimizing the policy of the ruling oligarchy. Group selfishness supersedes the strategy of safeguarding national interests.

There is nothing unusual about this: it is a rather common type of behavior under progressing moral and economic crisis. Suffice it to recall the experience of many African countries. The superprofits gained by illegal means enable a number of the present rulers to satisfy not only their own and their children's material needs, but also to guarantee the fulfillment of the most exquisite whims of their descendants, who can expect to inherit the boundless wealth now being reaped from the selling out of their country.

There are no barriers which corrupt and mafia-type structures are unprepared to overcome; there are no rules of society that they dare not break. Nor can the world community fail to realize the serious danger of the further criminalization of various politically unstable, especially postcommunist, regions of the world. All this justifies the conclusion that in the foreseeable future the problems of corruption will remain a central political issue.

§2. Ukrainian Kleptocracy

Ukraine, like other newly independent states of the former USSR, inherited eviscerated and deformed social, political, administrative, and economic structures. This in turn created extremely complicated problems, which, in the face of the persistent territorial and other pretensions expressed by its northeastern neighbor, require quick resolution.

As American Sovietologist Moshe Lewin rightly described it, under Stalinism the Soviet state literally swallowed up civil society, including the economy. The First Five Year Plan, he noted, "was a unique process of state-guided social transformation, for the state did much more than just 'guiding': it substituted itself for society, to become the sole initiator of action and controller of all important spheres of life. The process was thus transformed into one of 'state building,' with the whole social structure being, so to speak, sucked into the state mechanism, as if entirely assimilated by it."[13]

In other words, Stalin was able to concretize the Hegelian idea that the state created society by creating (to use the Orwellian Newspeak of the period) a state superstructure which, in turn, created its own economic base. The creation of the command economy and its appropriation of the agricultural sector during the forced collectivization of the peasantry relegated the economy to a secondary role wholly dependent on politics. And in a state where 90% of the economy is state property, economic problems simply cannot be solved without political decisions being made.

American political scientist Alexander Motyl also vividly described what he called "post-totalitarian ruin," stating: "Ukraine is a land with people and things, but the organization of the people and things, the administration and arrangement of them, the relations between and among them, are still for the most part missing or undefined." In place of a state which, in Max Weber's classic definition, effectively taxes, administers, and polices a certain territory, Ukraine today has an "underdeveloped and dreadfully corrupt... pseudostate."[14]

After the collapse of the USSR, Ukraine, whose ministries and administration had been little more that mailboxes for orders from Moscow, inherited a much too small, intellectually weak, and largely vassalized state mechanism with responsibilities much too large for it to handle – from building apartment complexes to running grocery stores.

It was only natural that most of the mechanisms of planning and supervision rapidly disintegrated. Instead of privatization there was a feudalization of state enterprises, the managers of which had administrative control over state property and goods and began to open their own "private" firms. This, in turn, allowed the manager to sell items from "his" state factory to his private firm at such prices that any profits were sure to wind up in his pocket. Thus, there was a unique and nonviable process of partial privatization where only the profits were privatized and the costs by and large remained in the state sector. State industries quickly lost all incentive to produce efficiently and cost-effectively. In the final analysis this caused a structural economic crisis which cannot be solved without a fundamental rethinking of the state's role in society, the separation of the private and state-run economies, and the creation of effective incentives to produce marketable goods and services.

These structural problems were in themselves sufficient to create economic chaos, a catastrophic decline in industrial output and, as a result, a substantial decline in real incomes. Nomenklatura partial privatization led to huge monetary emissions (which are now almost impossible to control) to persons protected by high state posts and who have real influence on economic policy. Such people have an interest in continuing the policy of state credits, which cause inflation by producing a huge structural budgetary deficit. This deficit, in turn, gave rise to confiscatory taxation, which then created a situation where it makes little sense to do business legally. The state's monetary hunger tends to push economic down where the tax man cannot find it.

Another important factor also influenced Ukraine's economic disintegration: its instantaneous isolation from the so-called "unified economic complex" into which it had been integrated illogically and without regard for its regional national needs and interests. From the 1930s on, in order to combat the danger of "economic separatism" industry was often located far from its sources of raw materials and from its consumers. When state enterprises in Russia stopped sending goods to and paying for goods from Ukraine, the chain of production was broken. Examples abound. Due to the fact that Ukrainian titanium was processed only in Russia, Ukraine is now forced to sell raw titanium while the Russian plants that used to process it into titanium sponge stand idle for want of the raw material. Sometimes economics circumvented politics, restoring the severed links in round-about fashion. Russia, which used to send Siberian diamonds to Kyiv for cutting, decided to give this business to an Israeli firm. But the Kyiv factory was cheaper, and the Israeli firm contracted with Kyiv to do the actual work. As a result, Russia began shipping raw diamonds to Israel, whence they were shipped to Ukraine, then back to Israel as cut stones, and home again to Russia.

Lower production presents two alternatives, unemployment or inflation. The state chose inflation, a choice governed by the fact that most people in Ukraine, for all their dissatisfaction with the communist old regime, are still in the habit of looking to the state as their universal provider. Fearing that civil disturbances could accompany the inevitable costs of shock therapy, politicians simply lacked the political will to do what was necessary. And with time it became clear that the demoralization and economic hopelessness of the vast majority of the population do not bode well for reforms which will inevitably impact negatively on people's morale and living standards.

Today the sole model of a market economy with which the vast majority of the population are familiar is the black market. Unlike America, where organized crime infiltrates legitimate business, in Ukraine organized crime (bands which traditionally controlled, say, prostitution and fenced stolen goods) have themselves established major commercial enterprises which frequently come into competition with firms founded from the only other major source of domestic investment capital, the banned (now partially legalized) Communist Party and Comsomol. In fact, the parallels between the economic activity of ex-criminals and ex-communists are so close that most people see no difference between them and use the same word, "mafia," for both. The growth of a market economy out of the black market has led to an economic culture closer to Al Capone than to Western business. Bankers cannot survive without a group of bodyguards recruited from former *spetsnaz* members because disagreements, which in the West would be solved with the aid of lawyers, are more cheaply and effectively solved here with guns and explosives. In Ukraine being a banker is very hazardous to one's health. And so on down the economic food chain. One cannot even open a kiosk without paying unofficial taxes to unofficial "authorities."

When criminal structures grew into legitimate business what took place was a simultaneous legalization of the mafia and "mafiaization" of business in general. On the one hand, former criminals set up banks and other big businesses without giving up what were, for them, their traditional spheres of activity. The inability of the state to adequately pay the police and other internal security agencies enabled organized crime to "infect" small business by demanding the latter pay the unofficial taxation known as the "protection racket." The vast majority of small and medium-sized businessmen are well aware of the fact that the cannot safely work without paying "insurance" to some sufficiently powerful Godfather.

Ex-party officials have their own structures of contacts and associations which assist them conduct their current "business."

It became a fact of life that no one could live on his official income. On the one hand, the need for a second "under the table" income fostered a less than serious attitude toward one's official job, where one has to show up or face problems with the authorities. And this led to substantial economic losses. On the other hand, the pauperization of certain strata of society inevitably led to widespread corruption, which has assumed a structural character justifying our employing the term, "kleptocracy." This does not mean that all officials and bureaucrats take bribes or steal, but rare is the person who, for example, cannot on his official income afford a new pair of shoes for his child and will eschew all not quite legal ways of supplementing his income. In this sense one can discern a venalization of the whole structure of public administration.

Misappropriation has also assumed a structural character, most prominently in the area of state and state-guaranteed credits. Here perhaps the best illustration is the case of the nomenklatura agricultural cooperative, Land and People, headed by former Agriculture Minister and current Deputy Speaker of Parliament Oleksander Tkachenko. As we know, in 1993 Mr. Tkachenko obtained for his cooperative a state-guaranteed credit line of $70 million US from Citibank in New York, ostensibly to buy seed corn. A relatively small quantity of corn was actually purchased, while much of the borrowed money went to buy 32 American automobiles, TV sets, computers, faxes, furniture, and other easily resold items. After the cooperative declared bankruptcy, Ukraine was forced to repay $53 million and still owes over $20 million to Citibank.[15]

Since Parliamentary Speaker Oleksandr Moroz cannot retain his fragile majority without Tkachenko's support, this illustrates how the need to protect specific political figures impacts upon the whole political structure and shows that theft has assumed the character of public policy.

Ukrainian kleptocracy is an important factor fostering economic and political instability. But as a form of government it is inherently nonviable because it cannot halt mass pauperization and the state's loss of effective control over the army and police. I see two alternatives for unraveling this Gordian knot. Either Ukraine will opt for radical reforms, privatization, and destatization to reduce the state's responsibilities to a point where the state can fulfill them and through the formation of a civil society become a direct and equal member of the family of nations (this might be called the Polish option). Or Ukraine will become a second class nation capable of participation in world civilization only through the mediation of a Russocentric CIS, which will swallow it up and impose on Ukraine what might be called "the Belarus option."

§3. Corruption and Corporate Interests

Most judgments on the economy and politics now current among scholars and practical politicians, economists, experts, political scientists — assume the existence of a certain object — society, economic life, relationships — which has only to be correctly understood and studied, about which correct conclusions have only to be drawn. Then, based on this knowledge, good transformation programs can be worked out, and the transformations will eventually take the right path. That is, it is assumed that there is someone who wants to make something good out of that object. But nothing ever comes of such wishful thinking. And excuses are always found that this or that plan was not adequate, this or that project was not quite perfect, *etc.*

Society, however, is not a passive, lifeless object. It is an active agent that contains its own dynamics of economic life. We all talk, for example, about the influence of politics on the economy; but conversely, the economy exerts far greater influence on politics, even if this influence is not exactly advertised by the politicians themselves. To take an example, the Peasant Party is at the same time a faction in the Parliament and a mouthpiece of the majority of agricultural (so to speak) corporations and chairmen of collective farms in Ukraine (*i.e.*, it directly represents them in the persons of their members). Eighty percent of decisions which they do or do not support flow from their direct economic and corporate interests. Let us consider another aspect of this problem. If most people do not live on the wages and salaries they receive at their official place of employment, but survive on their connections in the countryside or other jobs, then why does the overwhelming majority of population still cling to their official jobs? Why do enterprises not close down and why do workers at the Artem plant, who earn wages on which they cannot live, still go to work there? Here we come to the main point.

If people begin to create economic relationships outside and apart from their main job – the place of their "employment registration" (*i.e.*, unofficially, in fact, illegally and illegitimately from the point of view of industrial legal norms currently in force) – then necessity has cast over us a rather powerful shadow of a corrupted society which overshadows us all. Corruption is being structured into the forms of corporate representation in the upper echelons of power – either in the government or as a lobbying group or faction in Parliament. In other words, through legitimate structures of production and power, corporate interests of other kinds – private manufacturing or private commerce – and, eventually, the corporate interests of criminal structures proper find their way to covert legalization. This can take place even without bureaucrats and top elected officials clearly realizing that they are representing such interests. But one can never know when this blessed innocence may evolve with time into intentional purposeful lobbying by this part of the elite of corporate (as opposed to public, societal) interests and, later, into their institutional consolidation.

This process has, on the whole, an objective nature. But what policy and what realistic economic programs can we speak about, if the very existence of powerful corporate interests among the ruling elite is overlooked? How can reforms be planned, if these half-legal and practically illegal interests are not bridled? In the case of the Agrarian Party, this process holds no great danger. Here in the final analysis interests do not go far beyond the limits of the law, and we know what the representatives of the collective farm feudal lords want. They cannot permit radical alteration of the existing form of land use. But along with this, there are other corporatist "programs" about which we know nothing. And these undercurrents are, of course, not taken into account when official plans are made.

Thus, following President Kuchma, one can speak of social partnership. This is clearly a progressive proposal, if only because it recognizes different social interests of different social groups. Earlier, nobody wanted to admit this officially. For example, a director was assumed to represent interests of his workers. A director, who went with his family on holidays to Switzerland, was thought to have the same set of interests as a worker of that enterprise who earned about $5 US a month. And now the different interests of different social groups and classes are at least acknowledged. But what conclusion does the President's program draw from this? That it is necessary to raise most people's wages and salaries. In other words, it is recognized that there are people whose earnings should be reckoned with, *i.e.*, earnings of others should be brought up to the level of that political-economic incognito. However, nothing is said about the latter. Although from a public relations standpoint it would be worthwhile to plan some kind of law adopting a luxury tax.

Of course, it is quite possible that this spontaneous process of the corporatization of postcommunist society is unlikely to constitute a threat in itself. Far more dangerous is the disproportionate representation of different group interests. Those of many covert and openly acknowledged corporate groupings are not represented at all in the projected economic transformation. For example, the interests of trade unions as a legitimate corporate entity are not provided for at all. On the whole, the program takes into account the interests of legitimate business and the state-owned sector.

But this also means that the interests of a rather large segment of the population, for example, those who are busy with shuttle-trading, who go to far-away regions to earn money and who bring foodstuff from their relatives in the countryside, *etc.*, are not in any way taken into account. But, more importantly, the interests of the above-mentioned covert social corporatist entities are not given explicit and legal expression. And this may bring even the best thought out program to a bad end and doom it to economic failure. In the final analysis, in Ukraine as elsewhere in the post-communist world, everything could end up totally out of control.

Chapter 3.

The Political Sociology of Postcommunism

- Tendencies of Social Stratification
- Adaptation Strategies of the Former Communist Elites
- Problems of Internal Political Geography: The Ukrainian Example
- Images of the Social Structure
- The Social Pathology of Postcommunist Society

Externally, the society referred to by sociologists and political scientists as postcommunist does not much resemble its so-called "socialist" predecessor. There are many surface indicators of social and political life which seem to testify that changes and transformations have occurred: the *"nouveau riches"* and the *"new poor,"* strata which have formed very rapidly, within a year or two; the unprecedented penchant for creating new political parties; the new or, to be more exact, "finally restored" pantheon of the real historical and cultural heroes of the nation and state; the reassessment of the past and the desired future – all these show that society is actively and steadily producing and accumulating its own idiosyncratic formulas of self-determination and self-identification. One could get the impression that it is hastening to assure itself and others of not only its craving to be transformed but also to demonstrate the genuineness and irreversibility of its transformation. "New" is just the word that is used most frequently to describe the processes under way. Moreover, attempts are made to present everything now taking place and happening as "new," as changes for better or worse. Yet, in all this supposedly "new" a keen observer can still discern invariables as well as traces and vestiges of the "old." And this is precisely the task of a sociologist, who tries to find continuity and succession.

At the same time, one must admit that emergent social entities – strata, layers, classes, institutions, and organizations – are sometimes difficult to identify and define in traditional sociological or political science terms and paradigms: they have no analogs just as there is no historical analog for the attempt to transform a socialist state system into a democracy along the lines of a relative separation of the state from the public, social, and economic spheres. For this reason some sociologists and political scientists suggest various terms: perhaps "social embryology" for the study of social forms which are in the process of being transformed into something quite different from what they are now, or something like "social parasitology" for monitoring newly emerging formations which are being produced *en masse* in the situation of economic and social crisis and genetically related to the latter, or else "social pathology" to account for the disintegration of structures of social and everyday life, the ruinous and murderous interethnic and international conflicts, and the degradation of moral norms and the system of social values.

This is why, within the framework of the political sociology of postcommunism, the following has now emerged as most urgent: a profound understanding and ideologically unbiased description of the process of social differentiation and stratification, and a development of promising approaches to the analysis of crises. Useful for understanding what is happening in postcommunist societies and whether they are making a permanent break with the past may be relevant to the interpretation of political discourse. As some observations show, the latter is very sensitive to current trends of social differentiation and is simultaneously extremely conservative, for it is connected with language and linguistic clichés and stereotypes which can reveal the superficial imitation of fashionable political rhetoric and disclose the underlying basis in the practice of mass discourse. The sociological import of verbal communication lies also in the fact that its production, dissemination and, not least, suggestion of images of social structure and stratification can either consolidate the masses into solidarity-based communities or set one community against another. Individuals and groups also make use of such images to define their own and other economic and political situations, their own and other social and cultural identities.

Tendencies of Social Stratification

If models of social structuralization and stratification are considered sort of semi-finished products created by civilization, which are then finished by nation-states with due account paid to their historical and cultural specifics, then Ukraine has not only been unsuccessful in such work but seems to have failed to start it. Continual pledges by the authorities of their devotion to democratic ideals and market economy have remained but political rhetoric, for these legal, economic, and social values and slogans have neither been translated into norms nor become models and examples of behavior to be followed. As a result, Ukraine's independence has already had its verbalized political history commemorated in symbols but still lacks its own traditions. Undisguised discontinuity in actions, promises, appeals, and most important, discontinuity in responsibility – these are all the most prominent features of the past few years. Only curves of production decline and inflation are stable. We see all the signs of a process which Joseph Schumpeter would unhesitatingly call non-creative construction and non-creative destruction: whatever is creative or destructive can in this period only aggravate the situation.

The causes of this situation are clearly objective in origin and lie inside the bounds of the history of independent Ukraine rather than in malicious plots of some outside forces. In order to make clear what has happened since the referendum of December 1, 1991 on Ukrainian independence, one may use the following image. At the close of that year rich in political developments, Ukraine suddenly discovered that it had, so to say, the relative muscle mass of Gulliver in Lilliput, in the form of giant military-industrial, metallurgical, coal-mining, and other complexes. All of them had worked earlier for the whole Soviet Union, while presently the new-born sovereign republic acquired them as an anticipated inheritance. The industrial hypertrophy showed through immediately and inadvertently. On the other hand, as a state, Ukraine was a sort of Tom Thumb with a midget sociopolitical skeletal frame in some parts, inadequately formed and without any experience of independent and self-sustained existence, nor without any clear-cut idea of statehood that could sum up the expectations and orientations of the public at large.

This chimerical hodgepodge of the gigantic and the miniature, of obsolete and unformed structures, knocked Ukraine over and made it bedridden. Such a position is fraught with bedsores. And such was the case: to use philosophical terms, opacities and impenetrabilities formed in the socioeconomic body which divided autonomous areas of self-organization living according to their own rules and norms and producing models of development only for themselves. At the same time, the social body as a whole does not reform and progress, *i.e.*, it remains historically motionless. There are many indications of this on the surface of social life. Most indicative in this respect may be claims of the second President in a row for creating the "power hierarchy." Noticeable in these are easily inferred allusions to the mutual alienation of the central and local authorities – parties which cannot communicate and must be enabled to do so. The president's decrees are revoked, the government is puzzled by the quaint responses of commercial and production structures to the decisions it makes – life, in all its obviousness, goes on according to its own rules, which are quite different from the legally established ones.

Moreover, the organizations and structures to be formed are reproduced according to patterns and models of a bare-faced bureaucratic and totalitarian vein. Here is one example from the field of science, but similar things happen in other spheres, too. In Ukraine it did not take long to set up the Supreme Attestation Commission (SAC), which approves all post-graduate degrees granted by Ukrainian institutions of higher learning. And it has convincingly demonstrated itself to be an institution no less conservative, inert, and prone to dictate its patterns of behavior to the scientific community and to control the latter, than was the former All-Union SAC. Such an institution is characteristic of a very centralized state and can function efficiently only within its framework.

For all the obvious socioeconomic ruin, one still cannot call Ukraine's economy a no-win game. There are, no doubt, people here who know the rules of the economic contest with a vague and unpredictable outcome. Large blocks of capital are being accumulated; new private enterprises are being founded, which manage to prosper under the strictest regulation; networks of equivalent and inequivalent exchanges are being established. Rather quickly, especially in the big cities, a particular "industrial-permissive class" is being formed from young and energetic individuals with high incomes, served by a diversified network of casinos, bars, restaurants, exclusive shops, *etc.,* and an infrastructure for spending hard currency earnings. And next to them, dragging out a miserable existence, are zones of economic anemia, tissue decay, and the irretrievable loss of work motivation.

These are not social contrasts; they are completely sovereign enclaves in the economic arena of postcommunist Ukraine where tendencies for further isolation and seclusion prevail. The individuals belonging to them hardly come into contact. They go to different stores. The downtowns of the cities, hitherto the traditional residence of the high-ranking state and party elite, are quietly being resettled by the *nouveau riches,* who are also actively building exclusive suburbs. And the bedroom communities of the less privileged are pushed farther and farther from the business center; their inhabitants use various transport, some private and others public, which operates more and more poorly. This separation of life spheres and the lack of immediate contact obviously fosters the diffusion of social tension and is a certain "cunning" of the socium, like an instinct of self-preservation, trying to prevent the concentration of social energy. But its weight is felt more and more in mass and political discourse, and it is precisely in this that the two societies are juxtaposed (for more, see section four below).

The new social division results from the uncertain workings of the mechanism of recreating the social structure. This is why in what results from these workings, large social groups and strata, it is difficult to find certain things we were quite familiar with in the past, practically nothing of what we hoped for the future, while new, often unexpected traits abound. In the elements of social structure which are taking shape before our eyes, so much unforeseen, the old and the new, the nonviable and the vibrant, combine or coexist that it becomes difficult to ignore or even deny the idea that a spontaneous structuralization into zones of imperviousness is taking place in Ukrainian society.

This is to some degree caused by the fact that a certain autonomy has been acquired by certain sections of the mechanism responsible for the reproduction of a normal or socially necessary social structure. Three such links have distanced themselves from one another: social institutions (primarily the state); the normative value system which provides for a certain degree of solidarity and accord among population groups and strata; and finally, the actions of individuals and groups which in principle should be governed by one or another social institution and oriented toward legitimate, universally binding, and normatively confirmed behavior patterns and models.

That is why the state is isolated and undeveloped market elements (*i.e.*, the other emerging most important social institution) have undoubtedly failed to cope with their structure-forming and structure-supporting roles. Moreover, a normative value system, obligatory for most people and supported by them, can be formed only in accordance with the new goals of social development and dominant political rhetoric. Only in highly developed forms will it be able not only to exert a decisive influence on the degree of inter-group solidarity and accord but also to give birth to new social strata and population groups unaccustomed to the old ideas (socialist and older) myths and thus adequate to the socioeconomic reality.

Against this background of feebleness, inertia, and the extremely sluggish response of the principal social institutions, when recognized systems of values and ideals are lacking, the structure-forming, socially-differentiating roles of the state, market, and other social institutions have practically passed on to the spontaneous activity of individuals and their corporativist associations, which assume the form of a survival reflex in conditions of adaptation to crisis circumstances. One can argue that situationally temporary and often purely accidental factors in the formation of the social structure have prevailed over the long-term (or, to be more exact, "systemic") ones typical of dynamically developing economies functioning stably and also over legitimate values and norms.

As a logical result of the emergence and establishment of areas of impermeability in the mechanism of reproducing the social structure, the molding of societal entities capable, under optimal conditions, of becoming the basis of a market economy (businessmen, financiers, managers, financial intermediaries, and commercial middle-men) takes place very slowly. At the same time, the emergence and shaping of "non-systemic" elements of structure is rapidly speeded up, elements which lack any perspective for development but have the ability to reproduced themselves, to defend their interests, and satisfy their needs thanks to their access to both deficit resources and thanks to the creation of new, including illegitimate and illegal, possibilities to satisfy economic, social, and political demands.

A tripartite division of society into the weakening elements of social structure (layers and categories of population), those growing stronger and thriving, and those holding their own in preventing the decline in their material and social status seems, at present, to be most prominent and is clearly felt in the arena of social life. They have different destinies and different prospects for the immediate and medium-term future, and hence, those who belong to them display very different social attitudes and conditions. Those who fall into the category of weakening elements are experiencing a crisis of state dependency and a crisis of their self-identification with it. The crux of the matter is that education, competence, and experience cannot guarantee one's security in this society nor prevent the decline of one's living standards. Today, the rules which govern the distribution of social and material wealth, and which regulate access to such wealth, have nothing in common with either a planned or market economy.

For many, these rules are vague and ambiguous at best; at worst, they are unfair and humiliating. An important result of this trend is the progressive destructuralization and destratification of that segment of the population which is economically active in the state sector of the economy. Growing anxiety, a feeling of social degradation, and a decline in one's identification with previous economic interests characterize the feeling of this category of Ukrainian society. From this flows a crisis of community status, for the state fails to meet their social expectations. Moreover, this crisis of community status is accompanied and compounded with the crisis of professional and personal identity, developing against the background of a general inability to resist, individually or jointly with colleagues, lower standards of living and consumption.

By contrast, the layers of population which are thriving, growing stronger, and rapidly accumulating material wealth still lack a level of social respect and recognition which could normatively affirm the legitimacy of their own existence. These are the bearers of socioeconomic competence, and they know the rules governing the distribution and exchange of scarce resources. Differences in clothes and life-styles bespeak the social distance between them and other social groups. Satisfying their value claims is possible if normative values completely different from the old ones are confirmed, old ideas whose bearers are the weakening elements of the social structure.

Heterogeneous is the category of population which

manages to preserve its social and material status. A segment of it is obviously interested in preserving the *status quo,* for its main source of profits is derived from the opportunities to acquire and exchange resources, and these opportunities are reproduced by the crisis. By actively participating in systems of economic management and circulation of wealth, which exist parallel to the official ones, they inevitably engage in competition and confrontation with the state and market economy structures, but no less often they enter into agreements on division of spheres of influence and proportion of distribution of profits and privileges. Another part of this category seems not to be inwardly inclined to take advantage of the crisis situation, but is forced to yield to the pressure of unfavorable circumstances.

Disorder and chaos, as well as uncertainty as to what model of social distribution should be chosen, can cause the social whole to become unstructured. The same effect might also result from the deep structuralization flowing from the existence of zones impenetrability and opacity. To be sure, in Ukraine we are dealing with the latter phenomenon: the social fabric is not whole, it is torn to pieces. And the division of the social whole is both a result of the general crisis and a prerequisite for its further conservation.

Thanks to the action of various factors, a bipolar image of the social structure is taking shape in the popular consciousness fixed by various oppositions: "upper/lower," "strong/weak," "those getting richer/those getting poorer," "situationally competent/situationally incompetent," "winners/losers." Thus, a contradictory social structuralization and stratification of postcommunist society is taking place. The most competent and active have changed profession, taken on additional work, and are trying to prevent the lowering of their living standards. Others still expect assistance, protection, cultivate paternalist attitudes and expectations, and they vote accordingly at elections. Becoming even more essential among the factors of stratification are the ability and capability to take advantage of opportunities to upgrade one's status and to cope successfully with non-traditional varieties of activities. Thus, at the initial stages of the transformation of a state socialist society into a postcommunist model of structuralization and stratification one is reminded more of a conflict model than of a functional one.

Adaptation Strategies of Former Communist Elites*

§1. Which social class was the revolution for?

If we wished to apply conventional Marxist reasoning to explain the revolutions of 1989, we would have to ask: Which social class was the revolution for? Or, put more simply, who profitted from the crumbling of the former communist regimes? Was it the new entrepreneurs? They still hardly exist. Was it the "working class" which, through the actions of Solidarity, dealt the decisive blows? It seems almost certainly destined to live precariously and undergo a deep restructuring, resulting, primarily from the obsolescence of the former industrial bastions that created it. Moreover, it is scarcely probable, in an ideological environment dominated by "market" principles, that the founding myths which the working class has now rejected will reemerge. Are the beneficiaries the former bosses? Surely not, for their nonexistence as a social class and the diverse problems which now prevent them from reclaiming what was theirs does not place them in a very favorable position. Finally, most paradoxically of all, yesterday's dissidents, who until recently were still present in the forefront of the post-1989 governments, are now being progressively asked by a confused electorate to return to the anonymity of civilian life.

* This analysis is based on the data of sociological polls in Poland, Hungary, Czech Republic, and Slovakia.

Who, then, stands to profit from the revolution? We must conclude that the revolution took place for a class that does not exist, even though we can already clearly distinguish that, of the new winners in society, many are strong, even dominant economically. Thus, the few capitalists, those who dispose of accumulated capital and put it to work – either productively or speculatively – are also those who now undeniably profit most from new post-revolutionary freedoms. This is all the more true since they hold the three trump cards that are so cruelly lacking in Eastern Europe, namely capital, know-how, and the ability to hire labor.

It is common knowledge that among these *nouveaux* capitalists and other private entrepreneurs is a large section of the previous political elite. By various methods they managed to acquire political and economic power, and despite losing the former they have nevertheless managed to hold onto the latter. This leads us to another paradoxical situation: it is wholly possible that the ex-nomenklatura could play a leading role in structuring the future owning and leading class, and consequently exchange its position as a class swept aside by history to that of an elite regaining its dominant position, albeit by adapting to new standards.[1]

This reasoning also has a political dimension: is there or is there not a reconversion strategy of the former communist parties, passing through the establishment and control of an economic area, able to reinforce a national and international political network and finally become able to hold their own and even reconquer power?

§2. The Barrier of 'Decommunization'

It is far from easy to check these hypotheses, and we therefore first need to develop a methodology. Certainly, no "confrontational" approach would be of any use in breaking through the necessarily discrete and often undercover methods of people who are keeping increasingly low profiles as political campaigns are stepped up for the radical "decommunization" of the new Eastern European democracies. No one yet knows what the future holds for these attempts at decommunization and it is wholly possible that they will be reduced to witch-hunts. Nevertheless, this hypothesis must be taken into account in our line of investigation.

We should also clearly define the nomenklatura in question, for the category is extensive, and can be applied to just the upper echelons of the former State/Party, the upper levels, plus some of the lower rungs on the political ladder, or even the whole Party structure. Insofar as we are concerned with the nature and modalities of reconversion strategies, we will focus on the nomenklatura that has been able to build on the privileges and positions of power held under the Old Regime in order to attain for itself a private economic capitalist base.

The various national nomenklaturas are, moreover, distinct from one another, a heterogeneity that can be traced back to the differences in the history and political culture of each country. Their future evolution, despite common and uniform origins, nevertheless appears to have diverged since 1989. The strategies of political and economic adaptation are directly related to these historical differences. Their individual approaches to the changes in regime also have varying effects on the conversion strategies, their possibilities to change their status, and to consolidate any change in their favor.

Consequently, we must distinguish between *two types of nomenklatura*:

- *The "rationalist" nomenklatura* that almost deliberately gave up political power over society, and which managed to achieve a transition in the economic space that was all the smoother for its having been prepared earlier or, which at least, seemed to have been prepared. Poland and Hungary fall into this category. We will note that these types of nomenklatura are closely associated with two factors: (a) a long-established private sector (with 20 years sustained growth) and (b) a long tradition of openness to the West (political and economic migration), with the effect that the rules by which liberal systems work had already been learned;
- *The "reactive" nomenklatura* that were taken by

surprise by the sudden overthrow of communism and were powerless both politically and economically. The case of the Czech Republic is a perfect illustration of this type of structure. Economically, the emergence of a proprietary class from the nomenklatura was all the more unlikely as the economy had been totally state-run. For most of these countries the lack of capital will probably lead to the eventual money laundering. From this point of view Poland and Hungary differ largely from other former communist countries in their comparatively early legalization of the private sector. The relationship between political power and the private economy goes back sufficiently far for the influence of the nomenklatura to be considered, if not beneficial, then at least desirable. Will the same situation arise elsewhere, where the constitution of private capital will visibly be the result of the acquisition of public property (the Czech Republic, Ukraine, Bulgaria, *etc.*)?

It is interesting to note that an opinion poll carried out simultaneously, and with the same set of questions, in the three Central-European countries (Poland, Hungary, and the Czech Republic), showed a correlation between the differentiation of the nomenklaturas and in how they are perceived by public opinion. In response to the question "should the former nomenklatura be removed from major governmental posts?" 80 % of Czechs were in favor of a radical purge as opposed to just 40% of Poles and 35% of Hungarians.[2]

§3. The Invisible Transition

This movement of appropriation came within more general framework of the anticipatory phenomena that characterized these two countries, the spectacular culmination of which came with the break-up of the regime. In retrospect, it is easy to pick out these structural characteristics, scarcely compatible with Soviet-type societies, which preceded the 1989 implosion and which flourished in its aftermath. The previous decade had been marked by major movement towards economic autonomy by private actors. There was a progressive growth of private schools, the development (sometimes illegal) of an independent health service, a proliferation of garages and restaurants, plus growth in private agriculture. It was in this context that the last governmental teams of the old regime pushed through measures for the privatization of public-owned business to the clear advantage of the managers, company executives, and more generally to those responsible for the state economy. While it may be an exaggeration to say that the former elites deliberately passed a series of custom-made laws, they certainly profited considerably from the situation.

In Poland, on December 23, 1988, the Rakowski government passed a law generally held to favor appropriation of state property by the nomenklatura, and which was severely criticized as such. The gist of this law was that private companies could be created if they were partnered with state-run industries with the aim of revitalizing them. According to this law, state industry could sell, rent, or transfer management of its assets to private companies. For their part, the new companies were allowed to set their own prices (unlike the socialist-run sector that was obliged to follow a fixed price system). Managers could therefore sell-off state assets, machinery, and installations at greatly reduced prices to a private company, a company which, in all probability, they either owned or in which they had a controlling interest. For example, the manager of a state-run company could transfer to himself or to a group of associates whole factory workshops or departments. By then taking orders from the same production sector as the original company, the new company became a provider of services which concentrated on maximizing its own profits. On the other side of the fence, no manager-shareholder was concerned with increasing production costs inside his company, which he turned to the benefit of his private enterprise. He simply minimized energy costs, outlay on pollution control, factory rent, transportation, and communication. As the manager of a state-owned company he could legally incur costs, simultaneously feathering the nest of his private concern.

Foreign investors took an interest in these private companies, not least because of the fact that although the state was providing the industrial plant (buildings, machinery, tools, and transportation) it was not financially involved. The value of this material contribution was underestimated, consequently increasing the relative value of foreign cash investment and resulting in a greater share of the profits for foreign capital.

Ostensibly aimed at revitalizing the public sector, it would appear that the negative effects of this law outweigh its positive ones, especially when we consider that the deliberate crime was not exposed in time. Instead, it was allowed to spread, assisted by the fact that, at least initially, there was no limit to the number of managerial posts that could be held in state-run industry.

The results were:

- exchanges between publicly-owned companies and the new limited private companies never favored the former.
- private companies, contrary to their initial claims, almost never worked in the production sector. Most of their activity was purely commercial.
- the managers, the economic nomenklatura, were able to take advantage of financial operations, either directly, or indirectly through figureheads and this brought them rapid wealth.

The movement of state assets into private hands had the effect of converting a large section of the former economic nomenklatura into private capitalists. Consequently, during these few months of transition (between the end of the old regime and the beginning of the new), many of them began a primitive accumulation of capital which could prove decisive in a society on the threshold of the market economy. Obviously, we must now examine what role in this process was played by spontaneous movement (every man for himself) and what role was played by organic relationships (networks).

Hungary saw a real surge of privatization. From the beginning of the 1980s, the flourishing second economy had already led to a law legalizing company autonomy. Then, in 1988 and 1989, two successive laws, creating true private economic actors, laid down rules for public companies wishing to privatize.[3]

Hungarian law first imposed an increase in company capital before transformation could take place. Sellouts were encouraged for the injection of new capital into the company, which would, if it was sold, become part-owner. The company could also choose its buyers and set its own price.[4] In this way every encouragement was given company managers to profit from these legal "instruments." For example, the managers of a hotel chain (Hungarhotel) were suspected of having sold at a knock-down prices some fifty hotels, including the famous "Forum" and "Intercontinental." We should also mention that, up to 1989, the State encouraged entrepreneurs with tax incentives on sales.

Therefore, in the case of Hungary between 1988 and March 1990 — when a law was passed for the "protection of national property held by the companies" — the possibilities for primitive accumulation were similar to those in Poland, benefiting the Hungarian economic nomenklatura. Hence, it is valid to ask how this still concerned the nomenklatura — not only in Hungary but in other postcommunist countries as well — now dispersed in a new social configuration, despite the fact that public opinion constantly connected their increased wealth with their current activities and initial political status. The Hungarian press certainly took a weaker stand against the nomenklatura's abuses than its Polish equivalent, except where the issue concerned real estate held by the Communist Party and its organizations. This leads to the hypothesis that, in the context of increased privatization in the economy, the Hungarian economic nomenklatura vanished "into thin air" behind legal-economic machinery with greater adeptness than their Polish counterparts. We also still have to determine which device, Hungarian or Polish, was most effective for the development of "capitalism" in general and the enrichment of the nomenklatura in particular. We must also take into consideration the fact that just 4% of national property had been sold since the end of 1991: buyers were not tripping over each other in the rush; it is the sale of a state-owned company that makes it possible for its managers to become part-owners. Accumulation of capital also took place before 1989: during the constitution of the second economy, when inside the companies, private companies were set up in a situation similar to that which resulted from the Polish law of 1989.

In the accounts of the partisans of the integral "decommunization" and in the stereotypes put across by a section of public opinion, we are presented with the conviction that the actions of the ex-nomenklatura members, today holding positions in the private sector, were totally premeditated, and wittingly concerned with the theft of public property in a wave of "every man for himself." In reality, the laws of 1988-89 were not aimed at a deliberate political capitalization but the search for a rational economic solution in a closed system. Our interviews clearly show that when the laws were made public, the managers of state-run companies who finally tried the private way, were not always thinking of this. Their initial motivations were rather more closely linked with political calculations than the realization of an opportunity for a change in status.

Among the reasons for founding a limited company, foremost was the urgency to transgress the rigid barriers of the industrial policy of the communist government of the time (the reform implemented by Polish Premier Z. Messner, for example). Designed as a deflationary reform as far back as 1987, the industrial policy, obeying orders of the IMF, was an attempt to stop inflation by controlling prices and wages. Thus, it was impossible to stimulate production to any extent by giving companies free rein in setting their own price and wage policy. Company managers were to see the law of 1988 as a real godsend, and they simply had to graft production or workers onto the private company to find a competitive position again. And if they themselves did not see the immediate advantages of taking such a step, it was their workers who took on the job of showing them the example of the company next-door that had been able to increase wages thanks to the creation of a new legal structure arising out of private commercial law. To these motivations we can add another, more existential reason, relating to their own professional future. The "modernist" decision taken by the communist authorities, attempting to generate mobility for company managers by taking on Solidarity's idea of organizing competition for the top jobs, immediately brought out the self-defense reflex in these same managers. They preferred to increase their chances of holding on to their jobs by creating a private legal and independent structure where they were responsible only to their shareholders, rather than the uncertain verdict of open competition where meritocratic criteria could come into play together with trade union pressure. These three motivations taken cumulatively, and the type of behavior that they resulted in, were certainly not perceived by their authors as anticipatory action designed to counter the events of history.

§4. Who Are They?[5]

With the help of some thirty non-directed interviews in Poland, we tried to throw some light on the economic route taken by the new company bosses, all of whom held important posts prior to the events of 1989. We settled on an approach that effectively gets around the spontaneous mistrust evinced by the group in question, carrying out our study under the guise of research into the new economic elite. From just one interview we were able to reconstruct the former networks and trace the new bonds of solidarity. In addition, we tried to avoid the major cities, concentrating instead on provincial towns.

These interviews, which were undeniably easier to conduct with the former Party reformers and who, as a result, are over-represented in our sample, confirm and serve to illustrate the fact that a process of legal appropriation of public property had been concluded by a section of the nomenklatura. This process had been made possible by laws passed shortly before the downfall of the Communist regime, particularly in Poland and Hungary.

a) Educated and Modernist

The individuals in the non-representative sample studied are characterized by a sufficiently large number of common features for us to be able to speak of a relatively precise profile. Within the Party, they represented a modernist, educated, and reformist trend. Between ages 35 and 50, they had often joined the Party during the Gierek period and were influenced by his economic program. Frequently of working class origins, they had achieved a double social goal: higher education plus a career in the Party structure. It is also symptomatic that their professional credentials couple management training with a technical degree.

We should not be surprised that in postcommunist Poland the members of this group became private entrepreneurs, for they were already skilled in building a company structure. They became the new captains of industry who treated the state-owned company as a field of action: obviously, having their own company enabled them to better express themselves.

Gierek's policy had been very beneficial to competent performers, and his ideological risk, based on bonding competence, would, according to its promoters, lead to a society where all needs were satisfied. Indeed, it was under this "umbrella" that the nomenklatura could develop hitherto unknown levels of racketeering. With Gierek the money was earned legally. It is clear that it was much easier for this "economic" nomenklatura to instrumentalize the party now that the first secretary was speaking their language. The future historian will doubtless explain to what degree their aspirations were met by the strategies implemented by the government, but what interests us is the interplay between a modernist group and its ideology and the evolution of the system in which the private company made its way.

For it was under Gierek, and then later in the 1980s, that the private economy began to develop with bridges to the nomenklatura (a phenomenon already observed in Hungary)[6] and the conditions for accumulation were born. We know that, at the end of the 1970s, there were already regional information cells that were designed to make it easier for individuals to create "agencies" (as the private commercial enterprises were christened). Here we have a form of support for the creation of businesses, a phenomenon that would only take on wider dimensions in 1991. So, who knew how to make use of these devices? The "economic nomenklatura," people like this Katowice shop owner who, during the 1980s, at the peak of social crisis, doubled his role as a manager of a state-run company with the management of his own shop, without displaying any particular role:

"In Cracow, in the Voivode offices, I was given much advice on how to start up my own business. At that time (1979), an office like that was a real revolution. It was anarchy, no control at all. Thanks to the network, I was able to import foreign goods for the whole of Poland. It was a mixed status shop: the walls were owned by the state, but the merchandise was private. The Voievode office put me in touch with suppliers and buyers, including foreigners (Yugoslavia and East Germany). I ran the shop from 1979 to 1986, and was then appointed to manage a state-run company, leaving the shop to my wife, to live. After six months I had paid for a car and a trailer. Prices were like that in '79-'80: maximum profits! I built three-quarters of my house in '80-'83."

b) Reformers

Moved more by a feeling than by real preparation, the future capitalists of the nomenklatura, like everyone else, could not have imagined what was going to happen. They considered themselves reformers battling against conservatives, although still in a monocratic country, with only a partial market economy. The more the Party became reformist, the more their continued flourishing was assured.

They spontaneously felt closer to the elite of Solidarity, and hated the *betons* (concrete blocks, a Polish metaphor for the CP conservatives) against whom they at the time waged divisive war.

"Solidarnosc was a danger for the *betons*, but not for us." "Here, most Solidarnosc members were also Party members." "We believed in the Party slogan of renewal."

It is certainly easy to rewrite history in retrospect. Nonetheless, the reformers place great importance on their role in events, as if, blinded, they needed a legitimating device permitting continuity between a before and an after:

"We didn't want power, such as it was." "It was we who did everything: the opposition in 1978 was just a handful of people." "From 1979 on it became clear that the system was crumbling. Previous governments lacked courage: prices needed to be freed. People were being treated badly." "Changes in Poland came as the result of several influences, and above all from the progressive option of the POUP. That was an option that came from the well-supported basis for reform. In 1980 there was no difference in basic thinking between Solidarity and Party reformers. They wanted to throw us out in 1980. We wanted to introduce free elections within the Party. People have forgotten our role in the changes. If there was reform, it was thanks to us."

Where reforms were concerned, they mention precisely that they had been organizing market economy training courses for businesses since 1985, and that they were employing greater numbers of non-party members to positions of responsibility simply because they were competent. In a word, they see themselves as the fathers of neo-capitalism.

"We made the greatest qualitative leap forward during the 1980s. The new rules do not date from today, but from the time of Rakowski (the last communist premier) who let anyone create a private company. No one says it now, but it was the Rakowski government that made it all possible. If it had happened ten years earlier, maybe communism would have had a better chance of surviving, whatever you think of that." "The 1980s were the years of the peaceful abandon of power and transition towards a market economy."

c) Elites in Search of an Identity

Elites they were, and elites they remain. But they regret the fact that the postcommunist authorities are not aware of the fact. Having anticipated their future dismissal by opening up in the private sector or just simply being sacked, most of them created consulting firms (usually specializing in reconversions) or trade outlets, or a company directly related to their skills (including networks). Some of them also became the informed plenipotentiaries of leading Western companies (for example, in the banking and insurance sector).

Now captains of industry for their own profit, finally giving free rein to the spirit of enterprise without hindrance, they found themselves in a schizophrenic role, missing their former role as political leaders, regretting the fact that they now have only the economy.

"A lot of good people were got rid of, and they ended up in the private sector. Nowadays only the weakest managers are left in the State sector. A public sector manager only earns about as much as a private sector laborer. A lot of these managers have been chased out of state-run companies. But the movement to the private sector represents a waste of human resources, since a guy who can run a 5000-man factory ends up managing just five. Today, society treats us very unfairly. Poland is going to miss our generation, and it will take quite a few years to replace us."

Since 1989, this group has had to adapt and alter its world view. This is a group of bosses who know how to use and structure the old networks, particularly on the regional level, in favor of economic and political activities. In this process of identity construction, they aspire to find the values of an economic and national elite. With a taste for hard work they can boast of having made risk part of their way of life, and they accept instability and the feeling of stress. They know stress very well: before, in the Party machinery, they were in constant fear of changes in a direction that might exclude them, and now they are getting used to living in the climate of decommunization.

Already they are becoming dissatisfied with their enhanced economic status, and want to play a role in the life of their towns, their region, their country, to have representatives and create a political lobby. Yet, still they come up against a barrier, a contradiction that has its roots in their origins: by their tradition, habits, and sense of reform, they constitute potential clients for social-democracy, but the instant their own companies come into the reckoning (having a trade union in their factories), they immediately become very liberal. They would like to become society bosses and be perceived as such. While their votes and sympathies lie naturally with the new Socialist (formerly Communist)

Party, the "social-liberals" would also appeal to them: they admire the likes of Kuron and Kiss.

§5. Consolidation of Political Status?

The "classogenous" process may take different paths. It is probable that certain elements of the former communist elite truly do wish to organize and give the whole process a political expression. The political organizations that were offshoots of communism would be useful for this. On the one hand, there would be a political group in need of financing, and, on the other, an economic group in need of political representation, or even a pressure group, the social-democratic ground being the ideological link.

The meeting of the political and economic actors of the old regime could take place naturally because of these logical convergences. But it could also be the object of a well thought out strategy. In November 1991, the Soviet press revealed the existence of documents stating the hypothesis of an international concentration of economic conversion strategies, where the pre-August putsch CPSU was to have had the coordinating role. For this reason, a seminar had been held in Warsaw in March 1991 by the CPSU, which, as one of the participants wrote in a private letter, was to have: "given priority to the creation of structures that had no formal links with the Party, like joint stock share companies, foundations, and limited companies. In other words, it was to create institutions that could not be expropriated for political reasons."[7] At the same meeting, on the proposal of L. Miller, head of the Polish Social-Democrats (SDRP), a database was to be set up along with a coordination center for the business and industrial activities of the communist parties.[8]

The behavior of the former communist elites reveal at the present time, rather more adaptation strategies, especially in Central-Eastern Europe, than reconquest strategies. Doubtless the surprise of the general collapse of the system, which the communist leaders wanted to control up to the very last minute, thanks to power sharing (the "Round

Table" compromise in Poland and the "Triangular Table" in Hungary), upset the sophisticated constructions and led instead to survival reflexes. However, no keen observer could have failed to notice that in the midst of the uprisings (December 1989/January 1990), both in Poland and in Hungary, ritual, theatrical ceremonies were held to end the communist past and to herald the new social-democratic era (for example, carrying the flag out of the POUP congress). The manipulation of symbols could mean that there was, if not a ready-made script for the bowing out of communism, then at least the wish for it to go out in an orderly way.

The publication of documents concerning strategies for the coordination of the economic activities necessary for the reconstruction of a (non-communist) left, shows that the hypothesis is possible that anticipatory strategies were made up of several phases, following the watershed that introduced the "Gorbachev effect" into Central and Eastern Europe. The political conversion towards a social-democratic formula was boosted by the reformist triangle (Moscow-Warsaw-Budapest) before 1989. After the wave of revolution, its was the conservatives who took the initiative for coordination in most of the ex-Soviet bloc countries (in the same way that Gennady Yanayev granted a loan to the SDRP, it was most of the representatives of a hard line policy who were wise to financial movements, such as L. Miller, *etc.*).

However, there are historical reasons that clarify the leading role of Poland and Hungary (in addition to the various above-mentioned aspects): the tradition of competition with a dynamic opposition whose peaceful political plans "rubbed off" onto the morals and behavior of the communist elite; the nature of the reformist trends and the weight of a kind of invisible network made up of successive layers of communists excluded for reformist views; the frequency of the renewal of generations and the existence, on the eve of 1989, of a younger generation, educated and attracted by heterodox economic or political activity; the degree of political openness towards the liberal systems of the West and the tradition of contacts with "Eurocommunists" or Western social-democracy. In general, it can be said that the deeper the awakening of civil societies and their political cultures, the more sophisticated were the attempts of the elite at anticipating the change in regime. The real strategy of political conversion consisted in transforming programs, structures, and names in order to come as close as possible to the social-democratic model.

Other formulae have but a residual nature, most often revolving around the negation of the process of "social-democratization." Thus, some people are tempted by national-communist ideology or even nationalism. It is particularly true in those areas where ethnic and national antagonisms rise to the surface (for example, the problem of the Turkish minority in Bulgaria, the German in Poland or even the question of Slovak separatism). This tendency is particularly strong where the former powers had managed to arouse nationalist feelings in certain classes), today filled by organizations such as, in Rumania, Vatra Romaneasca or Romania Mare, where former members of the Securitate are used, or in Poland with the heirs of Moczarism, such as the Grunwald group, supporters of the 'X' Party of S. Tyminski. In Slovakia, separatist pressure has led ex-communists like Vladimir Meciar to espouse radical nationalist doctrines.

Another metamorphosis in this recomposition of the communist machinery are the orthodox. Largely in the minority, they cultivate continuity with the communist heritage, referring back to the birth of communist ideology, which they claim has been betrayed (for example, the Union of Polish "Proletariat" Communists), or to the legendary leaders such as the Hungarian Workers' Socialist Party (Kadarian) of K. Gross, or the Association of Enver Hoxha Volunteers in Albania.

Undoubtedly most ex-communists who chose the social-democratic path are looking to find in it ideological inspiration, a new legalization which will enable them to make connections with certain aspects of the past, without, however, risking on the electoral level the negative effects of a heritage towards which public opinion remains very sensitive. Social democratization as a repositioning strategy on the political chessboard, however, makes it difficult for them to have recourse to populist social demagogy. For the new social-democrats are in search of a European identity and international recognition as being on the side of Western social-democracy (see their repeated attempts to join to the Socialist International), which would have the effect of giving them a legal identity, disputed internally by much weakened historical social-democratic parties.

The hard core of reformers remains a group who will deny nothing of their past. Quite the opposite, in fact, as they continue to claim "author's rights" as the destroyers of communism and speed the move towards capitalism of a regime they considered outmoded and reactionary. An ideological conflict could ensue in the not too distant future between these economic actors and their political neo-social-democrat partners, a conflict whose ingredients are already to be found in the vision of the sociopolitical battlefield that we have been able to reconstruct from our series of interviews. The cohabitation of two contradictory syndromes (a social-democratic vision of social relations on the world scale and a liberal vision of professional relations on a local level, in particular at company level) must logically lead to a political social-liberal choice, i.e., towards the establishment of ideological and institutional affinities with the socio-liberals, such as the Democratic Union in Poland, the Szdsz in Hungary, the Union of Democratic Forces in Bulgaria, the Civil Alliance in Rumania, and certain trends close to Vaclav Havel from the former Civic Forum in Bohemia. This phenomenon could in turn have a carryover effect in the traditional field of influence of social-democracy, where a break in the social-democratized postcommunist formations could logically serve to strengthen social liberalism.

The remaining question is therefore whether the congruence of the status attributes that this social group, necessarily located at the intersection between the new proprietary class and a political group in competition for power, will revive discord with the tradition and ideological components that are pushing former communist parties towards platform functions for the underprivileged classes. In other words, this former communist nomenklatura, still fragile, will have to navigate the reefs that postcommunism creates for it. The first of these is decommunization, with the former nomenklatura representing the perfect scapegoat. Second, its political identity may fluctuate: it may be rejected by its original family for being too liberal, and by liberals for being still too connected to its former communist family. These possible rejections underscore the fact that this is a group with a very strong personality, ready and able to play a political role. In any event, in the new race for power, the former nomenklatura has the best starting position and the most advantages, not only in the private sector, but also in the state sector where its skills could one day once again prove to be indispensable.

Problems of Internal Political Geography: The Ukrainian Example

One of the most noticeable traits of the states created after the collapse of the USSR is the rapid formation and deeply underscored heterogeneity of the political landscape. In but a few years monoparty homogeneity was replaced by a variety of movements and parties. But they are but one component in the mosaic of the political field; they are in turn conditioned by the political likes and dislikes of the population which inhabits specific regions of a given country. And those preferences are governed by very deep factors.

In contemporary political discourse the use terms of geographical opposites is both widespread and inconsistent. Juxtaposing East/West, North/South, and New World/Old World indicates in a condensed, metaphoric form a complex of socioeconomic and political constants, which constitute the relief or "geography" of the sociocultural landscape. It has long been recognized that political geography uses historical-cultural geography as its matrix, but acquires legitimacy and completion only through the mobilizing work of active subjects interested in the articulation of sociocultural differences in order to gain access to power.

§1. The Historical Basis of Ukraine's Political Geography

Ukraine's social and cultural heterogeneity is the result of the capricious and free-ranging play of historical circumstances. Ukraine's western region, Galicia and Bukovyna, were under the Habsburg Empire for a long period of time. Then it went to Poland and Rumania, and during World War II was joined to Ukraine. The northern and eastern regions of Ukraine had belonged to the Romanovs, and after 1917 they became a part of the USSR. The eastern and northern regions of present-day Ukraine have been inhabited by both Russians and Ukrainians peoples, forming a rather mixed population over the last three centuries. The industrialization of Donbas and steppe regions resulted in new waves of migration, accompanied by an interaction and transformation of cultural models. The present borders of Ukraine were fixed in 1954, when Crimea became a part of Ukraine. Most of the Crimea's inhabitants are first or second generation immigrants to the peninsula.

The historically conditioned "nationalization" of the western part and "internationalization" of the eastern part have been important, yet distinct, trends. They have formed mutually different "ways to feel, to think, and to act" (Durkheim). On the level of everyday life images of "real" and "false" Ukrainians have taken shape. The Galicians of Western Ukraine see themselves as the only "real" Ukrainians and look upon their compatriots of the Dnipro basin as denationalized "Little Russians" (*malorosy*). Ukrainians of Central and Eastern Ukraine view Galicians as ultra-nationalistic "Banderites," "Westerners," and in the East one often hears that even the Ukrainian language and national symbols are not "ours" but "Galician" and thus somehow "foreign." Thus a deep schism has evolved between at least two Ukraines within one Ukrainian state.

This estrangement has also made itself felt on the interpersonal level. For example, Ukrainians who were taken to Germany in the 1940s treated each other with distrust and vestiges of their mutual "otherness" persist in emigration in America and Europe.[9] Thus, in Ukraine the geographic opposition "West/East" is overriding. Here, "East" also represents Ukraine's North and South, because in a physical sense Galicia and Bukovyna constitute Ukraine's "Far West." Certainly, it is accidental but highly symbolic that a central feature of Slavic mythology is this same geographical axis —

the sun's movement from the bright West to the dark East.[10] While the ancient Slavic world view the border of East and West had its place and was fixed on a certain center, the discourse of present day politicians and sometimes that of the mass media also tend to confirm this duality based on the different content of the two Ukraine's national self-identification.[11]

How did the Presidential election reflect Ukraine's political geography?

Observers without great respect for sociology, have stated, not without irony, that the *de facto* function of this discipline is to wear itself out in pursuit of authentic corroboration of what everyone already knows. And, in fact, everybody in Ukraine knows the East and West are different. Sociologists, however, insist on more strictly grounded arguments when making their findings.[12]

Ukraine's geographic heterogeneity became clearly evident in the late 1980s and early '90s. It has become evident that all those newly-organized movements and parties which pretend to represent nationwide Ukrainian interests lean on particular regions for support, nationalists on the West and socialists on the East.[13] At the same time, nationwide polls have measured significant differences in the political activity among inhabitants of western, eastern, and southern Ukrainian inhabitants. Galicia and Crimea are the two zones where the population is most active in political life.[14] In these regions sociologists have measured the highest level of readiness for various forms of protest.[15] Moreover, even a lay observer can understand that the energy level of political passions in the regions has its source in different, at times mutually exclusive, goals and values of the state system and the guarantee of sovereignty.

Observers and commentators have correctly pointed out the tendency of political and cultural-historical regionalization. However, only election returns can illustrate and precisely measure political watersheds and ravines. First of all, through expression of their preferences — Durkheim would say "their mode of political action" — the population has drawn new parallels and meridians, expressed their attitude toward the past and present, and pinned their hopes and expectations on their particular candidate. The pre-election data paint a picture of similarly homogeneous politically opposed poles, of separate arenas where neither of the main candidates had real positive support. Thus Ukraine's center of political gravity is this arena of political ambivalence.

Both the voters and candidates through their actions defined the political geography of Ukraine. In the election campaign the candidates' very names came to allude to not only historical-cultural differences, but also differences in the ability to overcome the economic crisis have been articulated by their real names in the pre-election competition. In parts of the one-industry hyper-industrialized East and South there were limited resources to halt factory closings and chronic hidden unemployment. The candidates paid this special attention, exploiting it to maximum political advantage. The question remains to what degree the difference in choice of who to vote for was governed by differences in the candidates' programs, how long a given presidential candidate spent campaigning in a given region, what was the content of their campaign rhetoric, and how was it received. It became clear to us that each of the main candidates appealed mainly to his own spatially localized political base, that the structure of political geography made it possible for the struggle for votes could be successful only in areas of political ambivalence, but not in the other candidate's territorial base. The structure of the political space forced the candidates to stress differences between "us" and "them," between eastern Ukraine and western Ukraine.

The high level of voter identification with their particular candidate shows that the goal of attaining high state power, was accomplished by means of instilling in the popular consciousness images of quite different political aspirations, pretensions, and attitudes. Thus, political structuralization was created not only by joint actions of the population but also by the actions of candidates themselves. The latter gave legitimacy to existing cultural and socioeconomic differences and based their campaigns on them. Thus, in the second half of the 1990s we have a situation where political capital in Ukraine is mobilized, among other things, by intensively exploiting regional differences. And then, having unreserved support in one part of the country, someone can completely neglect the other part. This is what really happened during the presidential elections.

Currently these differences have become a tool of every politician's spade-work, an instrument of his everyday troubles and concerns. The regions as such, in voting for their candidates to Parliament and high government office, have begun to compete for domination of a politically, culturally, and socially heterogeneous Ukraine. The ability to differentiate and identify became the stock in trade of both the politicians and population of the regions during the second presidential elections; this was understood and became a fact for every astute voter and politician.

§2. Conclusions from Political Geography for Sociology

Sociology, like politicians, is sensitive to differences. Within a difference in the mode of political action, a sociologist can see (to use Durkheim's terminology) differences in "ways thinking and feeling" or differences in *mentalitet* (using a modern term of the French *Annales* school). In other words, the sociologist tends to view a "region of residence" as a factor, which determines in advance the individual's ideas, emotions, everyday verbal reactions, and physical responses. The sociologist recognize that this factor can hamper or neutralize the influence of other factors. It has been noted that Russians living in Galicia react to and evaluate events according to local trends. Ukrainians living in the East and in Crimea on the whole reproduce the way of thought and action widespread in these regions as a whole.[16] Not ethnic identification, but immersion in and subordination to the general atmosphere, has become a major variable, reducing considerably the role played by ethnic factor.

Data from sociological surveys[17] in particular indicate that inhabitants of the western, more agrarian oblasts have a higher level of appreciation for the prestige of occupations which traditionally involve mental labor, such as teacher, professor, scientist, engineer, military officer, and nurse. The calling of medical doctor ranked fifth place, above those of lawyer, member of parliament, and businessman. By contrast, these professions receive lower ratings in the eastern and central regions. In the highly industrial East occupations involving physical labor are more highly regarded. Among them are seamstress, construction worker, locksmith, and machine operator, but even there they place in the lower part of the rank hierarchy.

These data indicate that each region has its own distinguishing characteristics, which reflect the specifics of how the occupational world is seen (way of thinking). In the western oblasts, evaluations of prestige are less exalted and extreme. Respondents avoid giving extreme ratings to highly prestigious and non-prestigious occupations. The dominant theme is moderation in evaluation, which stems from ideas about the undoubtedly good features of all callings. But the respect retained concerning mental labor indicates an obvious distancing from how the state currently evaluates them, reflecting a dominant way of thinking. In western Ukraine the population tries to preserve the scale of prestige, not to inflate some occupations and denigrate others in extreme fashion. In the Center and East more radical assessments prevail. This coincides with state actions during the crisis period with regard to professions of high-skilled mental labor and of low-skilled physical labor, to economize on remuneration in the state sector of the economy across the board and thus accord representatives of mental and physical labor the same esteem.

The West differs from Central and Eastern Ukraine by demonstrating greater orientation toward individualism and less affinity for collective ways of achieving success. Here, income differentiation is perceived with less pain and more tolerance. The need for such differences is more often understood and accepted as a norm of democratic society. Less frequently voiced is the idea that income differences are undeserved and that government action should equalize them.

The combination of political action and ways of thinking and feeling assume the form of a more or less definite trend, observed where the issue concerns democracy and economics as well as the nature and goals of individual or group behavior. This combination is of historical origin, but it is also influenced by the present situation, the structure of the economy, and burden of crisis, which various regions, according to their population structure, feel and understand differently. In this sense we can speak of "region" as an independent differentiating factor, which determines in advance not only the heterogeneity and tension of political and social arena in Ukraine, but also how the inhabitants of different regions interpret current events and strategies of development.

§3. Conclusions

Thus, the years of independence have witnessed Ukraine's political structuralization and stratification, the evolution of its "political geography." This means that historical, cultural, economic, and residential differences have acquired a political form and have been debased to the level of a weapon in the political struggle for dominance. Accenting them has become one of the rules of the political game. Politicians – *i.e.*, people who in the real world practice the art of divide and conquer, use intimidation, and apply force – have already fallen prey to the temptation of emphasizing and exacerbating such differences for exclusively their own political gain. In Ukraine the main problem is not one of nationalism but the hardening of its mutually opposed fields of economic, social, cultural, and political differences. This problem may assume different guises and manifest itself in heated discussions on, say, the status of the Russian language, the level of Crimean autonomy, or federalization. And one would have to understand nothing to not see what lies ahead if this is viewed only as a problem of nationalism.

Images of Social Structure

Among the most important products of a living and active society associated with various forms political of political discourse are variegated images of stratification and social structure. Such images are continuously produced by sociologists and the mass media, by politicians and political parties in speeches and programs, by state officials and ordinary citizens. The seriousness, steadfastness and even inspiration with which this is done testify to their deliberate character or, possibly, to the exceptional utility of these images. In any case, one can not deny their ability to create and serve the single communication space, where subject of political actions and interactions have a chance of coming to mutual understanding, to common definition of terms and circumstances, manifesting their intentions and future behavior as something foreseeable and consistent. In other words, they can create the single political community – polity or, on the contrary, divide and differentiate it in accordance with the earlier defined criteria.

Especially rich in images of social structure and stratification are the programs of political candidates. Politicians manipulate such images so confidently that there may be no doubt about a certain lofty goal for the sake of which they are ready to sacrifice themselves completely or motives and values which impel them to do so. It is also reasonable to assume that there are rules according to which images of social structure are produced, disseminated, or manipulated. But while an active political player is concerned only with the efficacy of the images he uses, a sociologist looks for trends: that which are recurrent and that which determines the recurrence and direction of the course of events.

§1. What is Structure and How Is It Reproduced?

Sociologists usually regard a "structure" as something invariable and unchanging, something that predetermines the course of social processes and behavior of individuals, that enables him methodologically to introduce explanatory schemes and fix the contexts of understanding; but which is, in and of itself, rather inert, stable and, most importantly, incapable of changing radically in historically short periods of time. This kind of notion may have originated and been consolidated in the course of studying what Claude Levi-Strauss called traditional "cold" societies which evolve relatively slowly. But even in the late twentieth century it has not exhausted its eurystic potential, setting methodological benchmarks for theoretical and empirical research. There are at least three statements summarizing various approaches to and interpretations of the notion of "structure" in sociology.

Statement One: a structure is something that existed before and continues to exist after individuals and is independent of them.

It does not matter in this case whether structure is regarded as the ideal type of Levi-Strauss' binary cultural oppositions,[18] Giddens's social "rules and resources,"[19] as a material and real formation – class-conscious "positions in the production of material wealth as understood by Marxism, "contributions" to society's survival in structural functionalism,[20] "situations" on the labor market and at a given workplace[21] or as "cities."[22] It is classes, strata, categories of individuals, social groups, categories of individuals (*i.e.*, societies and communities), as well as mental patterns and normative value complexes, that is most often meant by sociologists when they speak about structures in sociological terms.

Statement Two: a structure is not simply given or assumed; it gives birth to various forms of social life, supports, formulates, combines, and reconciles them. In other words, structure is in itself a generating and originating principle in any kind of individual and collective behavior. Every active member of society has to adapt to a structure, whether or not he/she is aware of the limitations the latter imposes. As an originating principle, it is known to determine the character and content of the processes and tendencies it initiates irrespective of the opposition of individual persons and groups.

Statement Three: structure, *i.e.*, the aggregate of individuals joined together and their interrelationships, functions as an explanatory principle to which everything is reduced and from which everything flows. Thus the political (and in substantial measure general and mass) consciousness of a statement about the reality of an existing social structure is understood and interpreted beforehand on a pragmatic plane, *i.e.*, from the perspective of the possibility of changing it in order to improve the social whole or rectify its shortcomings. The innate resistance of such independent and inescapable constructs and their resistance are usually ignored in such cases. It is evident that a social structure is the product of the hard work of history, sometimes clear and open, at other times quiet and secret, inaccessible to traditional social science methodology. Why this happens is a complicated question requiring special study. But since it cannot be ignored entirely, let us recall, for the sake of brevity, a remark by Norbert Wiener, who once said that there was an aphorism engraved on a stone slab at Princeton's Institute of Strategic Studies, which was headed by Albert Einstein: "The Lord God is cunning but not malicious." In other words, it may be extremely difficult to uncover the secrets of nature, but the latter resists the scientists' understanding unintentionally, without ill will.

However, sociologists cannot state anything of this kind in respect to societal "nature." On the contrary, here it is by design, whether good or ill, that so much is kept secret or hidden in the human world. And it is not seldom that something scarcely probable or altogether improbable may be explained as existing here and now merely by someone's whim or will, which must be happening in each point of the intra- and inter-group relations space. The suggestion and social reproduction of facts and artifacts (probably, in a larger number) are essentially biased, value and ideologically laden actions which, as a rule, do not meet the Weberian requirements of being value-free.

In society, facts and artifacts not only coexist but also enter into complex combinations. As a result, it becomes problematic whether it is even possible to separate "reality" from its interpretations or a social fact from its ideal symbolic reproductions. Of course, this flows not from the sinister designs of social agents permanently reproducing a secret space and keeping strangers out, but in a special, sensual-supersensual (in the words of Marx), the nature of the social subject matter. A sociologist proceeds from the fact that individuals and groups perceive and interpret situations and processes not only according to the latter's objective properties, but also in compliance with expectations, claims, errors, and stereotypes cultivated in a society or group. And, as was noted long ago, if they define a situation as real, its consequences are recognized as being just as real.[23] Therefore, the behavior of individuals and groups is conditioned not only by a "real" sequence of facts, but also by the subject-matter of the sensual-supersensual kind composed of a rather random combination of truth with what is recognized as "true" at a given time and place.

This is equally valid in respect to a social structure. It is reproduced by the whole complex of social, economic, and cultural circumstances. In this sense it may be referred to as an "objective" phenomenon, an object of sociological research. However, a structure is intensively formed by the activity of the interested social subjects, such as political leaders, individual politicians, parties, independent and dependent experts, as well as professional and amateur sociologists. The knowledge of structure is thus another product of its social reproduction. According to P. Bourdieu, this is the production and gradual legitimation of a vision and perception, which the above social subjects find desirable, of a socially divided world through an act of symbolic suggestion.

The more precisely the subject of this suggestion corresponds to reason and expectations widespread in society, and the more forcefully it is pressed by interest and will, the more certain is this legitimation of success.[24]

The intensity of producing a symbolic social structure grows dramatically during election campaigns, which are primarily a planned and announced time of intense political discourse. Precisely then, contenders for new vacancies in elective bodies of power are active in structuring the social space, giving it labels and meanings. Perhaps this is inevitable, for their programs are above all calls for as yet unrealized plans of transforming the existing order. In turn, this order is also represented by a social structure, *i.e.*, the organized distribution of the most important vital resources among institutions of society, groups, and individuals. And from this, one may assume that the candidates' ideational social structuralization, which is simultaneously a means of legitimizing their political demands with the help of the imposition of a desired vision of society and the creation of, if only the appearance and illusion of political discourse, meets the requirements of the notion of social structure formulated above.

For empirical confirmation, the programs of 49 candidates from three electoral districts in Kyiv in the Ukrainian parliamentary election of March 27, 1994, is used. Statements mentioning directly or indirectly, positively or negatively, groups, strata, communities, and categories of individuals, that is, concrete divisions and partitions of the social unity, were recorded. There were 209 such utterances, and the relative values given below were calculated on the basis of this figure. They are not representative of the positions of the Kyiv candidates, because the objective was not to form a representative sample of their programs but to find the rules by which candidates made socially structuralizing statements.

§2. *The Suggestion of Stratification Defects as an Important Component of Election Programs*

As is most often the case in political struggle, a defining characteristic of social structure is seen in the programs' division of "ruling elite" and "people," a division which assumes pathological form. Statements about the inadequacies of the existing authorities and, hence, the need to replace them was the main theme and a fundamental thesis of the pre-election utterances of new candidates for political elite status. In their view, the open cynicism of legislators, who have ignored the interests of "the people" and used them for their own private and essentially egotistical ends and brought society to catastrophe, has become intolerable. As a result, society has been split, polarized, and lost its integrity, while the silent majority must bear all the costs of this situation. Moreover, this majority has lost control over the elite and has been *de facto* excluded from political life.

Accusations against former deputies are represented by a wide range of verbal symbols ("mafia in power," "the establishment," "democrats," "new hetmans," "the corrupt caste," "the party of power," "theoreticians of unemployment," "guilty of plundering Ukraine") and make up 19% of all utterances. This also includes indirect invectives against the privilege of evading responsibility for breaking the law. 5% of all utterances demand equality of all before the law, pointing unequivocally to the ruling elite and its satellites who do not obey the law and live according to rules totally different from those for the majority. Another 6% call for honest people, dedicated to the cause of Ukraine and competent, to be elected to the new Parliament (of course, this implies that the former deputies lack such qualities). The share of utterances about polarization and even opposition of interests, character traits and vital aspirations of the political elite, on the one hand, and the masses, on the other hand, amounted to 30%, while the spectrum of accusations was firmly fixed within the scale ranging from "incompetence" through "corruptness" to "ignoring" or even "betraying Ukraine's interests."

Those in power were held responsible for the state's anemia, which suddenly emerged and threatens to become permanent. The basic social institution has proved incapable of maintaining, let alone increasing, the economic and social status of the population's professional categories traditionally dependent on it: teachers, doctors, military servicemen and researchers (6% of the candidates' promises included pledges to provide a decent level of incomes). The state is also accused of having withdrawn its support from the disabled and socially underprivileged: the handicapped, old-age pensioners, veterans of war and labor, those who suffered the aftermath of the Chernobyl nuclear disaster, large families, young families, children, mothers with infants, and young people (27% of all structuralizing statements).

The alienation of the authorities in favor of a narrow circle of persons is treated as a structure generating another sequence of divisions in the social entity apart from those mentioned above. Some programs insistently drew attention to the polarization of wealth and poverty in the shape of a stratum of those who, on the one hand, rapidly enrich themselves and have access to limited benefits and resources and, on the other, to a stratum of those who are rapidly getting poorer and are, in fact, held hostage to the nearly bankrupt state (6%). A polarized representation is accorded to the stratum of honest but poor material producers and that of greedy, dishonest speculators, handlers, and bankers (6%) and also "haves" and "have nots" in terms of the opportunity to succeed in the privatization drive now underway in Ukraine (3%).

Thus, the pre-election programs of various Kyivan parliamentary candidates tried to instill in the electorate the image of a deformed political and socioeconomic structure, which needs to be fixed and made healthy. This was a deeply stratified and polarized structure — "ruling elite" *vs.* "long-suffering people," "rich" *vs.* "poor," "law-abiding" *vs.* "those above the law" — of things which could not be considered just; they did not correspond to popular expectations, they were the result of the self-seeking antisocial actions of those in power. This translates into a quite definite pattern of perceiving, understanding, and interpreting the existing situation. To convince the voters of the reality of a situation and inevitability of its consequences also means the legitimization and justification of one's own political agenda. It is the legitimation of the idea that the social structure is defective and that the processes of its stratification are anomalous.

Further, it is the legitimation of a radical will to change everything for the better. This is demonstrated not so much by the verbal determination to right the situation thanks to more competent leadership – there were practically no accusations of incompetence – as by the verbal radicalism which breathes references to implacable struggle against enemies and traitors characteristic of the first stages of building socialism. Radicalism also surfaces in pledges to be "a true servant of the people," that is, a return to naïve romantic stereotypes to which fairly numerous categories of the population remain susceptible.

Active use of labels from the sarcastic to the abusive terms, identifies the powers-that-be as a bunch of plotters ("fat-cat democrats," "Comrade socialists," or just plain "evildoers") and thus discredits an opponent and lowers his status. Here we see a method of political struggle used on the stage of political theater in virtually every nook and cranny of the world. But the social meaning of such an action is not restricted to this statement alone.

The privilege of giving evaluative references, names and definitions was formerly possessed only by the ruling elite and those it empowered to do so. This privilege was identified in the past with power. Now the ability to name, define, and evaluate things has become open, accessible, and attractive to a great many people thanks to elections. The relative ease of getting on the ballot involuntarily imparts a simulative, role-playing nature to the whole process (the participants' political intentions can remain, of course, very serious). The production of various kinds of socio-structural "simulacra" today, organically fits in with the scenario of an election campaign, reinforcing the pleasure of possessing the power to assign names. The struggle of classifications, in the words of Bourdieu, is naturally accompanied by the struggle for official nomination, for the monopoly to set a "correct" classification and a "correct" order.[25]

However, most rules of such a name-game, with all intentions to assert oneself in a symbolic autonomous area, are by no means arbitrary; they follow the unwritten principles of the unyielding social matter. The crisis and disappointing fall in living standards stressed in the programs are insistently declared as consequences of the established order of distributing positions and posts of authority and, hence, access to the limited material and social benefits (*i.e.*, the consequences of the inadequate organization of the social structure). The contenders for seats in a legislative body come out "for" the people and "against" those in power, "for" the honest and law-abiding, the downtrodden and those undeservedly deprived of state help, and "against" the greedy and prosperous, who cynically flout the state's interests and seem above the law. They claim to have taken sides with the suffering majority. It is on the social territory occupied by this majority that the candidates for a new political elite enter into contact with the former, and develop a discourse aimed at formulating mutually coordinated definitions of the situation in society. That is why selective appeals to the masses of the humiliated and downtrodden (the entrepreneurial strata were positively mentioned by only 3%) are determined by the norms of political rationality: the ruling clique, alien and (to be more exact) hostile to the masses, is to be removed from the political arena (the term "clique" being used in a sociological sense; it was not used in the programs).

§3. The Unheeded Warning of a Catastrophe

Undoubtedly, the materials presented indicate that the above-formulated statements about sociological interpretation of the social structure, function, among other things, as definite rules governing political rhetoric. The division of a social unity (social stratification) is the product of society's vital activity which, in its turn, pre-sets the rhythms of actions for the latter and determines the status of access to limited resources. An intensive value-related coloring of pre-election rhetoric justifies the necessity and obligatory nature of changing the existing structure, *i.e.*, the previous social order.

There is also no doubt about the following: the voters recognize the images of social structure relayed through the above programs. The structuralization of the social world repeatedly projected by these programs in the mass media corresponds to the everyday individual and group experience of a sizable part of the population, which can be stated to a high degree of probability, even without resorting to sociological examination of a given hypothesis. The crux of the issue is that in postcommunist society neither the rich nor poor hide themselves in seclusion from one another. They walk the same streets and physically see each other, and for many this is an unaccustomed and shocking personal experience. Today social stratification is easy to grasp; virtually everyone is subject to its symbolization and evaluation by politicians and the mass media. The forced receipt of new status, in the image of which people experience their new social condition, the comparison of the former with the statuses of closely-related or reference groups and strata — all this is easily understood impels people to some extent to act in various ways, including asserting and defending their rights. Today numerous occupational categories have amassed experience in labor conflicts, and this shows that those categories have carried out the "operation of identifying" their position in a structuralized society.

The images of stratification created by political scientists and sociologists do not run counter to the ideas used by politicians and in large-scale everyday awareness. At best, the latter only specify the general picture without great differences in interpretation. Sociologists are inclined to recognize the degradation of a social structure as a consequence of destructuring tendencies, the latter being the result of the first years of Ukraine's sovereign and independent existence in the post-Soviet and international communities.

Most radical in this respect is the view that modern Ukrainian society is an amorphous formation lacking any clear-cut social strata, while individuals have lost the criteria of social self-identification.[26] Statements concerning the polarization (dichotomization) of structure actually complement this view.[27] As stated above, crises may find their origin in the lack of structure of the social entity as well as in the existence of zones of opacity, which may be either structured or amorphous. And this hardly differs in any way from widespread notions of the "lumpenization" of a considerable part of the population which cannot be forgotten or banished due to the candidates' propaganda during the incessant political campaigns of 1994, as well as due to all kinds of support from the mass media. The latter are used by analysts, sociologists, and journalists as a forum for passing judgment on the degree of society's stratification status.

Many of those making a bid for power today warn, in terms of Levi-Strauss' dual classification, about an ever-increasing "cooling" in Ukrainian society, its transition to a condition dominated by the traditional, in many ways anachronistic, mechanisms of social reproduction. The only real perspective for this kind of society is to is to harden and ossify into intense oppositions incapable of resolution. In this case it makes no difference which sociopolitical ideals pervade the thoughts of the program's authors — that of a totalitarian-distributive or a market-oriented productive society. The threat of a final transition to the category of "cold" societies is being brought home to the electorate by the bearers of different political persuasions and ideas.

Ideas about the deformity and defects of a social structure turn into a stereotype and catch-phrase used by both experts and dilettantes. The obvious warps in the social space (warnings from all sides) engender structural tensions fraught with destructive or virtually unpredictable conflicts. The programs of candidates might be construed by the rank-and-file voter as, first of all, an appeal to use his ballot to prevent a war of social structures or social catastrophe.

It is a paradox, however, that the rank-and-file voter, by and large, did not take heed of the appeals: only five out of 21 vacancies in Kyiv were filled. In most cases the election was invalid because the required 50% of qualified voters did not go to the polls. The preoccupation of power-seekers, their ostentatious readiness to take responsibility and rectify the not-so-hopeless situation run into indifference or imperturbability of the electorate and failed to overcome them. Kyivans put off indefinitely the alteration of political and everyday life, as if not sharing the candidate's alarm over their own future and the future of their state.

What requires interpretation is precisely this transformation of rather realistic images of stratification into simulacra which are not capable of initiating and maintaining political discourse, as does political absenteeism. They are unlikely to be fully explained away by the fatigue and indifference of voters, their exasperation at the disconsolate picture of social stratification imposed insistently and impudently on them by claimants to power, mass media, and sociologists, by an unlucky choice of time, or by the intrigues of slick operators who have staked their bet on a revelation of political will. Rather, one has to admit the existence and influence of factors connected with the general rules and regularities of division and differentiation (as well as those of mutual gravitation) in the political and private spheres, the sphere of rigidly structured instructions and that of individual life worlds which struggle desperately to defend their sovereignty and preclude outside intrusion.

One should also not exclude the possibility that in the situation of impermeability and opacity an unspoken agreement on the division of competence, jurisdiction, and influence be concluded naturally. The state and politicians are confined in their sphere and immersed in their own problems. They fail to influence stratification processes in society and quickly lose any motivation to do so, if ever they had it. In turn, population groups and strata adapt themselves, with varying degrees of success, to an unusual socioeconomic environment where "asystemic" elements dominate systemic and stabilizing ones. Neither side expresses a desire to interact constructively and communicate or perhaps they do not know how. In Kyiv, images of social structure have not become common factors of the situation. Perhaps this is because politicians and voters were in "different" situations, had their "own different discourses" and each subject of the political discourse would like to remain in his own situation and discourse.

The Social Pathology of Postcommunist Society

§1. History of the Problem of Social Insanity

Many postcommunist states have had to pay too high a price for freedom and independence: civil wars and mass-scale violence, a drop in living standards and rising crime, interethnic conflicts and all-pervading corruption, degradation in the fields of science and culture.

This cannot but raise a question: have the on-going changes dulled the human brain and the people been seized by mass-scale insanity? And do the analysts of today have the right, like thinkers of the Roman Empire in the times of Caligula and Nero, of France during the Jacobin terror, of Russia during war communism, of Germany under Nazism, to call their peoples insane, who know not what they do?

"It was again the wrath of gods and human insanity that provoked them into fighting each other." Thus spoke Cornelius Tacitus about Romans destroying each other each other for the sake of a short-lived triumph of just another *princeps*.[28] A millennium later the Byzantine historian Leo the Deacon wrote about the insane plot of Phocas and his sympathizers who were "incurably ill with a cruel and inhuman desire to kill and plunder" and thus provoked a civil war.[29] Another millennium passed, and Ivan Bunin, a witness to the "fall of the Third Rome," the Russian Empire, characterized popular state of mind during the Russian Civil War as "overall madness".[30]

But it is not only wars and revolutions that are associated with mass psychosis. Analyzing the reasons for the loss of the spirit of resistance to the national oppression suffered by Ukrainians in the Russian Empire, Mykhailo Hrushevsky explained this phenomenon by the strong fear of and aversion to the cruel punishments administered in the Empire which were, in his opinion, "organically alien to the Ukrainian nature." Being raised from generation to generation in a fear of political terror, Ukrainians, according to Hrushevsky, finally lost any mental resistance to such terror. It resulted in a "sociopolitical demoralization of Ukrainian civil society, a 'splitting' of its soul".[31]

But if a split personality is a symptom of grave mental illness, then what consequences can a "split soul" have for a whole nation? Is the double nature (ambivalence) of mass political awareness in today's Ukraine noted in sociological studies[32] and manifested in simultaneous orientations towards the diametrically opposed political alternatives (the choice of economic freedom, on the one hand, and socialist paternalism, on the other; striving for political independence, on the one hand, and nostalgia for the Soviet Union, on the other, *etc.*) only one historical form of mass psychopathology which threatens to develop into complete degradation of the population in the postcommunist countries and disintegration of the latter as a result of the progressive mass psychosis? Or is this ambivalence, nevertheless, a natural and quite appropriate response of the human psyche to the real double nature of postcommunist society which has lost its social foundations after rejecting the old system of ideology, economy, political order and failed to find the new ones indispensable for the normal functioning of a social body?

The answer to this question is relevant not only for Ukraine, Russia, and other postcommunist countries. It is also no less important for the West European community which now enjoys relative prosperity. But what is the price of this current prosperity? And has the West forgotten political insanity forever? The present-day problems of the West may be far from the danger of an overall revolutionary neurosis which expresses itself in "contagious fear," "patriotic flagellation," an epidemic of suicides, and the triumph of the possessed and maniacal about whom certain researchers have written in an attempt to explain the pathology of consciousness and deviations in mass behavior during the French Revolution.[33] But what is much nearer to our epoch (and fraught with much graver consequences for human civilization) is another kind of insanity which began under the patriotic bravura of World War I, brought Communism to Russia, and gave birth to Nazism in Germany. And it continues to exert a deleterious effect on public life in the postcommunist world.

As an analytical method, a psychiatric interpretation of this form of social insanity and social pathology has generally proved to be most convincing. This interpretation was upheld most consistently by Karl Jung. As he wrote: "I have always held the opinion that the mass political movements of our times are mass epidemics or, in other words, mass psychoses... Germany suffered a mass psychosis which inevitably led to criminality... The psychic problems of the common man...making his way through the social and political field assume the form of mass psychoses, such as wars and revolutions."[34]

Erich Fromm also explained the spread of Fascism as a psychological pathology of mass "necrophilia." He associated not only the past but also the future prospects of civilization with the danger of mass psychosis: "I believe we have every right to speak of a 'mentally ill society'... If society generally produces people suffering from grave schizophrenia, it will endanger its very existence".[35] This viewpoint is shared by certain prominent representatives of the psychoanalytical school on the role of psychopathology in society. Similar opinions are aired by many European philosophers and cultural critics.

For example, Johan Huizinga came to a conclusion in a quite aptly subtitled work, *A Diagnosis of the Spiritual Distemper of Our Time,* that "any comparison in the social and cultural fields is no more than medical" and therefore he characterized the pre-World War II period as a time of "wild, delirious fantasies,...haunting hallucinations as a result of heavy damage to central nervous system. Applied to the phenomena of modern culture, each of these metaphors has its own specific sense."[36]

Of course, Huizinga primarily stressed not so much the medical as the metaphorical sense of psychiatric terms. But the obvious relevance of such metaphors for understanding processes detrimental to culture and civilization make it possible to find adequate analogies in the field of psychic norms and pathology. Using the vocabulary and concepts of psychiatry in analyzing sociopolitical processes, Gilles Deleuze and Felix Guattari developed the concept of schizoanalysis as an alternative to traditional psychoanalysis. They view the application of psychoanalysis to the problems of mass neurosis as a deviation from an explanation of the true pathological nature of social conflicts and upheavals. Drawing a line between clinical schizophrenia and the schizophrenic process of the revolutionary transformation of a social field, and purging it of the obsolete semantic codes, Deleuze and Guattari give their own interpretation of what they believe to be key problems of the modern world, capitalism and revolution: "We can speak about capitalist paranoia and revolutionary schizophrenia because we do not proceed from the psychiatric meaning of these words; on the contrary, we proceed only from the social and political determinations of their psychiatric application under certain conditions."[37]

Therefore, schizoanalysis, with its vocabulary saturated by psychiatric terms, maintains, above all, a symbolic aspect in explaining social processes with the aid of psychopathological language. It thus challenges the position of those representatives of psychoanalysis who apply the diagnosis of mass psychosis to mass political movements, wars, and revolutions in a strict psychiatric sense.

Is social and political insanity a metaphor or a mental disease? This question is of paramount importance for an adequate understanding of not only the past follies of humankind. We think it is extremely important in assessing the prospects for the postcommunist world to escape from the desperate social situation in which it finds itself after the first tempting steps towards a society of freedom and individual initiative.

§2. *From Metaphors and Psychiatric Labels to a Theoretical Analysis of Social Pathologies*

With all respect for the authority of Jung and Fromm, it is hard to take on trust their belief in the psychotic nature of revolutions, world and civil wars in the twentieth century. One must take into account that Jung and Fromm, though differing from their teacher, Freud, in understanding the guiding motives behind social behavior, still were always staunch supporters of the psychoanalytical paradigm in understanding and explaining social phenomena. Freud's daring idea of curing a society of mass neurosis by psychoanalytical methods was transformed by his disciples into a desire to explain the horror and absurdity of World War II as mass psychosis. Freud's followers have transformed this doctrine into a hope of showing humankind a plausible way of overcoming the disease of modern civilization which manifests itself in uncontrollable outbursts of political violence and social aggression.

However, this road diverts society from solving political problems and conflicts rather than promoting their "cure." The point is the problem of diagnosing mental diseases, even applied to individuals, still awaits commonly accepted solutions in psychiatry. The variability and uncertainty of the boundaries of psychic norms and pathology (as a whole and between mental diseases) are so great that the supporters of "anti-psychiatry" generally consider psychiatric diagnosis as a kind of label attached by society, in violation of fundamental human rights, to people experiencing various difficulties of social adaptation (Robert Laing, Thomas Szasz, *et al.*). But even if the anti-psychiatric school is to be treated as necessary in obvious cases of individual mental disfunction, further extension of psychiatric diagnoses to a society is nevertheless justified no more than serious discussion of the question of "digestive disorder" or "heart disease" in this same society.

Finally, if wars, bloody revolutions, and other social deviations initiated by people and carried out by them are to be treated as outbreaks of psychotic epidemics, one has to admit that these mass psychoses are entirely different in nature from individual psychotic disfunctions. Otherwise it would be impossible to explain the indisputable fact that in periods of "mass psychosis" the rate of individual psychosis need not rise. For example, no increase in psychic disorder rate was ever noted in the former USSR during the decline of perestroika or in the chaotic life of the "post-Soviet" countries. And if individual and mass psychoses have nothing in common, it is quite legitimate to conclude that social insanity must be regarded not as traditional psychosis but as a specific pathology of a social organism which develops according to its own laws and is not subject to psychiatric interpretation and intervention.

Yet, it is psychiatric terminology which has occupied a key place in the current vocabulary of the social and political sciences. It has become a matter of good taste for representatives of the political and intellectual elite to state publicly that the country has gone crazy and that what is happening verges on delirium.

Wide currency is enjoyed by both everyday-language "diagnoses" (insanity, irresponsibility, *etc.*) and specialized psychiatric terms (psychosis, euphoria, apathy, hysteria, neurosis, phobia, *etc.*). Diagnoses of this kind are easily transformed with respect to society as a whole and acquire legitimate diagnostic status in mass awareness. Some concrete examples of the "diagnostic creativity" of politicians, sociologists, and political pundits were cited in our previous publications.[38]

§3. *Social Pathology as a Problem of Postcommunist Society*

The issue in question is the existence in society of a specific form of pathology which is entirely different both from mental disease as a subject of psychiatry and deviation from the social norms of behavior as a traditional subject of sociology and political science. This form of pathology has been defined as *social insanity*. Unlike psychosis and deviance, social insanity is not a digression from acceptable norms and values in the form of the psychological disorders, immoral or antisocial behavior which exist in any society irrespective of its specific historical and cultural conditions. It is, first of all, a mass phenomenon associated with the destruction of a value- and standard-related regulation system of social behavior.

Unlike psychopathology (mental illness) when an individual has his social adaptation mechanisms disturbed (*e.g.*, his orientation in time and space is lost), social insanity is a pathological form of behavior brought about by the destruction of the adaptation object, with the previously developed adaptive mechanisms preserved. It is the "wholesome" striving of people with fully preserved adaptive mechanisms to become accustomed to the uncertain and unstable system of norms and values of a transitional society which provokes the sensation of chaotic impulsive activity, resembling somewhat the behavior of a mental patient. Hence a haunting desire to discuss things like the "insane society," "mass psychoses," *etc.*

Social insanity is not a metaphor or an allegory, nor is it a heuristic pattern of symbols used essentially by the founders of schizoanalysis to denote "revolutionary schizophrenia" and "capitalist paranoia." It is real-life social pathology which we describe as social pathologies, *i.e.*, mass-scale disturbances of social adaptation caused by the absence or excessively rapid change of an adaptation object, with the old adaptive mechanisms fully preserved or changing with insufficient speed.

§4. General and Specific Social Pathologies

Social Pathology is a specific subject of sociological research which cannot be expressed in psychiatric terms as a matter of principle. Moreover, the substitution of the psychiatric terms for the sociological ones is by no means harmless. For example, constant use of the notion of an "insane society" gradually instills in politicians and at the grassroots a complex of irresponsibility: "What's it got to do with us? The society is crazy!" It is in this way that the mentality of a "mental patient" is formed: the latter can bite the first person he bumps into and go scot free.

But especially dangerous is the use of psychiatric diagnoses in a literal medical sense to characterize mass social subjects. For example, Ukraine has already become a true victim of and participant in the abuse of mass psychiatric diagnosis for quite unseemly ends: radiophobia, a diagnosis which gained great popularity when official attempts were made to explain the influence of the Chornobyl disaster on the health of millions of people.

It is beyond doubt that the Chornobyl disaster became a powerful stress-inducing factor for those who suffered through it, and the very fact of raising a question about the effect of this stress on people's mental health was not inappropriate. But when the population of affected was proclaimed radiophobic on no real grounds, the political purpose of this diagnosis was demonstrated, i.e., to shift responsibility for the most grave aftermath of the accident from the direct participants of the campaign in order to deliberately misinform the public and shift responsibility onto the latter by labeling it "mentally deranged and crazed with fear."

However, psychiatric experts failed to find any mass symptoms of phobia among those affected by the accident, while sociologists exposed the hidden political agenda behind the term "radiophobia" as applied to these people.[39] Yet, the abuse of psychiatry for political purposes still continues and the diagnosis of "radiophobia" is still employed by advocates of a psychopathological interpretation of Chornobyl's influence on public health.[40] The current disdainful attitude toward disaster victims who are forced to resort to actions of mass protest may have been caused largely by the purveyors of such false diagnoses. Their unprofessional psychiatric "investigation" groundlessly accused hundreds of thousands of people of manifesting a pathological reaction to compulsory resettlement or to health-threatening radiation doses received during the Chornobyl clean-up.

In studying social pathologies within a given society a distinction must be made between locally specific and general social pathologies. The latter may occur whenever there is social instability, radical changes and a dramatic drop in the people's living standards. When the old system of values and norms is ruined and a new one is not yet formed, a situation arises which Emil Durkheim called *anomie* (lack of norms) and which is reflected in the awareness and behavior of people who lose firm social support and experience alienation from the present and uncertainty about the future.

Robert Merton showed that in the condition of anomie there is no conformity between the socially significant goals of human activity and the socially acceptable means of achieving these goals.[41] As a result, some people try to achieve new goals by old means, while others – to reanimate the old ones by new means (*e.g.*, the communists appeal to democratic norms in an attempt to lift the ban on their party). As shown in studies, this pattern thus is revealed in postcommunist society: the majority of the population, being oriented toward the new democratic values and goals, prefer the old totalitarian means of achieving them. For example, while supporting the building a law-governed state, most respondents in public-opinion polls favor such clearly unlawful measures as granting law-enforcement bodies the right to take into custody officials suspected of bribery for an indefinite period.[42]

What also constitutes a general social pathology is the social intolerance which arises whenever living standards drop and people start looking for those they can blame for their current hardships. During the first years of perestroika public-opinion polls unambiguously showed that the role of "scapegoat" was meant for the Party apparatchiks and employees of the "socialist trade system." As hardships increased, intolerance acquired a more indefinite nature extending to representatives of various socio-professional and ethnic groups. True, this phenomenon is not at all specific in comparison with other countries and nations which were or still are in the grip of an economic or political crisis. The specific social pathologies of our society stem from its specific history and are somewhat unique. The analysis of mass awareness and behavior patterns in postcommunist society allowed the singling out a number of specific social pathologies which broadly determine the relevant manifestations and potential of "social insanity."

Nowhere in the world, except the former Soviet Union, can there ever have been in such a comprehensive form as the confrontational strategy of reaching social harmony according to which any constructive process was regarded as struggle. It was not only a struggle against the ubiquitous external and internal enemies but also struggle "for" — for meeting and exceeding production targets, for peace and friendship among peoples, for a rich harvest, *etc.* The principle of fighting on all front-lines formed a peculiar "trench mentality" which even now tells those who want to stand up and raise their eyes that this is an extremely dangerous thing to do, and that it is better to wait until an "all-out attack signal" is sounded. And woe betide that sovereign part of the former USSR where this signal is given by the unscrupulous politicians obsessed with self-assertion by affirming the idea of their nation's grandeur. For, until recently many people considered the values of struggle more significant that those of creation.

The specific social pathology of our society is also exemplified by the phenomenon of an acquired social helplessness rooted in the long period of total state paternalism which formed a basic type of personality unable to assume responsibility not only for the society in which he lives but also for his own life in that same society. The system of social links formed by communist theory and practice still continues to reproduce the phenomenon of an acquired social helplessness. True, the thoughtlessly accepted idea of an "almighty Party leading us to a bright future" has given way to a no less popular idea that it will suffice to exorcise the "communist devil" to bring us to the democratic pastures of heaven without untoward effort.

One can also highlight the socially pathological culture of contacts, which means a method of interaction among people whereby the participants in direct and mass communication are not interested in establishing feedback. This style of contacts was formed during the triumph of "democratic centralism" meaning in fact two unequal lines of communication: orders from top to bottom and reports from bottom to top. At present the most vivid example of a residual lack of interest in feedback among the subjects of communication is the steady unwillingness of the authorities to take serious account of the public-opinion poll returns. Not knowing public opinion as a whole, politicians are only guided by those forms of its manifestations which involve the most politically active strata (rallies, demonstrations, petitions, *etc.*) and often create a resonance incommensurate with their true influence on the broad masses. Hence the increasingly strong impression of an "overall madness," when the few but vociferous followers of an unbalanced political leader take part in clearly anomalous actions. In fact, the mass occurrence of psychiatric labels also testifies to a socially pathological culture of contacts which cannot express itself without using a psychological diagnosis.

In addition to those reviewed above, the following social pathologies are worthy of note: the postcommunist ambivalence of political awareness expressed by conformism and nihilism, deprofessionalization and confusion of the status-and-prestige criteria of human interaction, as well as by the deactualization of values. These still await detailed study.

Social pathology as a specific pathology of a postcommunist society can destroy the "social body" or check its democratic development. To overcome the former it is to necessary to foster the feeling of self-respect in society and the personality. Without this feeling, an individual country can create an anything but civilized state worthy of the civilized world community's esteem and interest in its future development.

CHAPTER 4.

GEOPOLITICS IN THE POSTCOMMUNIST WORLD

- The New Geopolitical Situation after the Fall of Communism
- The Contradictions of Geopolitical Self-Determination
- Geoeconomic Problems Facing the Postcommunist States
- Geopolitical Implication of Ethnopolitics
- The Realities and the Logic of Myth in Inter-Slavic Relation
- Ukrainian-Russian Relations and Western Policy

If the universal and global phenomenon of communism and hence, of postcommunist changes might require evidence concerning the internal situation in a given society, it is self-evident in terms of geopolitics. The communist ideology in its Bolshevik version underwent political development and best expressed itself as a "creative doctrine," in international politics. The postwar period witnessed the USSR's inability to win the underlying economic competition or demonstrate its internal qualitative advantages; the USSR's attention was concentrated more often than not on specific issues of global rivalry, on provoking any revolutionary movements which might be conducive to its historic and, hence, final global victory. The socialist camp created by Moscow was a powerful factor affecting virtually the whole structure of world military and political relations.

Expansionism is not a communist invention. But as distinct from a once traditional Western strategy of ensuring by force economic activities based on market expansion (including territorial), the Kremlin endorsed the originally expansionist extra-economic and far-fetched idea of world revolution and used even the slightest opportunity to promote it artificially. There were undoubtedly two aspects to the Cold War, the arms race and the long, drawn-out international tension, and, hence, two actors. But, as the course of international events bears witness, the communist bloc most often took the initiative. Of identical origin is another mass-scale factor which aggravated tension in international relations from the late 1950s to the late 1970s – Maoism.

By its very nature, the communist world also repeatedly displayed an "intraspecific" aggressiveness. The latter was profoundly experienced by Yugoslavia, Hungary, Poland, and Czechoslovakia; it was expressed in clashes between the USSR and China and in the Chinese invasion of Vietnam. The export of communist ideology along with weapons and various forms of military presence resulted in sometimes different but always tragic and logically motivated events in Cambodia, Afghanistan, Angola, Mozambique, Yemen, Nicaragua, the Horn of Africa, and other regions. Moscow's global strategy exacerbated and ideologically colored the national-liberation and later internal political struggle in third world countries and, even to some extent, influenced political processes in Western states through its support of leftists. Profound qualitative differences, an obvious asymmetry of vectors, let alone methods, actions, and roles of the two poles of force, distorted the geopolitical landscape for decades. In modern conditions this governs the complex, multifaceted, and somewhat amorphous processes of the postcommunist transformation in the world system of international relations. It is not a question of the mere restructuring of relationships but of the internal evolution of dozens of countries, of essential changes on the political map of Central and Eastern Europe, Central Asia, and the Transcausasus, and, on this basis, of fundamental change in the content and direction of the foreign policies pursued by countries of this vast area. A noticeable change has taken place in the qualitative characteristics and balance of the world's political and economic landscape, which necessitates geopolitical reorientation and forces the most stable and successful international entities to seek new goals and objectives.

The New Geopolitical Situation after the Fall of Communism

§1. Restructuring Global Relationships

The main feature of a new geöpolitical situation is its staid and amorphous quality. The postwar world community became accustomed to certain standards and comprehensibility in any given situation. The latter has now been complicated primarily by the tension and dynamic correlation of forces, and not by unpredictability in the intentions and actions of the chief protagonists in international relations. The old brutal determination exposed threats, simplified analysis, and in the long run precluded uncontrolled developments and full-scale clashes. Today, there is no longer any simple answer to the question of who is who in international politics.

It is symptomatic that most commentaries on geopolitical change and assessments of its further evolution contain attempts to find a "customary" version of the world structure and thus are reduced to building N-pole models. The staunchest traditionalists have N as equaling unity (*pax americana*); close to this are forecasts of reviving an arbitrary bipolarity/polarity (in case Russia reasserts itself as a great power and thereby offers an alternative global center of gravity). "Innovative" approaches to analyzing the geopolitical landscape and its inherent trends increase the number N to three, five, or eight, thus simultaneously attempting to illustrate both the real complexity of global situation and deliberately simplify and schematize the object of study. In the past this could be largely justified, for there were not only two powerful poles but also two systems cemented by global ideologies. The latter, often accompanied by intensive politico-diplomatic, economic-financial, and often military action, shaped the foreign-policy attitudes of dozens of states, checking expressions of alternative regional, ethnic, or religious views.

The new horizons of the modern world are associated with the disappearance of bisystemity rather than of bipolarity, along with the disappearance in principle of systems as primary components in the structure of global relations and bearers of the latter's relative orderliness.

A system like this in the full sense may be represented only by the Eastern community of states where, under strict centralization, there was perhaps, here and there, internal discord and heresy but no plurality of geopolitical attitudes. It is the intensive strategy of this community that also imparted systemity to Western international relations, albeit with internal contradictions and claims for the establishment of separate power centers remaining intrinsic.

Let us assume that the model of two mutually opposed systems played a, by no means, unambiguous and not altogether negative role in postwar history. It was at its most dangerous by far when the gap between the levels of scientific-technological and socio-political development, and hence, between the threat of catastrophe and the possibility of finding civilized solutions, was pushed to the limit. Bisystemity demonopolized in a peculiar way the influence and potential of ambitions to global domination, which were kept in check by mutual deterrence, and simplified the negotiated settlement of strategic issues in a period when there was no alternative to force as a factor in international politics and when the capabilities of that force increased dramatically. The competition of the two systems exposed the dangers of their irreconcilability, stressing the importance of common human values and the need to deideologize international relations. In the 1980s the erosion of the old model was adequately compensated for and in some cases stimulated by the strengthening of international law-and-order and by a qualitatively new, more natural, and more constructive pluralism.

The late 1980s – when the Cold War was petering out and new conflicts still looked like fleeting episodes and problem-free exceptions – gave birth to almost unanimous euphoria over the dawning of a new age of security, stability, and rapid progress in international cooperation. But the emerging transition period of international development could not, axiomatically, avoid various risks, complexities, and uncertainties. Soon, the Persian Gulf war, escalation of the Yugoslav conflict, dramatic events in many areas of the former USSR and, finally, Russia's controversial policies outlined a new tension-laden geopolitical situation.[1]

A lack of system and adequate structure characterize international relations today. The old artificial orderliness and rigid dualism of forces characteristic of the bipolar system has given way to polycentrism and multiplicity of criteria. The substance of the notion "world community" has changed in fact and in essence. And it is not only and not so much a question of the significant increase in the number of international entities as that of ever-expanding opportunities to select and pursue one's own strategy of being and foreign policy. Gone is the subordination propped up by global ideologies and forces, and so too is the uniform and externally governed quality of the postures and actions of states.

The old world structure was jointly created by a few great powers. It was their interests that until recently largely determined the rules of the game in the international arena. True, these interests have become harmonized with the interests of other members of the world community to a much greater extent than at the time of Teheran, Yalta, and Potsdam, but it is only recently, after the collapse of the communist system that the overwhelming majority of "non-western" states have been given the chance to turn from passive objects into active subjects in modern international life.

For the first time in history states, which formerly had to adjust their foreign policy to "systemic" discipline, have at least the prerequisites for expressing themselves freely in the international arena. Moreover, this pluralization has been supplemented by the emergence of new and potentially rather distinct states in the former Soviet Union and Yugoslavia, by a change of contours, and even by the initial formation of new sub-regions. New and more powerful impetus is being given to the life of Slavic states almost half of which have at last acquired a real chance for independent development. Slavic and Orthodox factors may become noticeable in the future on a sub-regional level (but only if the Russian factor is overcome and the problem of giving the relationship true parity, naturalness, and mutually beneficial quality of relations is solved). Concurrently, the eastern borders of Catholicism are being modified. The Baltic countries are expanding and diversifying the sub-region of Northern Europe. It is rather difficult to forecast what characteristics might be assumed by such new subjects of international relations as the formerly Soviet Central Asian and Caucasian republics. In any case, the world community is now distinguished by such essential general features as diversity, a considerable expansion of the circle of ideas, motions, and approaches, that can and should influence the creation of a common human political philosophy, of an effective system of international law, general world order, and the world community's search for a new dynamic balance.

Let us note that when it comes to nations, peoples, and countries, specificity is the norm and can be treated as an inherent and obligatory feature of sovereignty. However, this certainly does not require atomization and anarchy in world relations. The collapse of the bisystemic model eliminated the artificial and *de facto* authoritarian structure which had emerged from geopolitical confrontation, a structure which as early as the 1960s began rapidly to evolve into an anachronism, an obstacle to true harmony in global relations, and in no sense serving the interests of most states and nations.

Of course, the problems of achieving order, stability, and predictability in the modern overly pluralistic world are growing ever more complex; they require significant improvement of the legal institutions and mechanisms of interaction along with an overhaul of existing international structures. These should be democratic and, hence, sophisticated mechanisms. It will not be easy for them to achieve efficiency. These problems are likely to be solved on two levels: further development of universal mechanisms of cooperation along with the restructuring, and change in the essence of bilateral and multilateral relations. Regarding the former, one can foresee a more active discussion of ways to democratize the UN, to expand the spheres of activity and functional powers of intergovernmental organizations, to develop vertical links and the institutions to supervise the observance of general principles and norms of the rights and duties of states. One can also expect a far deeper awareness of the values and interests common to all civilizations and the need to safeguard them. This gives the global system of international relations a real chance to achieve order and assume a qualitatively new structure.[2] It is clear, however, that the liberation of international relationships from ideological shackles and the spread of general democratic principles has not yet freed the world community of the complications of uneven development, from the unequal objective capabilities of different states to perform duties as subjects of law or even to resolve their own problems. All this even now to some extent pervades world structures, exacerbating the questions of the place, role, and utility of "social motives" and the principles of liberalism in international relations. It would seem possible to resolve this global duality only within limits required for stability and security and not more. The differences remaining between the strategic interests of donor and recipient states mainly affect bilateral and group relations which have a much more active immunity to the virus of dependency and are directed at an original pragmatism.

It is the sphere of direct contacts among states complemented by the actions of NGOs that has the main potential for solving specific problems. Qualitative global changes certainly influence this level of relations as well, thereby lowering the probability of some obtaining artificial advantages over others. However, there is no diminution in its to objective advantages. Differences are growing in the capability and viability of individual states. The conditions of internationalization, the increased importance of international factors of development, formulate relations of unequal mutual dependence. Dozens of countries, with due regard for their own limited potential, map out a long-term strategy of relying on certain powerful partners. It is this reliance that creates international poles or centers of gravity. It is essential that in modern conditions such poles should not constitute an alternative to world structures. Nor do the latter operate in a finite space or set special, entirely different rules of the game. They are only a component of the world system and are oriented toward cooperation to no lesser extent than towards rivalry.

An essential feature of the new geopolitical situation is the cohesion and growth of a highly-civilized core in the world community, *i.e.,* the highly-developed Western countries, which thus unite the main poles of force. This may be illustrated by the stable activity of G7, a deep mutual interest in maintaining a dialogue between the latter and Russia, the dynamics of the general European process, and the strategic choices made by the countries of Central and Eastern Europe. Preconditions exist in this super-region for attaining high standards of international cooperation still inaccessible to other areas. Concurrently, the global influence of this core may gradually reduce the level of uncertainty in the geopolitical situations of other regions. However, this first of all requires general stabilization of the economic and political situation.

Today we witness an upsurge of crises and conflicts as another feature of the new geopolitical situation. The dawn of the new era in global relations was marked by basic changes in the structure and manifestations of threats to international peace and security. The danger of world conflict has receded to a purely hypothetical level and has in fact vanished. Orthodox aggressive strategies have been discarded by the states of not only the first but also, so to speak, second tier of viability. The problems of security have become deideologized and more tractable to logical and purely pragmatic approaches, as have international relations in general. It has been possible to deepen and consolidate a process conceived back in the times of Gorbachev's "new thinking," that is, the process of settling those regional conflicts (or their components) where the effects of bisystemic rivalry were especially pronounced.

However, there were also negative consequences. First, numerous young and strident nationalisms in Asia and Africa began or intensified their "creative" activities. The emancipated endogenous political philosophy gave birth to local expansionism, formed unstable local balances of forces, new or renewed conflict situations, and areas of tension. Second, various factors reduced the influence and control exerted by states which had been involved in conflicts and now constitute the main threats to international peace and security: Iraq, Iran, North Korea, and Libya. Third, the dismantling of the Eastern bloc itself, beginning with the Soviet empire, gave rise to a series of new, acute, and highly unpredictable conflicts associated mainly with overcoming the results of past arbitrary decisions on borders, political system, varieties and qualitative features of national development. In this connection, the Final Communiqué of the joint session of the NATO Defense Planning Committee and Nuclear Planning Group in May 1994 stated in particular that "the threats to our security and European stability as a whole are today far more diverse and complex than those NATO faced in its first four decades" and that current security problems require a broader approach.[3]

The situation could be characterized, in general, by the end of conflicts between systems and termination of "class-based" confrontation as well as by the expansion and exacerbation of ethnically, religiously, socially, economically, and domestically based conflicts. And from a purely functional viewpoint, the global threat of a devastating confrontation of the two systems gave way to endless sub-regional and local conflicts, areas of tension, specific internal difficulties involving (not just potentially but in reality) dozens of countries. Therefore, global security has increased, while the national security of a great many countries in the former second and third worlds is now greatly endangered. This evidently also does not completely by-pass the first world states, for they not only run the increasing risks associated with security indivisibility or with the destabilization of economic exchange, they also face immediate threats of mass migration, international crime, and terrorism.

These problems are rather specific. Almost all of them stem from similar historical and geopolitical sources and are connected with the fact that the conflicting parties were formerly objects of superpower expansion and victims of arbitrarily imposed geopolitical structures. The parties had limited opportunities for natural development, and they are now solving, in one way or another, problems of national revival. And this exerts special influence the local relations among neighbors.

The possibilities of maintaining peace and security in the former Eastern bloc territory depend on a complex combination of external and internal factors. In terms of classical peacekeeping through mechanisms of the world community (UN, CSCE), we witness, as with general problems of underdevelopment, a situation where available capabilities and will to act far are inadequate to the intensity of the problem. Russia, by means of its alternative peace-making proposals, attempts to fill the power vacuum in the region, outline a wide area of its own vital interests (the CIS), and seek an international mandate to keep peace throughout the CIS. This is obviously unacceptable, for it would have clearly breached the principle of the neutrality and disinterestedness of the peacekeeper.[4] The newness of the situation lies in the West's very cool reaction to it. Very few things remind one of the former rivalry over influence in the Central and Eastern European region. It makes clear the current NATO strategy: gradual, cautious movement eastward and, hence, extension of the existing Western continental security zone into states enjoying a reputation of being the most reformed and stable, which have resolved their main foreign policy problems, and managed to shake off the burden of Russian tutelage. It vividly illustrates one of the chief current geopolitical uncertainties – the uncertain Western policy towards Russia and the wide range of strategic options open to the latter.

After all, in spite of Russia being a legal successor to all things Soviet, it is a new, different state which has not yet fully solved its own problems of national self-image and self-determination. Its search for solutions is ongoing and dramatically effects the domestic policy in this Eurasian colossus. The world exerts limited influence on giants and therefore must wait and see. At the moment one can only state that Russia has not abandoned its old great-power methods in foreign policy, does not care to establish relations of trust with its "near-abroad" neighbors, and is carefully surrounding itself with a field of force traditional for geopolitical entities in periods of confrontation. Russian politicians try almost openly to express their lack of desire to further maintain a beneficial and equal dialogue with the West as compensation for the "negative potential" of their own crisis- and conflict-ridden situation. All this creates additional major threats to peace and stability. As stated in a comprehensive report of the Institute of International Economic and Political Studies of the Russian Academy of Sciences, "the direction of Russia's foreign policy may deviate drastically from a normal course consonant with national interests, and the country could again be held hostage to the ruinous dynamics of imperial policy."[5] It is clear that the West's undefined policy towards Russia provides for alternatives ranging from close security cooperation to a return to deterrence. All this, unfortunately, exerts a negative influence on other postcommunist states, first of all those in the CIS, restricts their room for maneuver, and makes it all the more difficult for them to overcome growing dangers of isolation.

The influence vectors of the West and Russia create a certain line of demarcation and from this flows the danger of breaking up the relative unity of the postcommunist region along the western border of Russia, Belarus, and Ukraine. In these conditions only Ukraine is potentially able, given her geopolitical efforts and aspirations for equilibrium, to maintain a sufficiently transparent continental space, change the configuration of strategic links, and enlarge the European community by joining it. But to do so, both pretentious Moscow and the neutral Kyiv would have to harmonize their positions and find a reliable scenario for their synchronized rapprochement with the West. Zbigniew Brzezinski notes in this context: "It is surely in Russia's interest to become more closely tied to Europe, notwithstanding the complications inherent in Russia's Eurasian geography and identity. It is surely in the long-range interest of Ukraine gradually to redefine itself as a Central European state. The proposed arrangement would provide the needed historical pause and the requisite sense of security for Russia and Ukraine to work out a stable balance between close economic cooperation and separate political coexistence – while also moving closer to Europe as Europe moves toward them."[6]

The security structures being set up in the CIS are directed at consolidating the Russian military presence and serving Moscow's interests, not toward establishing real cooperation or creating multilateral mechanisms. The totally unbalanced relationship within the CIS and the complex role of Russia in maintaining security and stability in neighboring countries do not allow us to view what is now being built under the Tashkent Agreement as a collective security system compatible with modern international practice. Moveover, the situation is often governed by internal, especially intra-regional, factors.

§2. The Internal Geopolitical Dynamics of the Postcommunist World

One can agree with Russian academician Aleksandr Yakovlev that the communist regimes in the USSR and East Central Europe did not fall because of nationalism. They were ruined by a multiplicity of historical circumstances, with nationalism merely filling the vacuum left by the lack of other serious ideological and political trends.[7] It is only to a small extent that classical nationalism caused uncertainty, risk, and conflict during the first years of postcommunist national independence. The issue has been more one of complications and contradictions in a more general process of liberation from a painful legacy, of building a new society, and for most former Soviet and Yugoslav republics it is also a process of solving problems of identity and self-sufficiency. The inherited problems also determine the nature of relationships among the new states. An almost unanimous recognition of an "easy," less dramatic dismantling of the Eastern bloc and collapse of the Soviet empire is only a formality, while the fulfillment of a positive program, *i.e.*, the formation of separate fully independent and self-sufficient societies and the respective relationships among is an entirely informal thing of virtually unprecedented complexity and scope. From the viewpoint of civilized standards of international relations, we face (at least in the former USSR and Yugoslavia) somewhat pre-international relations which lack openness and a truly official nature, where foreign and domestic policies are closely intertwined, and where responsibility to a partner is so devalued that it no longer counts as an international obligation.

The postcommunist region remains largely unstable internally and even rather unpredictable (in the Balkans and some areas of the former USSR). It is undergoing a dramatic process of identifying internal and common problems, of defusing destabilizing factors which have accumulated for decades and now show themselves because the administrative command system, which kept them in check, has collapsed. Their scope, acuteness, and hence ways by which some of them might be settled are not yet fully understood. The degree to which they are catalyzed by economic crisis and the latter's depth also defy reliable estimate. It is only natural that one of the risks monitored by, say, NATO is international, territorial, and border disputes and possibility of mass westward migration. And here the postcommunist states rival the developing ones.

The specific characteristics of the postcommunist world, essential as they are, display themselves to different degrees in different countries. Equally heterogeneous is the level of various states preparedness for reforms and independent development. The gap between the Bolshevik model and a self-governing democratic society proved to be far wider than that between their levels of material development. In these conditions the transitional nature of societies, their internal uncertainty, is natural, even normal. At the same time, if one accepts the notion that the communist system's collapse was an inevitable result of internal processes, then one should expect those processes to continue under the specific conditions of social transformation, that a qualitatively new society is in the process of being created, and this is precisely what is meant by transitional society.

This transformation must also be supported by external factors which may be viewed as a geopolitical factor, earlier virtually non-existent but now influential under the new circumstances. An essential feature of the new modern geopolitical situation is the "discovery" of a vast region consisting, until recently, of closed and semi-isolated societies. These societies, once in a qualitatively new situation, began to experience and even actively attract certain external influences. This partly intentional and partly spontaneous process interacts in various ways with internal factors to define the parameters of development. What is now self-evident, that the postcommunist societies of, say, the Czech Republic and Tadzhikistan differ radically from each other, underscores the fact that the former communist world also was not internally homogeneous, it was only brutally made monotonous by the system and transformed by Moscow into an integral geopolitical area. The collapse of the system and then of the USSR exposed the real non-uniformity of the Eurasian macroregion, and this is also reflected in the different speeds and directions of internal transformations in individual countries and regions.

The authoritarian administrative command mechanisms which kept the communist model functioning and the very model of which has been completely discarded only by Hungary, Poland, and Czechoslovakia (the Czech Republic acting much more quickly and decisively than Slovakia, which accelerated their divorce), by the Baltic states as well as by Slovenia and Croatia, the most developed republics in the former Yugoslavia. These countries may be said to have identified quite definite tendencies of transformations which clearly bring them closer to the West and create a new geopolitical situation in Central Europe. The same tendencies are far less pronounced in the Balkan sub-region.

Hungary, Poland, and Czechoslovakia were internally capable of using the Gorbachev reform of relationships, bringing about goal-oriented fundamental internal transformations, and even pushing the Kremlin forward, thus causing the Eastern bloc to fall apart. Other "people's democracies" first achieved true independence and only then made the transition to internally governed transformations. This group of countries naturally constitutes only the second echelon in their rapprochement with the West.[8] A similar situation burdened with lasting foreign-policy implications arose in former Yugoslavia, where more advanced Slovenia and Croatia initiated the federation's dismantling and sprinted toward the West, not only to solve ethnic issues but also to accelerate internally their socio-economic reforms. Likewise, Latvia, Lithuania, and Estonia were the only former Soviet republics with a truly national and massively supported democratic movement, where the struggle for independence rested on a relatively well-thought-out strategy of independent existence.

A more complex and uncertain situation arose in the CIS, where anticommunism gained momentum only due to the contradictory perestroika, which triggered the disintegration of the Soviet empire and brought about a situation where the forces of democratic renewal were partially disorganized and partially let themselves be seduced by the process of gaining sovereignty in nationalist garb. Having as their goal the universal task of creating a democratic law-governed state, these forces in each former republic found themselves in situations with a different correlation of socio-political blocs and thus had to solve different urgent problems. Here the Soviet geopolitical zone was preserved at different stages of modification with unidentified tendencies of internal evolution and the deepest possible multifaceted crises. The elite's amorphous values and ideologies, absence of a civil society, along with internal political confrontations accompanied by criminalization and massive corruption set the stage for a new time of troubles and render it difficult to state with any certainty what kind of social system will replace communism in the countries of this region in the foreseeable future. In addition, the CIS countries have not yet solved the problem of self-sustained sovereign existence and self-determination in the current system of international relations. Many countries (to be more exact, their rulers) faced these problems quite unexpectedly, without due reference to the inherent logic of internal processes. This is most true of the former Soviet Central Asian republics which were not prepared for independence in either an official, political, or socioeconomic sense. They also lack traditions of statehood adapted to modern conditions.

After the Bolshevik attempt to create a new civilization failed, ethno-religious and historico-cultural factors caused the renewal and deepening of civilization boundaries between individual countries, groups of countries, and even within them (Russia, Kazakhstan). Resulting large-scale migrations raised the prospect of a substantial reduction of the Slavic presence in southern regions, diminution of diasporas, and the scale of mixing bearers of different cultures. Given the lack of prerequisites for the rapid formation of a civil society, the complex forms of multiethnicity in most new states constitute not only a problem of internal integration but also an essential element of geopolitical uncertainty in the region as a whole and in the strategic perspectives of individual states. The generally accepted principle of inviolability of borders, of a territorial status quo in local conditions, gives fixed status to borders drawn arbitrarily by Stalin. A picture familiar since the decolonization of sub-Saharan Africa is here far more complex because of greater interdependence and distorted ties which have to be reformed, no matter how difficult. For this reason, factors of geopolitical pluralism and relatively non-harmonious geopolitical integrity act simultaneously in the CIS, causing considerable internal tension. The actions of these factors along with external influences determine to various extents the situation in individual countries and determine their attitude toward ideas of reintegration.

Of paramount importance in outlining the new shape of the geopolitical theater is Russian policy. With neighboring states inadequately prepared for independence, forced to concentrate on internal troubles and having limited capabilities to pursue an activist foreign policy, Russia is the only agent capable of undertaking system-creating action and of deliberately influencing the international relations being renewed. Russia's size, resources, and military potential are complemented by a psychological orientation that can only be described as a great-power syndrome of complete legal succession to the USSR and its traditional messianism. Hence, its unconditional claims for a special role and positions in the whole region east of Germany, its return to a more natural purely Russian nationalism, various popular scenarios of gathering and strategically subjugating satellites, and constant displays of its special relationship with the West.[9] But in this case Russia, too, experiences a large-scale and painful effect of newness and uncertainty. It again faces, as before, the question of historico-cultural self-awareness and geopolitical self-determination. In prerevolutionary times the needle of the strategic compass always swung from one pole to the other. The mind was drawn to the West, while wealth came from Siberia. The tug-of-war of Eurasianism and the unending debate between Slavophiles and Westernizers illustrate, confirm, and define the status of a choice never made.

Only yesterday the problems of Russia governed the fates of dozens of peoples. Now this has formally and for the time being changed. After the disintegration of the USSR Russia supposedly became less "eastern." But its "West" also shrank (one need only recall the past civilizing influence of the former Baltic states), and the old balance of contradictions was maintained. Moscow's conceptual indefiniteness also has a flip side which provokes heated debates in European and world politics where Western leadership is a fact. For there is also rather wide-spread xenophobia, "anti-Westernism," and a search for external enemies which lay claim to becoming part of official ideology. Such sentiments are nourished by both internal cataclysms and national traditions. As was aptly noted by "official" Russian political scientist Emil Pain, "Russian nationalism in its mass manifestations is nothing but degenerating Soviet consciousness."[10]

With the death of the USSR, problems of self-identification and strategic choice were inherited by all the newly independent states. Under the new conditions the East-West alternative underwent mutation, lost its old algorithm, and assumed the role of a pragmatic issue of contemporary politics: upon whom could they rely for support against threats to their new statehood, from whom could one obtain security guarantees, resources, and such. For today, under conditions of almost insurmountable isolation, the geographical borders of the CIS seem to embrace a zone where the choice in practical terms has been made and simultaneously undermine the very phenomenon of the CIS.

Specific circumstances in this early postcommunist entity illustrate a semantic dilemma: either a civilized divorce (which is the talk of the town in, say, Ukraine) or a veneer legitimizing a system of Russian domination. A third scenario, transforming the CIS into a civilized integrated grouping which could actually accomplish the voluntary unification of independent states based on a harmony of interests is impossible, at least in a medium term, for there are no truly independent states or opportunities for choosing a partner.

The CIS emerged as an unexpected result of processes in the Soviet Union during its final period of existence. It is first of all the intensification of a power struggle and related worsening of relations between center and periphery, *i.e.*, the former Union and certain of Russia's autonomous republics, territories, and regions. In this case, Party and state elites exploited, in one way or another, the idea of national liberation and democratization, thus neutralizing or utilizing local national and broadly democratic movements. The latter assumed a mass character and won respect very slowly in most republics, and only in some of them (Georgia, Armenia, Ukraine, partly Azerbaizhan, and Moldova) did they approach a level where they could constitute a real opposition to the ruling nomenklatura. The power struggle and shared interest in bringing down the central governing structures determined the sovereignization of the Union republics outside the logic of internal processes which elsewhere by and large have been precursors to independence. The events of late 1991 did not yet signify transformation of the empire into independent states; they merely witnessed the disintegration of the strictly centralized, partially reformed Bolshevik monarchy into separate fiefdoms, most of which still have considerable hardships to overcome on the road to self-sufficiency and true independence. This process was directed by the top Soviet bureaucracy and served their ambitions, which had reached the level of statehood. These only more or less coincided with real-life social interests. Sovereignty was not won but obtained by a redistribution of essentially the same power. The only exception is the Baltic states, for they steered, quite naturally, clear of CIS processes.

It is the redistribution and restructuring of power "from above" that brought about the surprisingly easy and virtually conflict-free disintegration of the USSR, so puzzling to foreign observers. If there were any complications on the road to sovereignization, they were of a rather peculiar nature, *e.g.*, the inadequate readiness for governmental responsibility of the leaders of some republics thrown into independence almost by force. On the eve of the August 1991 coup Ukraine was the only obstacle to signing a new Union Treaty. In October of that year when federal structures were in fact paralyzed, the leaders of most republics again intended to sacrifice national independence and support the re-edited treaty which actually would have given local "parties of power" the right to uncontrolled freedom of action along with certain guarantees. As soon as December the aspiration to have something of the kind prompted the Central Asian leaders to run after the CIS created by Russia, whose leadership ruled out any parallel existence for Union authorities, by Ukraine where the dominant conservative neo-communist forces did not require any outside support and even hastened to dissociate themselves from the waves of democratization coming from Moscow, and by Belarus which let things drift. Kazakhstan's internal disunity explains Nursultan Nazarbayev's especially active role in attempts at reintegration. In general, the Central Asian states, where the ruling elite relies both on Soviet nomenklatura-led mechanisms of domination and local semi-feudal traditions, are very far from Western standards of civilization and are orienting themselves toward maneuvers between the Muslim world and Russia, using the latter as a guarantor against fundamentalism and all-out islamization. Moscow, in its turn, is interested in restricting the northern penetration of the Middle-Eastern states. This region as well as, say, Mongolia will apparently remain a periphery isolated from broad international links in the short and probably medium term. One can also foresee a gradual weakening of Moscow's influence and the establishment of a new geopolitical balance in this subregion coupled with growing differences in the political will of individual countries.

The new Central Asian states and Azerbaizhan are certain to get closer to the Muslim world, but they are also likely to occupy a special place in it. They are almost sure to retain the signs of "Europeanness" acquired in the past few decades, *i.e.*, a certain immunity against fundamentalism, and they will thus not only expand the Muslim region but also diversify it. Azerbaizhan has chances to "embrace Europe" following the example of and aided by Turkey. Moreover, given the solution of internal problems, Christian Armenia and Georgia gain quite similar prospects, especially with the aid of their diasporas.

After the collapse of the USSR these states, along with Moldova (relatively more organic and consolidated), acquired clear perspectives and pursued a much more independent policy aimed at changing their own geostrategic paradigm. The essence of postimperial relations in the USSR, in particular Russia's interests and role, stands out more prominently against events in the above countries. The attempts of the newly independent states to overcome their isolation and one-sided dependence ran up against hidden but easily-guessed at and sometimes even overt counteraction by Moscow. It is not only the lagging of general democratic transformations behind the dramatic course of emancipated interethnic relations that can explain the dimensions and impasse of the conflict between Armenia and Azerbaidzhan over Karabakh, the defeat of the Georgian central government in Abkhazia, and the phenomenon of Transdnistria. Quite revealing are evolutionary changes, full of forced pragmatism, in Kishinev's and Yerevan's attitude to the CIS as well as Baku's and Tbilisi's "radical" reorientation toward it after a not-quite-legitimate comeback to power of the Kremlin old guard in the persons of Aliyev and Shevardnadze.

By far the most intricate problem of the CIS is that it has become an arena for Russia's own self-determination, *i.e.*, of a state which traditionally doubts the boundaries of its possessions and even of its interests.[11] But this is a separate topic. Russia continues to confidently neutralize centrifugal tendencies in the CIS. The first years of independence did not reduce the new states' dependence on Russia, nor did they give any real alternatives to their geopolitical attitude. A well-known strategy of safeguarding Russian vital interests in the former USSR seems to have been pursued.[12] This also holds good, with minor reservations, for Ukraine, given its considerable material resources, policy of neutrality, and chances that the West will develop an interest in it. Ineffective socioeconomic policy and the nomenklatura-tinged patriotism of the ruling elite made the country so weak that it has to make all kinds of new and dangerous concessions in its bilateral relations with Moscow, bringing it closer to the Belarus status of a model "younger brother."

The CIS member-states note unanimously that the organization is far from effective. It does not seem to be performing its official functions, and in this respect, as three years of experience indicate, it is past repair. The sphere of its actions and jurisdiction is gradually expanding, but no system of balanced relations is being formed, and most problems are being addressed by bilateral agreements. Decisions "for all" accumulate but only those which suit Moscow are fulfilled. Moreover, the necessity to look over one's shoulder at Moscow complicates the development of bilateral ties outside CIS channels. These ties, as yet of narrow margin, are so far being developed by the Central Asian countries alone. As of today, the commonwealth primarily serves Russian interests, legitimizing Russia's strategy to unilaterally control virtually the entire former USSR. This can be seen only too clearly in the military field: Russian military bases being established, special functions to the Russian army and border security forces being delegated: weapons supply, personnel training, *etc.*[13] It is also essential that Russia, as a leader in economic reforms, is acquiring additional geopolitical advantages thus complicating, rather than encouraging, reforms in neighboring states. For the other states, if their aspiration for independence is any indication, the CIS personifies the lack of real alternatives in the transition period, the latter consisting in overcoming one's inner weakness, unbalanced quality, *i.e.*, the many handicaps inherited from Soviet totalitarianism. The CIS has no more real chance than the perestroika-period USSR to eliminate at least many of these problems. The economy, a sphere more prone to inertia than politics and incapable of instantaneous change, once stimulated not only reforms but the empire's dismantling; today it lags behind the new political conditions and, moreover, suffers from them. The CIS is cemented by the dependence of the "eleven" on Russia. It must be understood that what keeps them together is artificial and far from perfect.

The CIS has no chance of becoming a mechanism to harmonize the interests of member-states because, first of all, this is not in Russia's interest, and secondly, the interests of certain groups of new states are sometimes essentially different and have quite distinct, even opposite, vectors. From this postimperial entity one can observe the complexities of an evolutionary restructuring of local geopolitical landscapes without resorting to strong-arm tactics. The West is identifying its interests in the CIS area very cautiously and gradually; it is in no hurry to be an alternative to Russia. The latter is the only entity pursuing a strong and structure-creating policy in the region. Establishing a new, indirect mechanism of domination, Moscow will by no means be interested in the eventual dissolution of the "near abroad" in the system of world-wide cooperation caused by a gradual *rapprochement* of the postcommunist world with the West. Therefore, the CIS countries face the danger of preserving "special" relationships with Moscow in relative isolation from other regions except through Russian mediation. But this does not mean that the CIS has no future. Given the lack of real alternatives and limited viability of most new states, these states are very likely to dissolve and adjust to "Eurasian" realities rather than pursue their own national interests. The limited mobility of geopolitical entities in the CIS area is maintained by a rusty but not dismantled inner skeleton. A qualitative renewal of circumstances is possible only if Russian policies change their paradigm or if the new states speed up decisively their reforms and thus pass on to a new stage of geopolitical change which would lead to the final destruction of the vestiges of archaic structures.

The Contradictions of Geopolitical Self-Determination

§1. Eastern Europe, Ukraine, and Modern Civilizations

The states of the former socialist bloc and those which emerged from the ruins of the USSR, are seeking their geopolitical places in the world, as is Ukraine. All this, of course, threatens stability and increases the likelihood of regional conflicts.

Given this state of affairs in the contemporary world, let us examine the situation in the region of East Europe (and more broadly in the civilization of Eastern Christianity) and the overall geopolitical situation. First of all, it must be admitted that at the close of the twentieth century, less active on the world arena are individual nation states than groups of states which are allied largely, though not exclusively, on the principle of civilization. The most vivid example of this is the decades-old association of Protestant/Catholic Europe, which simultaneously preserves the system of transatlantic partnership.

More complex and contradictory is the integration processes in the Muslim world. But there can be no doubt as to a high level of what might be called "self-identification" among the socially active segments of the Muslim world. Among the forces representing the Muslim realm near Eastern Europe Turkey is most prominent. It is capable of playing both Pan-Islamic and Pan-Turkic cards in the Balkans, Transcaucasia, Central Asia, and with time quite probably in Crimea. Ukraine, as well as Bulgaria, Serbia,

Armenia, Georgia, Russia, and Belarus do not belong (to put it in terms of the civilization approach) to either the Occidental-Christian (North Atlantic) world or, the more so, to the Muslim or some other Asian civilization. At the same time, there exists, as an inadequately understood reality — a world of people on the territory of Eastern Europe, the Balkans, the Caucasus, the Trans-Ural Region up to the Pacific Ocean mutually related by age-old spiritual, historical, and economic ties. The structure of this civilization community is quite complex and, therefore, in seeking to identify it, we see two different approaches which we can provisionally call post-Byzantinism and Eurasianism.

The former lays in its emphasis upon common criteria of the post-Byzantine culture, while its weakness lies in its ignoring the no less significant presence of the old and profound interpenetration and interrelations of Slavdom (predominantly Russians) and Turkic Muslims (except for Mongol-speaking Buddhists — Kalmyks, Buryats, and Mongols). Eurasianism emphasizes the latter, but fails to pay due attention to the cultural and spiritual kinship of the Oriental Christian peoples.

In addition, it must be noted that some parts of Ukraine and Belarus west of the Dnipro — especially Galicia, Bukovina, and Transcarpathia — have roots closely connected to the civilization of the West. This, along with the dual position of Greece, gives the Oriental-Christian and Eurasian "space" an additional Western dimension.

The realization by Ukraine of its place in the above geopolitical domain emphasizes once more the importance of its maintaining stable and balanced relations with Russia. It is well known how organically interrelated the economic, social, cultural, and scientific systems of these countries have become. For each of them, it is difficult (more for Ukraine than for Russia) to find a similar alternative partner. At the same time, political instability and the likelihood of chauvinist great-power forces coming to power in Russia make it vital for Ukraine to pursue an extremely cautious foreign policy, whose cornerstone must be to preserve and strengthen its state sovereignty and to develop relations with all the influential forces on the world arena (Western Europe, the USA, Turkey, *etc.*). But this does not at all contradict the top priority of affirming Ukraine precisely in the Oriental-Christian and Eurasian regions, taking into account the geopolitical mistakes made in the first years of its independence.

Among those blunders, the following should be especially underscored. First, the naïve and futile hopes for broad support of Ukraine by the West and betting on integration into the European economic, political, and military systems. Second, the absurd from any standpoint (both economically and culturally) idea of the Baltic-Black Sea Alliance: the countries of the Vyshegrad group, as well as Croatia and Slovenia, on the one hand, and the Baltic states of the former USSR, on the other hand, are regarded by Protestant-Catholic Europe as belonging to it. Their policies are oriented – with cultural and historical basis – toward ultimate integration into the West (and, one might add, acting as its Eastern *cordon sanitaire*), a world to which Ukraine has practically no chance of admission. Third, Ukraine's whole approach to the Commonwealth of Independent States (CIS) turned out to be erroneous in that the latter was viewed as a temporary organization, necessary for the velvet smooth divorce of its eleven member states. All attempts to find alternatives to traditional links, especially economic (not to mention interpersonal) ones, proved to be unsuccessful. Moreover, the Ukrainian leadership's reliance upon bilateral relations among CIS member-states (motivated by fears of Russian domination in any international body) led in practice to Russia's ever increasing supremacy over each of its CIS partners in bilateral relations.

The above review of the geopolitical changes now taking place leads to the conclusion that at present and even more so in the coming century the normal development of Ukraine, as well as other countries, presupposes its seeking their new place in a certain civilization. For Ukraine, this is the so-called Eastern-Christian – "Eurasian Œcumena," and its identification with the latter must be such that this would not hinder an all-around development of mutually beneficial relations with nations of the West, the Muslim world and other civilizations.

§2. Ukraine in Twentieth Century Geopolitical Strategies

Ukrainian geopolitical thinking urgently requires analysis of the strategies which have been pursued in Europe and to which Ukraine in particular has involuntarily been an object. One may discern at least three such strategies, and today we are witnessing the formation of a fourth.

The beginning of this century witnessed the development of the first strategy, which reached its climax with the outbreak of World War I. The initiators of "imperial geopolitics" were empire-nations split into two hostile blocs: the *Entente Cordiale* and the Triple Alliance. The outcome of this strategy resulted in the ruin of the empire-nations and the imperial idea, as well as the emergence from these ruins of independent states including Ukraine (1917–1921), the latter falling prey to foreign intervention. While in Europe (as a result of the First World War) continental imperial systems disappeared, on the territory of the former Russian Empire the change was of a merely decorative nature. Ukraine once again, as earlier, fell victim to Russia's imperial strategy and geopolitics, this time in its Bolshevik variant.

The second stage of geopolitical strategy arose as a result of the world's division according to the criteria of universalistic ideologies and their corresponding political regimes. On the one hand, at first sight, these were Western-type democracies, including the USA, and, on the other hand, totalitarian systems of the fascist and communist types. In this division of geopolitical forces, Ukraine did not play an independent role because it lacked, in reality, the basic attributes of state sovereignty. Moreover, it was held hostage to Stalinist Soviet geopolitics.

The consequences of the geopolitical strategy of the second period proved to be tragic for civilization as a whole. For the culmination of World War II manifested an even greater gap between the political thinking and scientific-technological progress that begot the gloomy prospect of mankind's self-destruction. Genocide and ethnocide became hallmarks of this period of world geopolitics. As a result of World War II, only one, the more externally aggressive part of the totalitarian order – Nazism – was vanquished. However, the Soviet Union survived and consolidated its international position as the mainstay of the totalitarian system and aggressive geopolitics, causing the division of the world into antagonistic groupings and blocs. It was precisely this situation which determined the nature of world geopolitics in the third stage, marked by the atmosphere of the Cold War and the onset of the so-called bipolar global system, the stability of which was based on Mutual Assured Destruction thanks to stockpiled weapons of mass destruction. Created for waging wars, these weapons were transformed into the principal factor of geopolitical strategies of the third type.

Now we live though the fourth stage of geopolitical processes which signifies the emergence of a new geopolitical strategy not only in Europe, but for the world as a whole. This stage could be conventionally defined as a transient one – from the bipolar and bloc system to an integrated one, free from blocs. It is at this stage that Ukraine made its appearance as an independent state capable of playing an independent role in the geopolitical realities of the late twentieth century. But, thus far it is very difficult to precisely define Ukraine's geopolitical strategy. This is due to various external factors, its great dependence on its CIS partners, as well as internal political processes, which hinder the efficiency of economic reforms, thereby holding Ukraine back from the European economic and, ultimately, geopolitical system. Therefore, having become an active player in world politics, Ukraine now finds itself facing the challenge of opting between two geopolitical strategies, *i.e.*, a strategy of choosing priorities and one of balancing interests.

A choice of priorities strategy requires a high degree of independence by a country already in a position to unilaterally choose its strategic partners on a basis of mutual benefit and to directly participate in structuring the geopolitical arena. The second strategy, that of interests balancing, is, perhaps, the only one possible for Ukraine at present, because of both external and internal factors.

Unfortunately, the interaction of these factors makes Ukraine's overall geopolitical course dependent on the international set-up and momentary (quite illusory) advantages – which, in turn, testifies to the fact that Ukraine is only approaching the status of an independent actor in geopolitics, remaining largely an object of the play of external geopolitical forces.

The lessons of the outgoing century conclusively demonstrate that only if Ukraine becomes a full-fledged actor with its own geopolitical strategy will it have a future as a state and its people form into a full-fledged political nation.

§3. Europe or Eurasia

The independence Ukraine gained in the early 1990s remains illusory without its return to the common European civilization. No matter how great the achievements of Ukraine's first years of independence may seem (state symbols, the army, diplomatic recognition), the loss of sovereignty and a probable disappearance of the Ukrainian nation itself will be inevitable unless its socioeconomic and political systems are remade and geopolitical orientation is changed.

The pressing need for an immediate geopolitical discourse is caused not so much by long-term factors as by the circumstances of a very loose and unstable *modus vivendi* resulting from large-scale upheavals and collisions in the economic system and the macroeconomics of a great many countries and peoples inhabiting the expanses from the Oder to Sakhalin, from the Adriatic and Black Sea to the Arctic. It is becomes increasingly obvious that in spite of all the fireworks of independence following the tearing down of the Berlin Wall, this and other walls would have stood for ages, had Russia resorted to her only convincing argument – the use of brute military force.

An entirely unique and historically unprecedented situation has arisen in East Central Europe as a whole and on the territory of the former USSR in particular. It is that Russia is more interested in the economic independence of the non-Russian nations than the latter themselves. Neither the nationalists nor the advocates of the USSR in Ukraine seem to understand thus far that restoration of the Union with its previous level of economic well-being is next to impossible, despite the most touching eulogies of some and the most wrathful anathemas of others, for such a Union lacks the "fuel" on which this earthly paradise ran for the last two decades.

The reason for Russia's rather favorable attitude to the independence of Ukraine and the other European countries is the lack of food raw materials and shortages of foodstuffs in these countries. To change this situation would be economically ineffective and not justify the expense. However, given the drastic fall of hard-currency earnings and a considerable deterioration of living standards in Russia, her aggression against the "near abroad" and probably the Eastern European countries as part of an attempt to seek means of life-support becomes inevitable (a historical parallel may be drawn from the events of 1918 to 1920).

It is clear that the best way to keep Ukraine from danger would be NATO membership and all the collective-security guarantees associated with it. But this option is currently not possible, and this must be left as a future goal. In the conditions of brief and shaky inter-pact equilibrium it seems more realistic to try creating a joint alliance in Eastern Europe would not only meet common needs of defense and urgent economic restructuring as a step towards all-European integration, but would also eliminate the danger of Russia and Turkey blocking the Ukrainian Black-Sea communications. It would also reflect the historically established East European set-up which had existed before the disintegration of the Polish-Lithuanian (-Ukrainian) state as a more or less homogeneous ethnic entity based on the common or very close cultural, economic, legal, religious, and linguistic foundations. However, this would not yet have solved the problems of harmonious relations and *rapprochement* between the continent's Eastern and Western parts. What is key here is the position and interests of the West.

The analysis performed reveals two fundamental approaches worked out by Western geopolitical science in respect to Eastern Europe. The first, represented by English and French thought, proceeds from the need to transform this region into a *cordon sanitaire,* which is to separate the living space of the two antinomic civilizations in the East and West. According to this vision, the East European area is to act as a buffer to soften the East's pressure and to neutralize its expansionism. This kind of "splendid isolation" of the two worlds obviously dooms the East European nations to rapid exhaustion in an unequal opposition to the East.

Other approaches to the future of Eastern Europe were proposed in Germany; these may be roughly classified as East and West oriented. This multi-directional quality reflects the cultural and historical dualism of Germany, whose history has always been characterized by a constant dialog of the two – Eastern and Western – parts, depending on various socio-political, cultural and religious factors. This "West-East" juxtaposition is often one more of culture and civilization than of geopolitics. When the Eastward, Prussian orientation (so-called "Borussimus") prevailed, the world witnessed not only the consonance and rapprochement of Germany with another exponent of the Eastern tradition, *i.e.,* Russia, but also their complete concordance in joint actions against the rest of the European world, as happened during the nineteenth century and the first years of World War II. In the early 1920s the idea of *Ostorientierung* and alliance with communist Russia was advocated by the extreme right-wing (*e.g.,* Möller, von den Brock) and radical left-wing (national Bolshevik) forces; the overwhelming majority of Nazis, Goebbels in particular, greatly sympathized with Bolshevik Russia at that time. These plans, under the influence of the school of K.Haushoffer, did not envisage any role for Ukraine. It is an open secret that today's Russia does not lack certain politicians longing for restoration of a "Prussian" Germany which could assist in another partition of Eastern Europe and achieve joint hegemony over the continent. However, there is no influential political force in today's Germany which hopes for an anti-European alliance with Russia.

Compared to the Eastward pro-Russian course, orientation to West European values has been a more weighty trend in the German socio-political thought. It is in the stream of this democratic, essentially, liberal-conservative movement that Naumann's "Middle Europe" project ought to be placed. It is also most probable that strategic *rapprochement* between Ukraine and Germany is possible in this liberal-conservative system of coordinates. Therefore, friendly relations between these countries depend on Ukraine's return to the conservative values historically inherent in her, to its individualism, to private property, and to the principle of *laissez-faire*. After the likely failure of another attempt to westernize and modernize Russia (as calculated by A. Yanov, the fourteenth attempt), it will be difficult to find forces capable of providing peace in the East European frontier area and guaranteeing security in Europe other than by a strong East European alliance along the German-Ukrainian (German-Polish-Ukrainian) axis.

It is important to remember, however, that Ukraine's reintegration into the European community is only possible provided Ukraine's European cultural and historical identity is recognized and a positive answer is given to the first component of the "friend or foe" dichotomy. In this connection great importance attaches to the problem of Ukrainian society's typological proximity to its European counterpart, since the mere fact of Ukraine's geopolitical location does not automatically by itself make her a member of the European family. Even though resemblance between the post-Soviet Ukrainian and European socioeconomic systems is close to nil, the analysis of the Ukrainian national sociogenesis gives every ground to speak about the identity or, at least, parallel development of the socio-creative process in Ukraine and Eastern Europe throughout Ukraine's history up to the 1930s. According to the conclusions of European observers who studied Ukraine's social system in the nineteenth and early twentieth centuries, the European identity of the Ukrainian nation may be attributed to the existing institution of private property and adequate European legal standards, ethno-socio-psychological archetypes of individualism, conservatism, democracy, as well as similarities in types of political cultures and political awareness.

Thus, Ukraine's reintegration into the European community is feasible from this standpoint by reviving its traditional sociopolitical and economic structures and institutions, reactivating its historical societal heritage, evoking historical memory and, thus, rebuilding and healing its broken socio-cultural continuum. To slow progress along this path would mean the deformation of the historic factor in the existence of the Ukrainian community and cause the death of the Ukrainian nation both as a European nation and as a nation as such.

It is these consequences that will affect the course toward Ukraine's integration into the CIS and projects to create a Eurasian Union. It may be recalled that the Eurasian idea put forward back in the early 1920s was developed by Russian nationalist *émigrés* with financial assistance from GPU-NKVD as an alternative to anticommunism by explaining the Russian Revolution within the context of Russia's Turkish-Slavic geopolitical identity, its legitimacy being sanctified by the political and cultural inheritance of the Golden Horde, the Grand Principality of Moscow, the Russian Empire, and the USSR.

§4. Ukraine and the CIS

To assess the prospects of Ukraine's integration into the world community as a whole and into the European geopolitical system in particular, it is essential to determine to what extent Ukraine's participation in processes now underway in the geopolitics of the continent correspond to its national interests and ensure its independence and security.

With this in view, let us consider the Eastern vector of

Ukraine's integration drift — the Commonwealth of Independent States. We shall attempt to outline the geopolitical consequences for Ukraine, its security and survival as a sovereign state, which may arise from its further integration into the common Eurasian space into which, as its patrons claim, the CIS is going to be transformed.

Overcoming the current socioeconomic crisis is at the top of the national agenda. When we consider that most factors causing the crisis are in one way or another linked with fallout from the USSR's collapse (severance of old economic ties, breakdown of the ruble zone, lack of access to traditional sources of raw materials and markets, territorial issues, ethnic border problems, *etc.*), it becomes easy to understand the fact that proposals of establishing "a renewed Union" on the territory of the CIS, of restoring the USSR, and even of "reunification" with Russia not only find support but are seen by some as Ukraine's only way out of the crisis. Similar attitudes can be found in other CIS countries as well, and are often made use of by various leaders who hope to speed the CIS's evolution into a new, integrated association with conspicuous supra-state institutions, with managerial, decree-issuing, and even coercive functions.

Ukraine is obviously interested in both the re-establishment of severed economic ties and the establishment of new ones with CIS countries and, above all, with Russia. But the main problem is this: what kind of ties with what inner economic content should there be? The compatibility of nations' market economic structures is a solid foundation for democratic integration processes. Moreover, such ties need not necessarily be guided by supra-state regulative bodies and political directives. As is witnessed by the West European experience, the latter spring up only after a certain level of economic integration is achieved, based on highly developed democratic national market economy structures of approximately the same level and type.

In the case of the CIS, an artificial pumping-up of market economy structures that have not completely formed will result in a restoration of the "single economic complex" of the former USSR with all its inherent weaknesses: inefficiency, technological backwardness, economic dependence on the state, excessive centralization, *etc.* All these scorn the logic of market transformation and will undoubtedly retard reforms, "preserve" economic backwardness and institutionalize its isolation of the newly independent states from the world economy.

The acceleration of such a process would certainly bring economic and political losses to all the participants, whatever their level of economic potential. An example of this is the attempt to unify the monetary system of various CIS countries. It is this example which demonstrates the priority of geopolitical and military strategic factors in the integration process now underway in the CIS, along with certain fundamental obstacles to coordinating each others interests and of Russia's policy of asserting her traditional dominance. This argument is also valid for the Economic Union within the CIS. Some clauses of the Economic Union agreement prohibiting member-states from participating in other economic and trade unions are of a political rather than economic nature. The primacy of political motives is also evident in other clauses of the Union draft agreement. Given this, Ukraine's status as an associate member is its best option. Under the circumstances, orientation toward the East only retards overcoming the legacy of its separation from an integrated Europe by a sort of economic Curzon line which would only retard the reform of Ukraine's socioeconomic structures and prevent its joining the family of civilized nations.

§5. In Search of a Strategy

Today Ukraine is first and foremost a passive object of policies pursued by the other global players for two main reasons. First, well-defined global priorities of economic and political character are absent due to ill-defined strategic directions of social and economic transformation at the national level. Second, Ukraine currently lacks an adequate economic base and institutional infrastructure which could allow it to pursue its interests on the international arena.

This uncertain situation is extremely dangerous because Ukraine's spontaneous or forced integration into the world economy would preclude its effective attainment of its national interests, have negative fallout at the national level, endanger its distinctive nature, and perhaps even its independence. For this reason, Ukraine must clearly realize to what extent it needs to integrate into or approach various economic and political groupings. Today one should speak about "managed" integration and rapprochement. Waiting passively for results of integration processes is dangerous to Ukraine, for it could lose its existing opportunities for economic stabilization and transition to a new model of economic development.

After the Cold War it has become fashionable to speak about the end of the bipolar confrontation in Europe. Such optimism is premature. The evolution of a post-Cold War Europe is, and will for some time continue to be, very much influenced by the ghosts of the past decades.

It will be some time before the dream of all-European political, economic, and security structures becomes reality. In fact, given contemporary trends in Western Europe and the former Soviet Union, there is a very real potential for the reemergence of a bipolar system in Europe roughly along the lines of the old Cold-War standoff. This confrontation, unlike its predecessor, would not necessarily be an armed one, but its socioeconomic consequences could still be no less real.

Where does — and where might — Ukraine possibly fit into this scheme of things? Currently, Ukraine is very much perceived, both abroad and by many Ukrainians (gripped, it seems, by an almost paralyzing Slavic fatalism), to be a natural candidate for eventual full membership in the anemic CIS.

However, Ukraine should unequivocally persevere along the path leading to eventual integration with the West. By so doing, Ukraine would both offer its people the best long-term guarantees of their own well-being and also go a long way toward preventing a possible redivision of Europe, thus removing the principal obstacle toward the eventual development of truly all-European structures.

The aim of Ukraine's foreign policy should be to seek the creation of an external environment in which domestic socioeconomic institutions can flourish. The domestic roots of foreign policy seem obvious, but are all too often overlooked. Ukraine's progress toward "the West" should therefore be analyzed from the perspective of both its domestic and foreign policy components.

As for the latter, Ukraine's steps toward the West in 1994 have been encouraging. Progress has been made with both the European Union and NATO, despite an apparently grudging – but gradually increasing – Western acceptance of Ukraine's immense geopolitical significance. Ukraine now has its foot in a door that not long ago appeared locked tight. Every effort should be made to push open the door wider still. Thus, in foreign policy, there appears to be movement toward an eventual goal of integration into the West though the tactical expedient of close short-term cooperation with the CIS as a mechanism for a civilized divorce.

However, the organic link between contemporary Ukrainian foreign policy and its domestic base is tenuous in critical parts of the country. Very broadly speaking, Ukraine's pro-Western orientation appears to be largely an initiative of an executive branch that finds its natural constituency in Western Ukraine and Kyiv and among strata of the population. However, should the ascendant trends in the current domestic debate over the future development of Ukrainian statehood congeal into a coherent policy, it would become extremely difficult – perhaps even impossible– to maintain the present pro-Western momentum. The tactical expediency would then necessarily become a goal in itself.

It is difficult to be optimistic about Ukraine's long term future under such circumstances, regardless of whatever immediate economic benefits it might bring. Full and voluntary integration into a CIS dominated by a brooding, unstable, and assertive Russia would in no sense foster any form of meaningful sovereign Ukrainian statehood, notwithstanding arguments for cheap oil.

The arguments for a sovereign Ukraine whose domestic

and foreign policies have a clearly recognizable pro-Western orientation cannot easily be dismissed:

First, Ukraine's determination to chart a Westward foreign policy course would be a critical factor in dissolving the residual Cold War mentality and frames of reference.

Second, just as Lenin and Gorbachev realized that there could be no Soviet Union without Ukraine, a CIS minus Ukraine cannot evolve into a threatening, proto-imperial structure.

Third, a sustained pro-Western Ukrainian initiative would in and of itself force Russia to examine its own domestic and foreign policies. Thus, Ukraine would make a significant contribution to Russia's search for a (hopefully benign) post-imperial and post-Soviet identity.

Fourth, a domestic policy of steady and consistent market reforms would eventually and inevitably strengthen the links between Ukraine and the West, thereby easing the task of Ukrainian diplomacy in negotiating formal integration.

Fifth, and most important, history suggests that the Western model of socioeconomic development offers the best vehicle to fulfill the well-being and potential of the Ukrainian population. Neither the dynamism nor the relative success of this model can be reasonably disputed on objective grounds. Moreover, given its universality (should we even speak of a Western model which applies also to Japan? The term is actually more useful as an analytical concept than as a description of current geographical realities), there is no reason to assume that Ukraine cannot also eventually adopt and successfully adapt the Western model to its own particular needs. The major obstacles are a lack of political leadership, vision, and the unwillingness of many politicians to pay the political price that a fundamental, well-balanced program of economic reform would inevitably require. Ukraine's current politics – and not some kind of cultural, social, or historical determinism – are responsible for Ukraine's current plight.

There is little doubt that Ukraine will remain an independent state. The debate is now over the content and meaning of that independence — in other words about the well being of the Ukrainian and, by extension, European people. The foreign policy choices Ukraine makes today will inevitably affect and be affected by the course of this debate well into the next century.

§6. *The Problem of 'Returning' to Europe*

In order not to remain in semi-isolation, Ukraine must return to Europe; it must accomplish a *rapprochement* with the West. However, *rapprochement* must be recognized for what it is and it is not. It is the elimination of tensions and the fostering of goodwill between two parties. Ukraine's rapprochement with the West should not be confused with a process of integration into the latter. *Rapprochement* can still leave a country standing alone. Thus, the new challenge before Ukraine is to transform *rapprochement* with the West into real and accelerated integration into that community of nations and its leading European institutions, the North Atlantic Treaty Organization and the European Union.

This is a particularly difficult challenge in light of several geopolitical factors or dynamics that could loosen Ukraine's foothold in the European community. These dynamics make it all the more necessary for Ukraine to adopt a foreign policy that moves beyond neutrality and whose economic, political, and security components unambiguously foster Ukraine's integration into the West. An ambiguous geopolitical orientation will, at best, perpetuate Ukraine's position as a state standing alone between Europe and Eurasia. At worst, it risks allowing the emergence of a new division in Europe which could isolate Ukraine from the broad European community of nations.

The first dynamic pulling of Ukraine away from a larger Europe has been Russia's effort to establish its hegemony over the space of the former Soviet Union and East Central Europe. Russia's strategy to this end has been to strengthen and institutionalize the CIS, particularly its economic and security components. Moscow's policy toward Kyiv is an important element in this strategy and reflects prevailing Russian attitudes toward Ukrainian independence.

Prevailing attitudes in Russia will not rapidly shift away from the assumption that Ukrainian independence is a "temporary historical aberration." Ukraine was, and remains, far too important to Russia historically and strategically to assume otherwise. Moreover, Ukraine's integration into the Western community of nations would be a significant setback for a post-Soviet Russian foreign policy, whose principal objective is to reestablish a Eurasian zone under its domination. It is safe, therefore, to presume that for the foreseeable future Russia's intentions toward Ukraine will remain, at best, contradictory, at worst, bent on hegemony.

The second dynamic shaping Eastern Europe's geopolitical landscape has been the regionalization of its economies into four clusters. The first cluster is the Visegrad Group, consisting of Poland, the Czech Republic, Hungary and Slovakia. Except for Slovakia, these nations have demonstrated commitment to aggressive market reform, including fiscal and monetary responsibility and aggressive privatization.

The second economic cluster consists of the Baltic States: Estonia, Latvia, and Lithuania. Their policies are also characterized by rapid privatization, responsible monetary and fiscal policies, and an undisputed desire to enter the Western community of nations.

The third group consists of the Balkan states: Romania, Bulgaria, Albania, and the states of the former Yugoslavia. Stagnating economies and civil war have plagued this Eastern European cluster. Although, Bulgaria and Romania are associate members of the European Union, the pace of their integration into the Union lags far behind that of the Visegrad Group. Slovenia described as the emerging "Singapore" of Europe, stands out prominently above the chaos of the Balkan war.

The fourth group consists those of European states that are part of the CIS: Russia, Belarus and Moldova. They are characterized by a lack of market reform, as well as fiscal and monetary irresponsibility.

Despite growing recognition in the West, and the United States in particular, that its policy toward Eastern Europe has been excessively "Russocentric," and that a "Russia policy" is an inadequate substitute for a "Europe policy," it has still failed to produce a vision of post-Cold War European security which could serve to guide its relations with East Central Europe, including Ukraine.

In order to overcome the economic and geopolitical dynamics that are pulling Ukraine away from a larger Europe, Kyiv must more clearly assert its intention to fully integrate into that community. The basis of such a strategy must be economic and political reforms which transform Ukraine from a nation which the West regards as a potential dependent into one whose political and economic vibrancy will be recognized and desired as a strategic asset.

With regard to foreign policy, Kyiv must abandon the assumption that a clear geopolitical orientation toward Western Europe requires Ukraine to abandon or isolate Russia. Integration into Western security, political, and economic structures would significantly assist the development of Ukraine's economy, which is the most effective means of neutralizing the imperfections of Russian-Ukrainian economic relations.

§7. The Parameters of Foreign Relations Harmony

As for Ukraine, given its large territory and great potential, it has a real chance and urgent need to decide, independently of considerations of momentary political advantage, its natural place and role in the system of international relations, as well as to better define, individualize, and stabilize its parameters as an independent member of the European and world community. Obviously, the following should principles should govern such a self-identification: self-sufficiency, the unequivocal priority of its own national interests, independence from other states or groups of states, high norms of civilized behavior, and a responsible policy as well as vigor in the development of partnership on the basis of real equality and mutual benefits.

The Contradictions of Geopolitical Self-Determination

One might well apply Friedrich Gorenstein's famous description of Russia to Ukraine: "Its culture...is related to Europe, while its civilization — to Asia." Moreover, it is in Ukraine that the features of a peculiar "Asianism" were made more prominent by the Bolshevik rule over the past seventy years. To get rid of them and to join Europe seems to be an objective impulse of our society today. However, because of the actual absence of a Europe-or-Russia alternative, the problem of choosing priorities proves to be quite complicated.

The Ukrainian state that has arisen as a result of external events (both in their origin and nature), will need — now and in future — much from the outside, which can be found partly in the West and partly in Russia. Both Russia and the West are Ukraine's partners; they complement each other rather than substitute for one another. The current orientation toward Russia serves as an imperative, linked with top priority economic tasks, as well as with achieving the needs to preserve the whole domain of human ties. At the same time, the orientation toward the West reflects its need for political guarantees of its independence, of finding additional opportunities for economic modernization, and designing promising models of social development on the whole.

Such a policy, involving both the Western and Russian orientations, seems to be not only logically appropriate — taking into account the merits and drawbacks of such a policy, as well as the low probability of other alternatives being achieved — it also corresponds most appropriately to the tasks of the domestic integration and stabilization of Ukrainian society. A practical resolution to the problem of choice (either Russia or the West) would result in counterpoising one's own interests to those of others, and in artificially limiting the possibilities of international cooperation and interaction. Because of essential differences in social and historical experience, as well as the mentality of various regions of Ukraine, the policy of one-sided orientation cannot be truly national and, hence, efficient.

A question arises — is it, in principle, possible and adequate to formulate and pursue a strategy devoid of a clear geopolitical orientation in the unstructured domain of Central and Eastern Europe, which is far from harmonious in its international relations? Obviously, given the attitude of the two above-mentioned sides to Ukraine – the wait-and-see attitude of the West and the political/economic pressure that accompanies Russia's claims to domination – the following may be a good guideline to consider in the near term: a predominantly political and (insofar as possible) economic cooperation with the West; a predominantly economic and (insofar as possible) political relationship with Moscow. It should be added that the South also has to gradually take its natural place in Ukraine's foreign relations.

The essence of such a policy lies in the renunciation in principle of all confrontation, of all attempts to use anti-Russian feelings, and to juxtapose Russia with the West in the dynamic participation in Pan-European cooperation. By so doing, Ukraine can play an exceptional role in preventing the restoration of geopolitical bipolarity on the continent, by achieving its various long-term interests.

Giving up an unequivocal choice in matters of geopolitical orientation should not be considered as a sign of isolationism, individualism, or amorphousness in Ukrainian foreign policy. On the contrary, this policy has to be based on distinct normative reference points, principles, and priorities. And from this it follows that it has to advance Ukraine's image as an attractive, dynamic, constructive, and reliable partner. But, in so doing, it is important for Ukraine to not lapse into "messianism" and to not burden itself with the function of being a "bridge" or mediator in some utopian and futile attempt to artificially push West and East toward unification.

Geoeconomic Problems Facing the Postcommunist States

§1. Postcommunist Economic Disintegration

One of the most important factors of the communist system was its rigid double centralization – both within each specific country and internationally. This was expressed, above all, in the so-called unified national economic complex of the USSR, the system of mutual linkages within the Council for Mutual Economic Assistance (COMECON) as well as in the former quasi-federal states of Czechoslovakia and Yugoslavia. The only alternative to membership in these rigidly hierarchic centralized structures was in the virtually complete economic self-sufficiency, almost autarky, practiced by such communist states as Albania, China, and North Korea.

The collapse of the communist system could not but affect its geoeconomic dimensions. The disintegration of the communist geoeconomic structure proved to be a highly contradictory process. This process, albeit natural, evolved against the background of growing international integration and therefore seemed unnatural. It should be noted that most of the postcommunist states had highly specialized industries and sectors which cannot function normally without foreign economic ties. The economies of nearly all such countries (except perhaps those which had already adopted the strategy of autarky) depended to rather a high degree on external buyers and suppliers – primarily, within the USSR economic complex and COMECON.

Thus, the collapse of the previously existing structures of international cooperation has produced complex problems of geoeconomic self-determination in virtually all postcommunist states. What foreign economic strategy should be adopted? What attitude should be taken concerning the ongoing processes of international integration? Who can serve as short-term and long-term economic partners? These and related questions became an integral part of innumerable dilemmas which arose during the postcommunist economic transformations.[14] Inability to solve these problems and the tendency to put them off until the instability inherent in transitional economies is overcome may be a fatal mistake for any postcommunist state.

Of course, in contrast to the centrifugal processes which required from politicians not only thorough analysis and well thought-out decisions but also political courage and will, the procedures of geoeconomic self-determination require scientifically based strategy and tactics in the area of international economics. It is the latter that "first wave" postcommunist politicians lacked, which caused the process of the system's break-up to turn into a unique psychological complex of separation anxiety and postcommunist xenophobia first of all the economic sphere. Guided by the emotions and slogans of "anti-imperialism" and "anti-totalitarianism" in foreign economic policy, they failed to make any real progress in making their countries part of the international system of the division of labor on a new basis.

What are the likely alternatives for a realistic foreign economic strategy?

§2. Possible Models for Geoeconomic Self-Determination

The model of geoeconomic behavior for any country is derived from a rather complex aggregate of factors. The latter comprise, among others, comparative economic advantage, the mobility of economic, scientific, and technological development, long-term domestic and foreign policy considerations, the lessons of history, along with its contemporary social values, cultural and religious peculiarities, and psychological make-up. Starting from this, one can discern the main models of geoeconomic development for a given post-communist country.

Model 1. Preservation of the status quo. For the Newly Independent States (NIS) of the former Soviet Union, this means a priority orientation towards developing mutual economic relations within the CIS. For former COMECON client states, this pattern would mean a search for new alternatives which would allow the maintenance of the old ties to retain their top priority nature.

Model 1 is advantageous in that it represents for many countries the simplest and easiest solution to these economic problems they have had to face since the disintegration of COMECON and then the USSR. The economic risks are lowest in this case (although political risks are enhanced in connection with the economic dependence of outwardly sovereign states). For the realization of this pattern there are still certain convenient structures and skills of mutual cooperation preserved by the postcommunist nomenklatura from the past. Thus, in the short or even medium term, this choice may be the cheapest (in both the literal economic and figurative socioeconomic sense) geoeconomic strategic model.

For the NIS, this option has in fact materialized as a process of integration within the CIS Economic Union. The Long-Term Plan for Developing CIS Integration adopted in Moscow in late October 1994 envisages the step-by-step formation of a single economic space for member states. The establishment of the Interstate Economic Committee (IEC) and the Economic Union along with the signing of a Payments Union Agreement became the first practical steps. Another item on the agenda is the creation of a free trade area which, thanks to a coordinated and (future) unified foreign customs policy of the Economic Union member states, is bound to turn into a customs union. The integrating measures envisage a rather intensive process of liberalizing the flow of commodities, services, capital, and manpower (*i.e.*, a speeded-up transition from a customs union to a common market). They also include a wide range of issues to be discussed in order to coordinate the economic policies of the member states. According to schedule, this would allow practical solution of the problem of monetary union by 1998, which in turn would indicate (if one goes by the universally accepted criteria of stages in international economic integration) to the formation of a real economic union.

The decisions adopted are thus aimed at renewing the old economic complex of the NIS in a new form. It is a foregone conclusion that Russia would play the leading role here. The economies of the other participants would be bound to the Russian economy. It should be borne in mind that integration will proceed not only from above but also from below, *i.e.*, through establishing so-called international financial and industrial groups, in other words, post-Soviet multinational corporations. There is little doubt as to who would control the overwhelming majority of such multinationals. Russian finance capital has every opportunity to prevail in a new single economic space of the NIS (except the Baltic states), taking advantage of not only its higher economic potential but also of the fact that reforms in Russia have made more headway than in other Economic Union member-states.

One must admit that the short- and medium-term advantages of Model 1 may be offset in the long term by inadequate economic efficiency due to the priority of cooperation with countries also having insufficiently high parameters of economic development. This main drawback of Model 1 impels a search for variations on it which would allow simultaneously coordination of the general policy of economic integration within the CIS economic union and consistent diversification of foreign economic ties. This strategy of development is aimed at trade creation within the CIS coupled with a simultaneous intention to avoid trade diversion which usually accompanies processes of integration. There are reasons to think this strategy is to some extent being implemented by, say, the countries of Central Asia.

As to the former COMECON client states – the countries of the former socialist camp – Model 1 was never taken as a basis for any large-scale joint efforts during the disintegration of that organization. True, one may recall at-

Table 1

Geographic Structure of Exports and Imports of Various European Transitional States[16] (in percent)*

Country	COMECON		USSR/CIS		Countries with Developed Market Economies	
	1989	1992	1989	1992	1989	1992
Bulgaria						
exports	12.9	6.3	49.3	25.2	19.6	37.0
imports	12.0	6.0	34.0	28.6	35.4	44.9
Poland						
exports	16.4	5.8	24.4	11.0	43.2	73.7
imports	16.6	4.9	21.4	14.1	46.5	68.9
Rumania						
exports	10.2	5.0	14.5	13.5	47.7	47.6
imports	14.9	7.1	22.5	13.7	17.2	56.0
Hungary						
exports	15.9	6.0	25.1	13.2	43.1	70.0
imports	17.1	6.6	22.1	16.8	49.3	67.7
Czecho-slovakia						
exports	20.1	9.7	26.5	10.9	37.6	63.7
imports	21.9	5.5	25.9	24.6	37.6	62.6

* The 1992 data cover First to Third quarters.

tempts to locally apply this pattern to payments relationship of the former COMECON countries. This was primarily evident in plans to create a multilateral payments system in order to overcome the complications caused by the sudden transition to hard-currency payments. Strangely, however, there are only a few specialists[15] who worry about the probable detrimental economic downside to the abrupt reduction of economic ties between the ex-COMECON states and hence its generally negative impact on the overall course of economic transformation. These countries, especially those carrying out more successful macroeconomic stabilization and systemic changes (Poland, Hungary, and the Czech Republic), show a much calmer attitude to these difficulties. The latter led to, among other things, a virtual official refusal to consider any, even limited, initiatives within the framework of the above pattern.

Model 2. Complete Geoeconomic Reorientation. Its advantages lie in the ability to effect a dramatic structural maneuver while implementing economic reforms, the incorporation of modern technologies into the economy, orientation toward more challenging markets, thus accelerating and enhancing competitiveness. However, this option requires considerable expense and much time. It also requires certain pre-conditions: a process of intensive capital accumulation based on both internal savings and large-scale foreign investment, achievement of rather firm macroeconomic stability so that the economy can withstand the stresses associated with basic restructuring, and a high degree of market openness in the countries toward which exports are redirected.

This pattern has been adopted by the former COMECON client states. For example, a number of East European countries, the USSR/CIS and the developed market-economy countries experienced rather drastic changes in export and import in 1989-1992:

The above data indicate an essential reorientation of foreign economic ties toward the developed market economies by practically all the states of East Central Europe. In this case, the more successful the transition to a market economy, the more these states turn to markets in the developed countries.

Among the NIS it is the Baltic states are also attempting a radical reorientation. However, while this process has made headway in the former COMECON client-states or even been completed (Poland, Hungary, and the Czech Republic), among the NIS it has materialized only in Estonia, which in 1993 channeled 53.7% of its export production to the developed West which in turn accounted for 67.9% of its total imports. These indicators were significantly lower for the CIS countries: 29.0% and 21.8%. In Latvia this process is evolving, which has produced a unique economic bipolarity: in 1993 the CIS countries accounted for 45.8% of Latvian exports and 37.8 % of imports, while the developed market-economy countries accounted for only 34.2% and 29.6% respectively. In Lithuania, where the process of reorientation is in its infancy, the CIS countries dominate in both exports (62.8%) and imports (84.1%) (calculated on the basis of: Economic Survey of Europe in 1993-94, New York and Geneva, 1994).[17]

It is very difficult to identify true adherents to this pattern in the CIS. On the one hand, Azerbaidzhan, Moldova, Turkmenistan, Uzbekistan, and Ukraine intend to diversify the geographic structure of their foreign economic ties. On the other hand, this kind of diversification requires substantial expenses and time. For this reason, the geoeconomic strategy of these states displays a basic contradiction between long-term interests and inevitable routine activity. And nobody seems to know how to reconcile short- and long-term interests. Under such conditions, priority is given to short-term measures, ruling out any decisive geoeconomic reorientation.

Model 3. A Geopolitically Neutral System. This pattern is based on the necessity of a uniform development of foreign economic ties "in all directions." Its advantages consist in its laying the broadest possible economic foundation of a state's political independence as well as its ability to make foreign economic ties more stable vis-à-vis political expediency, that is, to maneuver among various countries in foreign economic policy and thus maximize economic returns.

The disadvantages of this strategy stem from its high risk of degeneration into a policy of isolationism and economic autarky, for in theory geoeconomic neutrality can be achieved in two different ways. The first way is a partial reorientation of foreign economic ties whereby the latter are not oriented towards any new priority but instead undergo a more judicious structuralization in terms of geoeconomics. The second one is an accelerated reduction of foreign economic ties with countries which enjoyed top priority in the communist era. The first way is obviously more complex. Therefore, the second way becomes irreversible, given the lack of sufficient prerequisites for reorientation of an ill-considered foreign economic policy. We already witness the consequences of this strategy in the case of, say, Azerbaidzhan, Armenia, Georgia, Moldova, and here in Ukraine as well.

§3. Patterns of Participation in Processes of International Economic Integration

The experience of postcommunist development has fully demonstrated how unrealistic is a policy of "economic independence" pursued at the expense of economic efficiency. As a result, all postcommunist states now face the problem of how best to join the processes of international economic integration. Several likely options for solving this problem have been drawn up in theory and in practice, for under present circumstances one can expect to enter the world economy only through active participation in some regional (integration-oriented) grouping. This has in turn called forth a wide variety of integration-oriented territorial economic organizations or, at least, the intent to create such organizations.

For example, Lithuania, Latvia, and Estonia agreed in 1990 to the gradual creation of a Baltic market. In 1991 these same countries established a Baltic customs union with the aim of achieving comprehensive economic integration.

At the same time companies and other entities of Bulgaria, Poland, Hungary, the USSR, and Czechoslovakia set up the international East European Cooperation and Trade Organization in order to renew the severed economic ties among the former COMECON client states on a market basis. The cooperation project envisaged the creation of an East European Stock Exchange, International Banking Clearinghouse, and commodities exchange. Another non-governmental organization of this kind, "For a Regional Market of East European and Asian States," was also created almost simultaneously.

In 1992 Azerbaidzhan, Kyrgyzstan, Tadzhikistan, Turkmenistan, and Uzbekistan (Kazakhstan opted for observer status) joined the Organization of Economic Cooperation

(OEC), with Iran, Pakistan, and Turkey having been its members since the 1960s. This allowed the OEC to become one of the world's largest trade blocs. It plans to reduce tariffs, set up an investment bank, a joint airline, a satellite communications link, *etc.* The Black Sea Economic Cooperation (BSEC) – an organization of 11 Black Sea countries plus Azerbaidzhan, Albania, and Armenia, was created in 1992 and provides for a gradual lifting of restrictions on the movement of commodities, capital, and manpower; the development of transport and communications infrastructures; maximum encouragement of mutual cooperation; and the creation of a joint investment and foreign-trade bank for the region.

1993 saw the birth of the CIS Economic Union (EU) aimed at the gradual formation of a homogeneous economic space, effecting mutually agreed-upon economic reforms and pursuing a coordinated economic policy as well as adjusting member-states' economic mechanisms to each other. It is significant that there were simultaneous attempts to integrate the CIS economies on a narrower basis. This was expressed, in particular, in the July 1993 declaration of the governments of Belarus, the Russian Federation, and Ukraine on taking urgent measures to deepen "economic integration," foreseeing a treaty on and organizational structures of economic cooperation with Central Asia and Kazakhstan.

In December 1993 Poland, Hungary, the Czech Republic, and Slovakia – the so-called Vysegrad Four – concluded the Agreement on Free Trade in Central Europe with the aim of encouraging mutual trading exchanges and coordinating their economic policies.

Throughout the period a number of states were also striving to establish relations with the European Economic Community (EEC). This resulted in Poland, Hungary, and Czechoslovakia acquiring EEC associate membership in 1991 as well as in the European Union (EU), which signed comprehensive partnership and cooperation treaties with Russia and Ukraine in 1994.

It will also be recalled that some political circles of national-democratic leanings have discussed rather actively the idea of forming a Baltic-Black Sea Union (or Alliance), *i.e.*, an organization which could, as some people think, counterbalance integration processes within the CIS.

The Baltic states pursue their own integration strategy toward the Scandinavian countries, while Moldova moves in similar fashion toward Rumania.

Also evident is a specific orientation of individual regions in large-territory states towards different foreign economic partners. For example, the Russian Far East clearly gravitates towards Japan and China. In Ukraine, Galicia is

Table 2

Pro-integration factors of Possible Regional Associations and Partnership Relationships

Regional economic association or partnership relation	Pro-integration factors							
	1	2	3	4	5	6	7	8
CIS	+/-	+/-	+/-	+/-	+	+/-	-	-
Russia–Belarus–Ukraine	+	+	+	+	+	+/-	-	+
Central Asian states and Kazakhstan	+	-	+/-	+/-	+/-	+/-	+/-	+
OEC	+	-	+/-	-	-	+/-	+	+
BSEC	+/-	+/-	+/-	-	+/-	-	+/-	-
the Baltic market	+	-	+	+	+/-	+	+	+
the Black-Sea–Baltic union	+/-	+/-	+	+/-	+/-	+/-	+	-
Joining the EU: - Central European countries - other countries	+	+/-	+/-	+/-	+/-	+	+	+

the Vysegrad Four	+	-	+	+	+/-	+	+/-	+
Regional organization of the former COMECON client states	+/-	+/-	+/-	+/-	+/-	-	-	-
the Baltic states – Scandinavia	+	+/-	-	-	+/-	+	+	+
Rumania – Moldova	+	-	+	+	+/-	+/-	+	+
the Far East: Russia-Japan	+	+	-	-	-	-	-	-
the Far East Russia-China	+	+	+	+	+	-	-	-
Galicia–Poland	+	+/-	+/-	+/-	+	+	+	+
Transcarpathia – Hungary	+	+	+/-	+/-	+	+/-	+	+

* + means presence of a respective pro-integration factor, – denotes an anti-integration factor, +/- means either the pro- and anti-integration factors cancel each other out or that it is impossible to determine their true balance at present.

traditionally oriented towards Poland and Transcarpathia toward Hungary.

The wide variety of unifying tendencies does not only indicate the importance of each postcommunist country finding its own "integration niche" in the global economic space. It also indicates the lack of a clearly stated foreign economic strategy in those countries, which provokes attempts to test various patterns of integration behavior and find the only correct solution by the method of trial-and-error. This, incidentally, explains the at first glance strange tendency to simultaneously join several regional groupings differing in their orientation and integration strategies.

However, it might be well to point out that a successful application of the strategy of economic integration requires the joint, coordinated, *i.e.*, synergetic, action of many integrationist factors. The most important of them are:

1) geographical proximity;

2) potentially mutually complementary nature of the products of the given national economies, giving a comparative advantage to mutual economic cooperation;

3) virtually identical overall levels of national economic and social development;

4) similar strategies of long-term economic development;

5) well-developed and diversified economic ties;

6) common long-term political interests;

7) a history of relations between the respective countries and a favorable psychological attitude toward their cooperation;

8) cultural and religious similarities.

How do the various integration projects look from the viewpoint of the presence or absence of these pro-integration factors? (see Table 2)

This analysis performed allows singling out three groups of integration or partnership possibilities. The first group consists of those having real chances of success. They are: a likely unification of Russia, Belarus and Ukraine, the unification of the Vysegrad group countries and their joining the EU structures, bilateral integration: Rumania – Moldova, Galicia – Poland, Transcarpathia – Hungary. The relations between the Baltic and Scandinavian countries and between the Russian Far East and China have somewhat lesser prospects.

On the other hand, the present-day conditions leave very few chances to the BSEC as well as to integration into the EU of the NIS, the geoeconomic revival of COMECON, and integration of the Russian Far East with Japan. Rather slim chances are left to integration within the CIS Economic Union, between Central Asian states and Kazakhstan, of the former Soviet republics within the OEC as well as to the idea of a Black-Sea Baltic union (alliance).

True, the results obtained should not be overestimated. The point is the above-mentioned gradation is based on the principle of equality of all pro-integration and anti-integration factors. This may not be so in real life. For instance, the economic integration of Russia, Belarus, and Ukraine has only one negative, namely, the historico-psychological, factor; but this may practically rule out this integration option in the short and medium term. The same is true of the Baltic market, the Vysegrad group, the Romania – Moldova integration because the lack of mutually complementary key production factors in the respective countries may bring to naught any kind of economic integration. With this in view, one can conclude that the formation of large-scale international groupings and complexes based on the postcommunist countries is rather problematic in the near future.

§4. East – West, North – South, or Something Else?

The problem of postcommunist geoeconomic orientation has not only a regional but a global dimension. From this point of view, it is important to determine the potential of the postcommunist states for integration into the world economy as well as the geoeconomic axis of which they could realistically a pole or a point. The former socialist-camp countries belonged to the category "East" as a counterbalance to the developed capitalist West. This kind of opposition is senseless now that communism has collapsed.

Let us again emphasize that different postcommunist countries have different objective geoeconomic orientations. Orientation towards the West has become realistic for Poland, Hungary, and the Czech Republic. These postcommunist nations are in fact becoming part of the West. A similar tendency is also typical of Bulgaria, Slovenia, Latvia, Estonia, and to some extent Lithuania, although their incorporation in the Western structures is still problematic and will require more time and effort. Other NIS and Rumania to a certain extent face a real dilemma: West or South?

The formation of a geoeconomic axis of the transitional economies of North-South is quite a realistic prospect for

Central Asia and Kazakhstan (even given the uncertain prospects for economic integration in this direction). This direction may also become an essential supplement to the Westward leanings of such European countries as Russia, Belarus, and Ukraine. (Incidentally, this is a direction of development that can save their manufacturing industrial capacity from ruin, since a substantial proportion of their industrial output will for some time remain uncompetitive on the markets of the developed countries).

Of special interest for the transitional-economy countries on the North-South axis are relations with the Persian Gulf oil-producing countries. This follows from the fact that it is this area that has amassed the greater part of capital free for profit-making investments. And it is the investment of this capital in high-technology industries, the upgrading of certain processing industries in the transitional-economies that can promote diversification of the structure of foreign economic relations the Gulf states and enable the latter to accomplish their own ambitious economic projects at a less cost. Moreover, the Islamic factor has to be taken into account, for it gives cultural and psychological impetus to forging economic ties with Muslim NIS.

An important direction in the geoeconomic strategy of many countries with a transitional economy may be the formation of an axis of transitional economies of West and East — Far East, where Far East primarily means the new industrial countries of southeast Asia. It is this axis that allows some transitional-economy countries (above all, Belarus, Russia, and Ukraine) to combine their considerable scientific and technological capacity with experience in the prompt introduction of new technologies and capturing the new markets accumulated by the new industrial countries of the said region.

* * *

Thus, one can hardly speak of only one specific pattern of geoeconomic orientation for the postcommunist states. On the contrary, more evident is the opposite, *i.e.*, an evergrowing structural diversity of economic ties. This may be accompanied by the further economic estrangement of former partners and the formation of new centers of gravity for these countries. This will be a quite natural phenomenon reflecting the establishment of international economic alliances based on geoeconomic factors and the comparative advantages of a given country in the world economy rather than on political and ideological considerations.

The problem of geoeconomic self-determination is growing ever more complex for certain postcommunist states in that they are not geoeconomically homogeneous. Their territories may be seen as divided by geoeconomic borders. This objectively causes different geoeconomic orientations of a country's different regions. Russia, Moldova, and Ukraine may serve as an example of states where the issue is one of both geoeconomics and domestic policy because any solution largely depends on internal political factors. This presents an especially acute case, for a high probability remains of certain economic decisions being over-politicized and subordinated to internal political considerations.

It is theoretically quite possible for different regions of a country to be oriented toward different foreign economic partners. In this connection, eastern and southern Ukraine could be integrated in the northeastern direction, while the West could take a westward path (Galicia would then take Poland as a priority direction, as would Transcarpathia with respect to Hungary and, to some extent, Slovakia). Given successful economic reform and the sufficiently dynamic development of new internal economic relationships, this geoeconomic pattern need not endanger national unity. And conversely, under conditions of growing economic hardship these said geoeconomic differences could become the first step toward disintegration. In a case like this we may witness the repetition of bitter lessons in the history of the Soviet Union, Czechoslovakia, and Yugoslavia on a new level and under new circumstances.

Geopolitical Implications of Ethnopolitics

To understand the ethnopolitical situation in the current postcommunist world, it is useful to divide it into four regions:

- Russia proper, with its particular ethnopolitical problems;
- The former non-Russian Union republics which were parts of the USSR before 1939 and lived through the full force of Stalin's "deconstruction" of the non-Russian nations in the 1930s;
- The territories annexed by the USSR after the Molotov-Ribbentrop Pact of 1939;
- The former so-called "people's democracies" which lost their independence *de facto* but not *de jure* (except for former Yugoslavia).

§1. Ethnopolitics as a Geopolitical Factor in the Postcommunist World

In the classical sense, ethnopolitics in a nation-state means the political relationship of the titular nation with other ethnic groups as well as the interrelations of various nations and ethnic groups among themselves. It also means the state's regulation of these interethnic relations and the pursuit by ethnic groups of their interests and programs (including control of or influence on the state). However, in the countries that emerged from the collapse of the USSR, general trends in ethnopolitics are governed more by external than internal factors. For this reason the problems of ethnopolitics are currently closely connected with issues of foreign policy.

It is common knowledge that nowhere in the world do the geographical boundaries of nations neatly coincide with state borders. Ethnic groups, which are the titular nation in one state, are often ethnic minorities in another. And, quite naturally, any state considers its co-nationals living in other states as an object of its legitimate concern, interest, and not seldom as a lever of political influence. Ethnopolitical violations of human rights or discrimination against an ethnic minority on the state level may often detonate an explosive response in the state where the group discriminated against is the titular nation. This, in turn, places on the agenda the question of border revisions, and this is extremely hazardous, for the inviolability of borders is crucial to international stability.

The history of practically every country is marked by border disputes. Redrawing borders can be an interminable process, and it is precisely here that interstate, international, and interethnic conflicts may erupt. Especially thorny are border questions in the postcommunist world, for the domination of the Russocentric Soviet empire merely submerged and did not solve age-old interethnic and international conflicts. This is one of several causes of tension between postcommunist states, which are capable of erupting into armed confrontations.

§2. The Historical Roots of Interethnic Conflicts

A group's feeling of sharing a common heritage and historical fate is an important component of what makes a nation. This is why difficulties, which at present may seem incomprehensible, irrational, or even insane, can be understood and explained by delving into the past. The war in Nagorno-Karabakh originates in the massacre of the Armenians by Ottoman Turkey in 1915. In the eyes of Armenians, Azeri Turks personify their old, hated enemy and carry collective guilt for an old and terrible crime. The mutual hatred of Serbs and Croats, which is the basic motive force of war in former Yugoslavia, is nourished by Croatian memories of their subjugation by Serbs in the interwar Kingdom and Serbian memories of the genocidal wartime Croatian Ustasha regime. Old seeds of ethnic hatred can take root and burst out into murderous blossoming in any corner of the world. The recent genocide in Rwanda can be explained by historically accumulated anger at the pre-colonial arrogance of the Hutu minority over the Tutsi majority. Not so long ago Argentina declared war upon Great Britain in order to recover islands taken by the latter a century and a half ago. But in the nations of the postcommunist world interethnic problems, long frozen by the Soviet empire, can explode and assume acute and extremely dangerous forms. Such conflicts are difficult to settle by the international community because they are essentially emotionally, *i.e.*, irrationally based and inclined to escalate.

Radical nationalist political movements in most countries seek to break the vicious cycle of interethnic competition by establishing a monoethnic state. In modern history, various Western states have attempted to do this but ultimately failed. The policy of expelling minorities from a territory where they had long resided has often led to economic catastrophes, social upheavals, and armed conflict. After 1918, in the wake of the creation of the Second Polish Republic and the disintegration of the Habsburg empire, the independent nation-state became the dominant principle of territorial-political organization in Europe. Alongside the creation of nation-states, the problem of ethnic minorities emerged and loomed large. In order to ameliorate this problem and prevent conflicts between the new states and their minorities (among whom Ukrainians were the largest in Europe), the victorious Allies imposed on the new states a series of minorities treaties, which proved singularly ineffective. All the newly created states, with the possible exception of Czechoslovakia, fell prey to one or another form of nationalist authoritarianism along with discrimination against and subjugation of their minorities. Adolf Hitler went to great lengths to make use of the distress and frustration of Germans outside the Third Reich (*Volksdeutsche*) in being transformed from a *Herrenvolk* into an ethnic minority. By exploiting the real and imagined violations of the rights of the *Volksdeutsche,* Hitler was able to destabilize the postwar Versailles European order and unleash World War II, which began, of course, with a fourth partition of Poland carried out in concert with the Soviet Union. In the interwar period, historical rivalries between Rumanians and Hungarians, Poles and Lithuanians, Bulgarians and Turks, etc., fostered a general trend away from democratic pluralism toward extremes of nationalist authoritarianism and ethnic discrimination.

§3. The "Russian Problem" as a Destabilizing Factor

Tsarist Russia entered the twentieth century encumbered by a host of ethnic problems. For centuries Russian culture failed to cultivate a particular Russian national idea beyond the simple expansion of borders which might explain its otherness toward Europe and rationalize Russian domination over neighboring nations. The seeds of the so-called "Russian idea" which ultimately did emerge, run back to the period when Muscovy, the cradle of Russia, was alienated (as were the Balkans) from Christian Europe at a formative stage of its historical development. After its liberation from Tatar domination, Muscovy continued to view Europe as something alien. Russia, which, in Stalin's words, was always beaten for its backwardness, looked at Europe with profound feelings of inferiority. In the nineteenth century, representatives of two competing trends in Russian intellectual thought attempted to face this backwardness. The Westernizers sought to adopt Western models and saw Russia's future as being a part of Europe. Slavophiles, who constituted the more deeply-rooted and powerful trend in Russian intellectual history, embraced a sort of megalomania as compensation for their national inferiority complex. They renounced the West's "materialism" and sought in materially poor Russia, the spiritual wealth of a "Third Rome" destined to create and lead a new, more spiritual, non-European, pan-Slavic civilization. And they simply could not understand those Slavs who did not want to take part in such a seemingly glorious crusade. Representatives of this movement, which generally enriched Russian culture, could never get used to the idea that other, less numerous, especially East Slavic, peoples did not (and do not) want to play the role of younger brothers to the Great-Russian nation.

Russian expansionism in the tsarist period produced a deeply ingrained idea of Russian messianism in everyday life. Russians have never considered themselves a nation constrained by any state borders and have never taken into consideration the national aspirations of other peoples inhabiting Russia as "resident aliens" (*inorodtsy*). Panslavism might be called the focal point of Russian political culture. Even the most democratic representatives of the Russian intelligentsia have never understood Ukrainian aspirations for national self-affirmation and self-determination. A vivid example was Sergei Bulgakov, who called Ukrainians "a nation which just thought itself up." In various guises this rather less than unbiased view has been echoed in allegations that the Germans invented Ukraine or that Lenin invented Ukraine (as Dmitri Volkogonov would have it).

Drinking deep from the well of their national myth, "the Russian idea" or "Moscow, the Third Rome," many Russians have dreamed of Russian domination over Eastern Christendom and lost themselves in reveries over Constantinople. It is a cliché of Russian historiography that Kyiv is "the mother of Russian cities," where Russian history has its beginning. If Kyiv is a Ukrainian city, that is, not Russian at all, then Russian history loses its beginning, and the Russian idea has to be essentially modified and transformed. Obviously, this can become for many Russians an intellectual and political catastrophe of far-reaching implications.

Of course, every nation has its national myth. But Russians have never developed a national identity allowing them to separate themselves from other Slavs. Hannah Arendt pointed out the difference between ordinary nationalism and tribal "Pan-movements," Panslavism, Pangermanism, and so forth. In her opinion, the difference lies in the ahistoricity of tribal nationalism, which depends on a holy task, a spiritual mission, and is unrestrained in its political, cultural, and military will to power.[18]

Leninism was essentially a particular mutation of the Russian idea on the basis of nineteenth century nihilism, an outgrowth of one of the dark undercurrents of Russian history for which Western Marxism proved to be only an external ideological cloak. Lenin himself was in no sense an adherent of traditional Russian messianism. He combined the Russian radical tradition with the classical Marxist formula: that the proletariat has no fatherland; and that for the proletariat, the nation, its culture and language, are without value. Lenin believed that nationalism was a manifestation of the bourgeois false consciousness produced by capitalism and that socialism would witness the coming together and amalgamation (*sblizhenie i sliyanie*) of nations. That is, that under socialism non-Russian nations would themselves understand (*i.e.*, would have to understand) the progressive nature of their assimilation by the more highly developed Russian language and culture. Thus, Leninism constituted the first Russian national communism which, as a result of the inertia of Russian history, almost inevitably evolved into the open Panslavism of Stalin, who used this "Russian idea" as political glue to paste together a totalitarian regime on the basis of Russocentrism.

§4. Ukraine's Main Ethnopolitical Problem

In the interbellum period, especially in the 1920s, the system had to demonstrate its toleration of the interests and aspirations of other nations which found themselves in the newly reconstituted, now Soviet, empire. In order to stabilize and consolidate Soviet rule in the non-Russian "borderlands" (*okrainy*) of the USSR, in 1923 the Communist Party proclaimed a policy of indigenization (*korenizatsiia*), which in Ukraine was called "Ukrainization." Ukrainization provided Ukraine's nationally-inclined cultural and political forces an opening and allowed them to demonstrate forcefully that Ukraine was capable — if allowed to do so, even without the fraternal assistance of Moscow – of solving complex problems directly concerning its statehood and nation-building. The year 1929 became a turning point in the process of Ukrainization. Ukraine witnessed a dramatic increase in the number of cultural and educational institutions representing the culture and scholarship not only of Ukrainians but also of other ethnic groups in Ukraine. There were Jewish, Polish, and other theaters; children of Moldovans, Greeks, Germans, Jews, Poles, *etc.*, had access to education in their mother tongues. Ukrainization was actively carried out in the Kuban, Don, Armavir, Tver, Maikop, Selsk, Stavropol, and other regions of compact Ukrainian settlement in the Russian Federation. There were Ukrainian reading rooms, clubs, classes for adult illiterates, high schools, and courses for workers (*rabfaki*). A Ukrainian teachers college was opened in Kursk. In Ukraine, enrollment in national minority language schools exceeded that of Russian language schools. Along with the creation on the territory of the Ukrainian SSR of an Autonomous Moldavian SSR (which under the name Transdnistria is currently occupied by the Fourteenth Russian Army), there were 25 national minority districts (8 Russian, 7 German, 3 Jewish, 3 Greek, 3 Bulgarian, and one Polish). There were hundreds of village soviets for various ethnic groups, and in Ukraine's schools could be heard the Armenian, Assyrian, Tatar, Jewish, German, Polish, and other languages.[19] Culture and literature witnessed a period of development unprecedented in Ukraine's history.

Ukrainization was halted in the 1930s. This is why the cultural revival of that period is now referred to as the "the revival that faced the firing squad" (*rozstriliane vidrodzhennia*). The terrible man-made famine in 1932-33 was in one sense a war against the peasantry, a war upon which Stalin and his henchmen consciously embarked. But at the same time, campaigns were orchestrated to exterminate the clergy, scholars, artists, literati – whole social strata which were the backbone of the Ukrainian nation and other ethnic groups in Ukraine. The Russian national pattern was sown in place of the Ukrainian. All this constituted a tragedy of apocalyptic scope. And it is the legacy of this period from which many, if not most, of Ukraine's current misfortunes flow.

The real ethnopolitical problem in Ukraine is not about Crimean Tatars, Germans, Greeks, Jews, or other national minorities. The main ethnopolitical problem in present-day Ukraine is the Russian question, but not – and this must be emphasized – the problem of Ukraine's ethnic Russians, who, despite propaganda to the contrary, do not experience any oppression or violations of their rights. In most of Ukraine it still is easier to find for one's children a good Russian school than a Ukrainian one, most books are published in Russian, and on television one hears a great deal of Russian. In the big cities, except for Western Ukraine, Russian is still the preponderant language of everyday life. Russian newspapers have never been in short supply. And so on and so forth. This is the primary reason that in Ukraine there is no social basis for creating such extremist Russian organizations as the Interfronts of the Baltic states or Russia's openly anti-Semitic Pamyat which seek to bring the newly independent states back to the bosom of Mother Russia. To be sure, in Ukraine as well one can also occasionally hear such things from certain politicians or political groupings in Ukraine, but they are not voiced on a large scale and certainly do not threaten Ukraine's independence.

The Russian question in Ukraine is really the problem of the northern neighbor, the problem of relationships with Russia as a power whose politicians are wont to make territorial, political, and other claims. Given the imperial ("integrationist") bent of Russian foreign policy, the destabilization of interethnic relations on Ukraine's territory is obviously in Russia's interests. Russia does not want to have ethnic Russians coming back to their homeland, as was demonstrated when Russian refugees from Chechnia sought refuge and asylum in Ukraine, Belarus, and the Caucasian republics, while Russia itself was very reluctant to give them shelter. Russia's political line in this sphere leads one to suggest that ethnic Russians in Ukraine are designed to play the part of a fifth column which can be taken advantage of in order undermine Ukrainian independence. Whether the Russian minority in Ukraine will agree to play this role will probably be determined more by the state of Ukraine's economy rather than by culture or politics. A rise in living standards would automatically lead to a decline in separatist sentiments among the Russian-speaking population of the Donets Basin and Luhansk and would eliminate any social basis for propaganda among Ukraine's Russians in favor of reconstituting the empire.

Thus far Ukraine has had to take into consideration the rather widely held notion that anything Russian is by definition superior. This is certainly not a specifically Ukrainian problem. In the state once called the USSR, there was no national enclave where after 1930 the slightest manifestation of national self-assertion did not call forth accusations of "bourgeois nationalism" (then considered equivalent to high treason) and a consequent blood bath. In a world where the least hint of disloyalty to the regime carried with it the threat of death sentence or repression, the Russian language (along with active vigilance in exposing any display of so-called "bourgeois nationalism") was an outward display of political loyalty and orthodoxy. The supremacy of everything Russian, cloaked by the high-sounding phrase, "proletarian internationalism," created an ethnopolitical situation in which everything Russian was always superior, better, more fashionable, and more progressive.

§5. Belarus: Two Paths to the Future

The bloodless revolution of 1991 brought statehood to peoples long accustomed to thinking of themselves as second-rate. Under such circumstances, the feeling of some that there was something artificial and not quite serious about this new statehood was simply inevitable. This was especially the case in Belarus whose capital still lacks a single school with Belarusian as the language of instruction. Belarus, like Ukraine, faced two alternatives: resort to large-scale privatization and the de-statization of society in order to stimulate the formation of a society capable of democratic self-government, a society where the habit of respecting human and minority rights would become ingrained, and in so doing to actually join the world family of nations; or to enter the family of nations only through the mediation and fraternal aid of Russia, that is, to give up a considerable measure of its independence in the hope that its stronger neighbor would unravel for it a whole knot of complex social and economic problems.

It is obvious today that Belarus has opted for the second alternative. The Belarus leadership agrees to change its borders, to the free transit of Russian goods and citizens through its territory to the West, and permanent Russian military bases on its territory. Belarus was the only country which openly supported the Russian invasion of Chechnia and announced suspension of its dismantling of military equipment, thereby calling into question the validity of the Treaty on Reduction of Conventional Forces in Europe, which is, of course, precisely what Moscow wants. The President of Belarus has sponsored holding referendum virtually renouncing Belarus's very independence and allowing its *de facto* incorporation into a neighboring state. But the greatest gift was presented by Belarus' President to imperial-minded Russian politicians when he publicly announced that the Belarusian language was inferior. This escapade of the Belarusian leader, even given the obvious weakness of the Belarus national movement, is extremely dangerous for Belarus itself, for it may dramatically destabilize the country's ethnic equilibrium. In the final analysis, this, in turn, would mean inviting greater Russian pressure not only upon Belarusians themselves but also on the country's ethnic minorities who, given Russia's record on the issue, cannot assume that their ethnic and cultural needs would be satisfied. In addition to its overwhelmingly Belarusian majority and insignificant Russian minority, Belarus is also populated by Poles, Ukrainians, Jews, and others who are very unlikely to obtain real rather than declared national cultural autonomy in a situation where the titular nation of its own accord renounces its own language and culture. Moreover, it is unlikely that the Belarusians themselves would agree to such a policy without any resistance or protests. According to the 1979 population census, 74.2% of all inhabitants of Belarus and 83.5% of ethnic Belarusians in Belarus declared Belarusian their mother tongue.[20] Powerful assimilatory processes have taken place in recent years, primarily in urban areas, but, obviously, Belarusian can never be rooted out from everyday, family, and cultural communication. The Belarus spiritual and cultural organism will inevitably come to the point where the question will arise of outright resistance to the policy of Russification rather than cooperation and interaction.

As far as economic advantages of this policy are concerned, very telling is the fact that Russian financiers and bankers are currently quite willing to cooperate with Ukrainian financial and commercial structures, explaining that the Ukrainian karbovanets is at present the hardest "soft" currency in the CIS, and the former are very reluctant to have anything to do with the Belarusian ruble. There is also the conspicuous fact that, while highly praising the policy of the Belarusian President in public, Russian etatists have as yet neglected to write off Belarus's debts for Russian fuel and other power resources.

§6. Risks of Future Tragedies

At present Russian politicians are also pleased with the policies of Kazakhstan, which is steadily and unswervingly moving toward integration with Russia. Until the 1930s, the Kazakhs were a nation of nomads, but their society was quite structured. They had their own religious and cultural elites along with a nobility. It was easier to exterminate national leaders in Kazakhstan, because of remnants of the feudal-tribal social system there, and it was not difficult to label someone who owned a big flock of sheep as a bay (rich landowner in Central Asia) or parasite. Moreover, a third of all Kazakhs perished in the early 1930s during famines and there was a massive Slavic colonization of the Kazakh steppe.[21] As a result, Kazakhstan became a country where the indigenous population became an ethnic minority, less educated and influential in solving crucial political and economic problems. But with time the "Kazakh question" may well become aggravated and loom large. Among Kazakhs in a country, where they do not have a decisive voice, there will always be the possibility of forming nationalist movements whose leaders may resort to extremist methods of struggle against the privileges of the Russian-speaking population. And the fact that the indigenous or indigenous language-speaking population is an ethnic minority in its native land does not necessarily imply that there will always be stability and accord ensured by "big brother." The experience of Northern Ireland shows that one small group, which never enjoyed substantial support even among Catholics, could intimidate and terrorize not only Ulster but the whole of Great Britain for decades on end. In Northern Ireland, the imperial policy of the powerful neighbor provided every opportunity for the painless absorption of this small country. Assimilatory policies resulted in the fact that English became the predominant language and even few Irish speak Gaelic. But a feeling of historical injustice remained there when immigrant Scottish Protestants decided the fate of their region by remaining part of the United Kingdom and discriminating against the local Catholic minority. This resulted in the emergence of the clandestine extremist provisional wing of the Irish Republican Army which resorted to terrorism in the struggle against the British (and local Protestant) authorities.

Failure to renounce the privileges of the so-called "Russian-speaking population" may well lead to similar results, even if this policy proves as successful as the British policy of founding Protestant colonies on the lands of Irish rebels in the seventeenth century. For the success of an imperial power may only persuade the indigenous population that their situation is hopeless and unless they resort to terrorism. Such "success" can only sow the seeds of future tragedy.

Events in Chechnia have also shown that imperial claims on territories annexed by tsarist Russia and reconquered by the Soviets cannot be maintained without assuming the role of a gendarme nation. Fearing Russian expansion, those Moslem states of the CIS, which were able to extricate their peoples from the Soviet melting pot, are noticeably turning toward the Moslem world. Active negotiations are underway with Turkey, the Arab countries, and anti-Russian feelings are on the rise.

One need not be a prophet to see what complications are in store for those Russians who have to live in a foreign language environment which they find culturally alien. Psychologically, transition from the status of *Herrenvolk* to that of a national minority which finds itself in a linguistically alien environment, can be neither simple or easy. Here much depends on national and ethnic policies adopted by the new Moslem states, and these policies are significantly influenced by Russia's policy toward the Moslem CIS states.

The Karabakh impasse is marked by Russia's permanent presence in the region, which is why geopolitically the Karabakh conflict, like the problems of the Transdnistrian Moldovan Republic and the Georgian-Ossetian confrontation, is in the interests of a Russia which continues to retain its political and military bases as potential levers for pressuring "rebellious" governments and states, while simultaneously demonstrating to the West its indispensable role as guarantor of order in the region. Ukrainian analysts have repeatedly noted that the West will never get tough with Moscow on behalf of former Soviet republics. Even the events in Chechnia have not led to a dramatic worsening of the US-Russian relationship, only to a slight cooling of the West's relations with Russia and a lower profile for Russia in the eyes of Western politicians.

In general, nowadays the West is guided in its actions by the principle "Let it be as bad as it is, if only it will not get worse." The playing of the "Zhirinovsky card" by the Russian mass media and politicians has produced the requisite and, very likely, well-designed and calculated effect. The West is ready to give up much in order not to lose all. Fearful of the threat that fascists might come to power in Russia capable of unleashing World War III, the West demonstrates very sluggishly and reluctantly its anger at the massacres in Chechnia, confining itself to slightly curtailing its economic cooperation with Russia. The West's fears of the possible collapse of economic and political reform in Russia are not groundless. There are forces in Russia itself which consider Western assistance and aid as Western attempts at economic and financial expansion. A reflection of these fears is an opinion that all foreign political analysts and scientists are employed by the CIA and that mythical Jewish secret centers are plotting to buy up wholesale "beloved mother Russia" and to cause something terrible to happen to it. This fear of the West is but the flip side of the same old Russian idea, and those analysts are likely to be right who prognosticate that, in case Russian reforms end in fiasco, Russia's imperial policy in its traditional sphere of influence will dramatically intensify. That Russia is beginning to recompense itself for its humiliation in Chechnia at the expense of its neighbors is already being seen, and rather vividly at that.

§.7. Political Double Standards

However, Western politicians who anxiously anticipate a quick settlement in the Chechen conflict are naïve. In Chechnia, Russia confronts not just a small people trying to gain independence: it is a political conflict between pro-imperial and anti-imperial forces on the territory of the former USSR. It is no accident that at the height of the Chechen massacre Russian government officials intensified their efforts to push through the issue of dual citizenship in Ukraine and that in Kyiv itself a congress of the Communist Party convened under slogans calling for the restoration of the Soviet Union, while in the Crimea a rally gathered under the slogan of Ukraine's integration with Russia, and a new series of pro-Russian political provocations concerning the division of the Black Sea Fleet began. In the Crimea, when Russian chauvinist forces step up their activities, Russia has not only political support but also a military forepost which could be used as the ultimate argument in any dispute with an unyielding Ukraine. Generally, provided the interethnic situation in Ukraine is stable, the Crimea may evidently be the only point of real threat which Russia is capable of manipulating and using as a lever to support a policy of intimidation and hegemony.

Ukraine's "Crimean problem" tends to become ever more complicated and aggravated. By giving up the information market to Russian chauvinists, Ukrainian officials lack the opportunity to directly communicate with the peninsula's inhabitants in order to win their support. Extremely important in this situation is continual explanation to the Crimea's inhabitants the real nature of the economic, ecological, and social problems of the peninsula, which, given Crimea's dependence on Ukraine for water, food, electrical energy, and such, should the Crimea break away from Ukraine, could lead to real catastrophe and mass migration from the area. This is the real threat the Crimea must face, not the mounting pressure of mainland Ukraine on the Crimea, the President's brandishing his mace or Parliament's threats. There is only one civilized way of settling the Crimean issue – to recover the lost information theater. There is only one kind of war to be waged in the Crimea – a war for "hearts and minds" of its people.

Incidentally, Russia's policy toward the Crimea itself shows how it employs a double standard respecting its own and somebody else's problems. Moscow actively supported Crimean ex-President Yuri Meshkov and conducted an undisguised anti-Ukrainian propaganda campaign in the Crimea at the same time it declared President Dudaev in Chechnia a criminal and invaded his country. But both Meshkov and Dudaev were elected Presidents by the local population in virtually identical constitutional or, rather, unconstitutional situations and under very similar legislative circumstances. One recalls Orwell's *Animal Farm*: "All pigs are equal but some are more equal than others." Moscow's interference in Ukraine's internal affairs under the pretext of "protecting the Russian-speaking population in countries of the near abroad" cannot but sooner or later lead to a further aggravation of Russian-Ukrainian relations at the state level, because Ukrainians, making up 25% of the Crimea's population and lacking their own schools, theaters, newspapers, radio stations, *etc.*, may create precedents contrary to the interests of ethnic Russians in the Crimea. Meanwhile, the indigenous population whose expulsion helped make room for all those Russians, the Crimean Tatars, on failing to tolerate the central authorities' helplessness in solving their problems, might ultimately opt for radical methods in the struggle for their rights. All this could in turn lead to a test of Ukraine's tolerance to violations of its laws on territory which is juridically part of Ukraine. The problem of the relationship of any Ukrainian government with the Crimea will inevitably put on the agenda the issue of limiting or even abrogating the Crimea's autonomy, because any autonomy is always constrained by the legislation of the country of which it remains a part.

Valeriya Novodvorskaya, a deputy in the Russian State Duma, writes: "National passionarias represent a floral culture which is grown in abundance in Russian patriotic hothouses and, therefore, is readily supplied to markets in the CIS, the Baltic states, the Kuril islands and to the 'political stock markets' of the civilized world by way of a little humanitarian blackmail: 'If you don't feed us and let us come to your discotheques, we'll give you away to Zhirinovsky'."[22]

After the events in Chechnia, this "little humanitarian blackmail" has already led to the fact that former so-called "people's democracies" are actively intensifying their efforts to gain admission to NATO. Polish President Lech Walesa has said, "We will try for join NATO and not ask any permission from Russia." East Central European and Baltic politicians are actively turning toward Europe. For them, Europe is an alternative to what may happen after the Chechen crisis in their own countries and a guarantee of their security.

§8. Democracy as an Instrument of Geopolitics

Within this context, Ukraine has found itself in an extremely complex situation. Its dependence on Russian fuel and other power sources and Russia's economy in general makes it impossible for it to turn away from its northern neighbor without suffering major economic and financial losses. Any possible destabilization of its relationship with Russia would also be unlikely to find support among the considerable segment of Ukraine's population having family ties in Russia. On the other hand, Western officials have become accustomed to having a relationship with Moscow and many of them do not even know where Ukraine is, traditionally perceiving its independence, in the words of Russian spokesmen, as a "very temporary phenomenon." The West fears Russia's self-isolation and the disappointment of hopes for Russia to reform and evolve into a democratic nation; that is why it is so difficult and troublesome for it to take Ukraine seriously. This is not a mere blunder – it is a political blind alley for which the West may have to pay dearly in the future. A strong, independent Ukraine is a guarantor of not only its own stability but also that of Russia itself and of Europe as a whole. There will be no new Russocentric empire without Ukraine. Without it Russia will have to till its own soil and put its own house in order rather than to count on solving Russian problems by "swallowing up" other peoples along with their lands. There is only one way to quell the expansionist instinct and cure the age-old disease of imperialism: for the West to pay serious attention to the problems of Ukraine, Belarus, Moldova, and of the newly independent states in general. Psychologically, this is difficult and expensive for the West to do, for it is also seeking simple solutions to secure its well-being. But under the present circumstances, there can be no simple solutions. Totalitarianism is a deadly disease which is characterized by the constant threat of relapse and of infecting others. The German people, dissatisfied with the democratic order in the Weimar Republic, the weakness of the central government, and rising street violence chose a path which led to the deaths of millions of Germans and others. Democracy has its limitations and weaknesses, but it provides a historical perspective which is obscure or entirely absent under despotic, authoritarian, or totalitarian systems.

Democracy in Ukraine means, to a considerable measure, democracy in Russia and constitutes a historical perspective for the West itself.

Beyond the boundaries of the CIS, where there is practically no Russian population, the ethnopolitical scene is fundamentally different. First, the forced population exchanges after World War II removed such complicated problems of the past as the ethnic German minority in Czechoslovakia, which was unceremoniously shipped off to Germany. The voluntary separation of the Czech Republic and Slovakia has given powerful impulse to their prospective *rapprochement* and ultimate merger on a voluntary and equal basis. Czechs and Slovaks may take pride in the civilized solution of their complex ethnopolitical problem, and this is the kind of political capital which in the future will amply compensate for the economic and political losses flowing from the disintegration of Czechoslovakia.

The experience of the armed conflict on the territory of former Yugoslavia vividly shows how the dark undercurrents of history may suddenly surface and with what danger they are fraught. Four hundred years of Ottoman rule left a bitter legacy of hatred toward Turks and Moslems in general, as shown the discrimination against Turks in Bulgaria and that euphemism for genocide, "ethnic cleansing," in Bosnia. Historical claims of Greece, Bulgaria, and Serbia on Macedonia are also fraught with the threat of possible conflicts. Serbia's aggressive attitude toward other parts of what once was Yugoslavia is a product of its return to the traditions of the interwar kingdom which was under Serbian domination and serves as an example of a dangerous tendency of Russia's relapsing to similar traditions. Since in the wake of World War II Poland almost completely lost its hitherto numerous ethnic minorities and Rumania's territorial claims on several districts of Ukraine's Odesa region are not of such proportion as to mortally damage bilateral relations, the only other potentially destabilizing ethnopolitical problem in Eastern and Central Europe is the "Hungarian question," for after World War I the Treaties of Trianon and St. Germain left one third of all ethnic Hungarians outside Hungary, mainly in Rumania (Transylvania), former Yugoslavia (Vojevodina), southern Slovakia, and Ukraine (Transcarpathia). Hungary has no territorial claims against its neighbors but, at the same time, it has a permanent and legitimate interest in the fate of ethnic Hungarians, especially in those countries where discrimination against them is probable. Even in the days of the Warsaw Pact, Bucharest's attitudes toward Rumania's Hungarian minorities often complicated its relationship with Hungary. Today, when the countries are becoming more democratic and local agreements on bilingualism has been reached in Transylvania, this potentially acute problem seems on the road to alleviation.

The ideal model for protecting ethnic minorities might well be the Law on National Minorities in Ukraine which guarantees all citizens of Ukraine, irrespective of their ethnic origin, equal political, social, economic, and cultural rights and freedoms along with state financial assistance in the development of their national and ethnic identity and self-expression. However great Ukraine's shortcomings and mistakes in other spheres may be, this can serve as an exemplary (*de facto* and *de jure*) model for other newly independent states interested in stability, the inviolability of borders, internal consensus, and harmonious cooperation in order to preclude a restoration of the former Soviet empire.

Of course, interethnic relations in Ukraine should not be idealized, but both at the time of the Ukrainian Peoples Republic and in the period of Soviet Ukraine's relative autonomy (1923-33) and in its new status of an independent nation, Ukraine has demonstrated that it is capable of effectively solving its ethnic minorities problems on its own, without outside pressure or guidance. Ethnic tolerance and respect for other nations are essential components of the Ukrainian national mentality, and one can argue rather convincingly that radical political trends of various political orientations will not find any broad support here, provided – to emphasize once more – the country's economic situation stabilizes.

To be sure, one cannot ignore the various problems and differences in political and party orientations among

Ukraine's regions. A great step forward would be made if the problem of the balance of regional rights and obligations were solved, regional autonomy in economic and cultural matters were extended, and bilateral relationships between regions were expanded – obviously, provided that not only a waitress in Drohobych (Western Ukraine) could give an answer in Russian when spoken to in Russian but also that an official in presently Russian-speaking Kryvyi Rih could speak Ukrainian.

Ethnopolitical relations in the postcommunist world are complex and far from uniform. The newly independent states strive for equality with the leading nations of the world; nationalities and ethnic groups strive for their national and ethnic self-determination and self-expression. Today not only Europe but the whole world faces basic choices concerning its future development and progress. For there is a real threat of its being trapped in the endless murderous ethnic strife which could shatter mankind's hopes for a better and more civilized future. But there is a chance, perhaps the final one, to realize the age-old dream of democracy, independence, and justice.

The Realties and the Logic of Myth in Inter-Slavic Relations

The present condition of the postcommunist societies occupying the vast expanse from the Kuril Islands to Dubrovnik offers rich material for new ethnosociological study. It is generally known that interethnic contacts were among the dominant topics in Soviet ethnology, and that from the outset everything was programmed to help strengthen the "unbreakable" Union. But there was also real deep seated antagonism to the unity imposed by the dominant tribe. This phenomenon was not noticed in the scholarly realm, but it was obvious in sphere of enforcing the system. Communist ideology was enforced in an area with ancient historical traditions having deeply archaic roots. These traditions refused to yield to ideological leveling; they fled from the pressure of propaganda and totalitarian repressions. With the fall of the regime supporting the system – and, of course, its ideology – the sense of tribal unity broke loose from its centuries-old (and sometimes even older) fetters, charging the national organism with fresh energy, directing it toward actions whose psychosocial roots extend back to pre-Christian times when instinct prevailed over the civilized dictates of Christianity. The communist system, opposed to this society by a number of cults and various other explications, demonstrated inherently pagan morals. Evidence of this is found in one vivid example – today's interethnic hostilities.

§1. Tribal Wars

Symptomatically, the reflex of interethnic enmity embraced the entire postcommunist archipelago, all the way from the Kuril Islands to Dubrovnik, manifesting itself in a comparatively equal measure among ethnic groups differing in geographical location and cultural-historical tradition. The reason probably lies in the anthropological roots common to all humanity, namely, the herd instinct, and in its common catalyst, the ideology instilled in all these ethnic formations. If we keep this in mind, the similarity of interethnic confrontations from the Balkans to the Caucasus becomes understandable. At the same time, one cannot but notice the marked brutality of interethnic confrontations registered in regions inhabited by ethnic groups with archaic traditions – and the territories mentioned, although separated by thousands of miles, are precisely such regions. To a researcher versed in ethnogenesis it becomes immediately clear that the geography of these localities is marked by age-old traces of various ethnic migrations. The territories of this archipelago are also rich in archaic signs indicating the deep roots of pagan culture. For us it is important that Ukraine is situated between these archaic zones, and so the question becomes to what extent are the atavistic reflexes peculiar to man living in our space? Ours is a society whose cultural tradition bears extremely old information encoded in well-known historical landmarks from the pre-historic Trypillian culture on down.

Communist ideology took deep root in territories with archaic traditions. This was no accident. The new-born communist ideas were interrelated with socio-utopian views; in fact, they served to lend Utopia its Marxist form – and there are numerous such variations in the history of Utopias. These ideas were best nourished in lands with archaic traditions and developed folk precepts. Hence the constant reference of communist ideologues to the "masses" with their positive response to Utopianism, the latter being reminiscent of folk tales, so very much alive in the consciousness of this category of society. And, remarkably, this tendency persists, even after the obvious fiasco of the ideology, discredited by purges, pervasive corruption, "the betrayal of its ideals," *etc.* It is also obvious that this ideology could take deep root in the Eastern Hemisphere, and not in the West, the former having a predominantly rural culture. There the proletariat, in whom communist theoreticians placed such hope, was made up of urbanized masses of pauperized former peasants who had been uprooted from the village but remained natural carriers of the folk mentality. Torn from their traditional settings, they formed the cultural medium for folklorism, preserving the "traditional" (in the sense Werner Sombart used the term) structure of cognition. This also explains the number of exponents of former communist ideologies in the city. Following the ruin of the ideological apparatus (Party structure), only the supervisory-punitive correlates of collective concepts disappeared, since the city, whose progress was affected by a series of mass "invasions" of peasants, shaped individuals with urban culture against a solidly rural background. The result was total deformation of the social structure; the village lost a legitimate component of its culture, its patriarchal ways and logic of myths, bequeathing them to the city. In the communist scale of moral values "nonurban" ways of thinking ranked high, and almost all public figures, Party functionaries, *Kulturträgers,* and the like made a special point of their worker-peasant background. The collapse of formal ideological structures left practically intact communalistic instincts. Hence, the postcommunist nomenklatura's quest for an institutional basis for such instincts, for new adherents; hence, too, the response of the masses. However, consolidating open Communist Party adherents, even using rather inconspicuous techniques, is not a widespread phenomenon, because neocommunism is no longer capable of effectively attracting the masses, exhausted by decades of unrelenting brainwashing. Here much greater influence can be exerted by public groupings. These do not propagandize solidarity with a particular ideological structure (communist or openly fascist), but bring forth the tribal reflex in calling for unity and for resisting the common "ethnic enemy."

This reflex is reproduced by the ethnosocium, which combines certain ethnic instincts multiplied by societal (in this case communist) tradition. *Homo soveticus* is a typical product of such reproduction. This ethnosocium is charged with the inertia of programs borrowed for the arsenal of communist propaganda (*e.g.,* for restoration of the USSR and the Communist Party, against capitalism, *etc.*). But all this acquires special importance only in the presence of yet another confrontation, the ethnic one. And thus the old communist arsenal fits with new "national aspirations" perfectly. Remarkably, it is in *homo soveticus* that the inherent antagonism toward the neighboring ethnic other is especially manifest, even though this neighbor is more often than not very close to him in historical and territorial traditions. Here a certain common thread is always present: the closer the ethnic bodies are to one another, the stronger their antagonism (given the breakdown of their "bonds of internationalism") develops, the Slavic example being the most vivid.

§2. The Myth of Slavic Unity

The Slavs, especially their southeastern branch, archaic by origin, were subjected to the strongest influence of communist ideology in its Eastern Orthodox variant. Later it was extended to the Catholic South Slavs who were habitually less susceptible to Bolshevism. The latter was most deeply rooted in areas dominated by the archaic principle of tribal fraternity where those with the strongest state structures were the "big brothers." This combination of archaic instinct and new communist ideology begot a "fraternity" based on coercion, violence, and fratricidal wars, planned and unleashed according to the Cain-and-Abel recipe. Given the USSR-socialist camp version of "proletarian internationalism" or Yugoslav "brotherhood and unity," these relationships were actually a continuation and a stronger variant of the early medieval supremacy of one ethnic group over all the others and its self-assertion by means of violence directed against those others. This can be traced in all the binary oppositions of the Slavic "fraternity," especially in the Russian-Ukrainian. Such relationships inevitably give rise to social neuroses, and history knows their various forms, ranging from mythical utopias, stories about a tsardom of powerful and equal Slavs, to the cult of revenge, an urge to get even with the cruel "big brother."

The myth of Slavic unity permeates all Slavic history, arising in different forms at different times, in the medieval period, with the earliest notions of Slavic-Rus' unity laid down by the forerunner of Slavistics, the Kyivan monk Nestor; the Renaissance, ranging from Dubrovnik-Dalmatian verse overlain with Slavic patriotism to the historiosophic phantasmagoria *The Kingdom of Slavs,* written in Latin in 1601 by Dubrovnik historian Maurus Orbini. The treatise was addressed to the Holy See, which blacklisted it, thus showing its attitude toward the idea of Panslavism. Later, Peter the Great ordered its publication in Russia. In fact, it was an overture to Russian political exploitation of Slavic patriotism. What Orbini actually did was to create the prologue of baroque Slavism in which utopian expectations relied on an appeal to the "sacral carrier of the Panslavic idea," the Muscovite Tsar. These expectation reached their apex in the activities of Croatian encyclopedist Jurij Krizanic. At the political level they were manifested in the Ukrainian utopia of the 1654 Treaty of Pereyaslav.

The idea of Slavism is mostly preserved in the folk and political memories of Slavs forced to confront ethnically alien neighbors, in Slavic lands bordering on non-Slavic territories. There the old Slavic antithesis "we and they" is lent the sharpest acuity. It was usually most evident in nations lacking statehood but possessing advanced literacy like Renaissance Croatia and baroque Ukraine. Here a political solution to the problem is traditionally inseparable from the "good liberator," a strong Slavic tsar. To the Croatians of the Renaissance, this was the Polish king and later the Muscovite tsar. One searches in vain for a single example throughout the history of Slavism, when the idea of Slavic unity as a political means of solving the problem of stateless peoples came to a positive end. All such attempts by various nations to assert the idea of Slavism proved abortive, at times with very tragic consequences for them. The time came when Maurus Orbini's book was entered into the Orthodox *Index Liborum Prohibitorum*; when Jurij Krizanic exiled for fifteen years to Siberia on orders from Alexis I Mikhailovich, the "Most Serene" Tsar of Muscovy; when numerous purges were levied on the Ukrainian champions of unity based on equality; when the Serbian colonies in Ukraine disappeared in the eighteenth century, because the country was colonized by the Russian Empire. And now the Yugoslav variant of inter-Slavic slaughter.

Essentially, the idea of Slavic unity is an ethnocentric utopia, with no chance of coming true, because mutual territorial claims have rather dangerous implications and because the Slavs are divided by traditions they had long ago acquired from the Greek and Latin variants of Christianity. Even religiously homogenous Slavs are under inner strain, which is by no means less fraught with danger, because the Orthodox Church, already politicized in the Middle Ages, was and remains a form of ideological surveillance; in its own way this Church reflected – and still does – the encounters of political trends. And currently the phenomenon of confrontational repoliticization of the Church is reemerging. Evidence of this is the discord in Ukrainian-Russian-Serbian-Macedonian-Montenegrin church relations.

§3. On Modern Panslavism

The "Slavic idea" lives on in the form of politicized myth. It is mostly used by smart political operators and talkative TV prophets to save the Empire, already in its last throes. At present, Slavism time and again surfaces as an attempt to restore the lost former "unity," in spite of the latter's complete and self-evident disgrace. It is presented in the form of all kinds of "demonstrations of unity." And history proves that the stronger the forced unity and the efforts to preserve it, the heavier the price paid when it falls apart.

Characteristically, signs of efforts being made to restore that "unity," nostalgia, and mourning its collapse are registered precisely in the former "imperial" centers. Hence the outbursts of Belgrade-Moscow "fraternity."

At the same time, horror stories about "Satanic Serbs" began to spread in Ukraine, written by people who seemed determined in every way to prove their Ukrainian patriotism, but who, on the other hand, remained captives of a public image and political choice made on the crest of the perestroika wave.

Sometimes political myths on the Balkan theme appear in print, adorned with pretentious "scientific grounding," mostly echoing the variegated Balkan folklorist repertoire. Here one finds numerous hints at a "conspiracy" against Orthodoxy, resistance against Ustashism, bulwark against Islam, *etc.* Some authors build a smart combination of dates to back their mythology, but it obscures one important thing: it was only after the complete destruction of the Croatian town of Vukovar (incidentally, home to the largest Ukrainian community in former Yugoslavia) and the barbaric bombing of Dubrovnik, that gem of Mediterranean civilization, that Europe had to finally recognize Slovenia and Croatia.[23] This procrastination only served to implement the idea of ethnically "clean" territories, cherished by the ideologues of Greater Serbia.

The Balkan experience demonstrates that to simplify the ideological justification of military actions, one needs to provoke direct interethnic conflicts among the populace. The rest is a just matter of propaganda techniques. The troops of the Yugoslavian People's Army started active operations in Slovenia and Croatia precisely under the motto of "defense of the state frontiers and preservation of the territorial integrity, which, given the level of concepts and norms of the period and fully conformed to international standards..." These "standards" also perfectly suited the obedient students of the Balkan war, all those who would follow the Belgrade scenario and destroy Grozny. After all, the Chechen campaign became possible only after the successful Yugoslav experiment in international law and the international community's vague response to the atrocities in Bosnia. (For the record, among the victims of bomb raids at Grozny and Vukovar were Serbs, Russians, and Ukrainians).

After the republics of the former Socialist Federative Republic of Yugoslavia realized they were not strong enough to face the armada led by the General Staff of Belgrade and in which hopes were placed for restoring the Yugoslavian "fraternity," they had no choice but turn to the stronger traditional allies. Trying to prevent Yugoslavia's breakup meant waiting for the tanks of the Yugoslavian army to crash Zagreb and Ljubljana. Bloodshed could be easily stopped in Yugoslavia if, following those same international standards, the right of the republics to separate, within the postwar frontiers, were recognized. However, to this Belgrade gave a resolute no.

§4. From the History of the "Balkan Knot"

The breakup of Yugoslavia was inevitable, and the reasons run deep. The Yugoslav (or rather, post-Yugoslav) situation provides a graphic example of a tight knot of archaic patriarchal traditions combined with modern political maneuvering. Here old and new myths merged in people's mentality so completely that it would be next to impossible to determine the origin of each. That is why it is anything but easy to reveal all the reasons of the current war, to present it only as a manifestation of either interethnic, religious, or political enmity. The turn of events there (and there is no end in sight) can be divided into several stages, and the historical vertical allows us to single out certain domestic mechanisms which triggered the current slaughter.

To begin with, it is a fatal conglomerate of mutual historical settling of old scores based on old antagonisms. Yugoslavia (literally, "South Slavia") was an artificial association of peoples, each with centuries-old problems. A number of indicators relating to the ethnogenesis of these Slavs point to a typological affinity to Iranian-speaking archaic ethnic groups which came in waves to the northern Pontic steppe and whose traditions were absorbed by Slavs inhabiting the Dnipro-Carpathian region. As a result of several such waves of migration, the South Slavs (*e.g.*, Slovenes, Croats, Serbs, and Macedonians) found themselves on the lands from the Alpine foothills and deep into the Balkan Mountains. Beginning in the early Middle Ages, they gradually lost their common political identity. Slovenia was German-ruled. Croatia, retaining only islands of independence (like the city-state of Dubrovnik/Ragusa) changed its territorial configuration constantly as the Ottoman invasion which extended a wedge into historically Croatian territory. Serbia gradually lost its medieval might, turning into a province of the Ottoman Empire, beginning in the fifteenth century, where Slavs from the Bosnia-Herzegovina lands also merged and dissolved. The only exception was Montenegro, a hereditary bishopric where power passed from uncle to nephew, religiously akin to the Serbs, impregnable and unattractive to the Ottoman Turks because of its mountainous terrain.

The cultural and historical development of the South Slavs was determined by their Greek Orthodox and Roman Catholic affiliations. The Catholic Slavs gave the world such famous attainments as the Dubrovnik-Dalmatian Renaissance and Croatian baroque, which placed quite some distance between them and the Orthodox Serbs and Macedonians in the Middle Ages. Therefore, the South Slavs had every right to regard themselves as ethnically related but historically distinct ethnic entities with different traditions and cultures.

A palpable role was played here by the religious factor. Meanwhile, Croatian men of letters, discovering for themselves Ukraine's intellectual treasure trove and its horrible history, strongly cautioned against Russophilism. Simultaneously, Croatian romantics actively propagated the idea of South Slavism. In fact, they conceived the country's name, Yugoslavia, and did their best to help establish it. The Illyrians – as they called themselves – volunteered to choose a dialect which was the closest to Serbian when the time came to form a literary language. This was a gesture of unity with an ethnically related people. It was thus that two ethnic groups with different names found themselves united by a linguistic umbilical cord in the course of spreading romantic Slavism. With time this caused historical grievances which are still very much alive.

The formation in 1918 of the "Kingdom of the Serbs, Croats, and Slovenes," renamed Yugoslavia in 1923, did not bring the non-Serbs the liberation they had expected. Instead, it signified a new stage of dependence, accompanied by a various of acts of terrorism, starting with the 1914 assassination in Sarajevo of Archduke Francis Ferdinand which set off World War I (the assassin, Gavrilo Princip, had been a member of the underground Serbian Black Hand, and the victim was alleged to be the initiator of the idea of creating a "triple" Habsburg Monarchy in which would include Croatia as an equal member alongside Austria and Hungary), an attempt on Radic, leader of the Croatian opposition (murdered in Belgrade in 1928), and the 1934 assassination in Marseilles by the Croatian Ustasha of Alexander Karadjorjevic, Macedonian-backed pretender to the Yugoslav throne. The result of this mutual animosity was the appearance of extremist organizations, the Serbian Cetniks (named for wartime anti-Tito Serb partisans) and the Croatian Ustashi. The latter saw a solution to the national question in an alliance with Mussolini's Italy and gained independence as a German satellite state during World War II. This fact was and still is widely used by postwar communist propaganda to build the Croats a negative "national image" among Serbs, despite the fact that Tito, himself of Croatian parentage, was at the head of an anti-Nazi (national liberation) resistance movement in which an important role was played by Croatian brigades.

Despite the official split with Stalinism (the Cominform decision of 1948), the outwardly liberal Yugoslavian regime was in actuality a microcosm of the Soviet Empire. The "Bare Islands" Adriatic concentration camp for Yugoslav Stalinists were little different, if not even worse, than its Siberian counterparts housing "Titoists." The Yugoslav League of Communists (YLC) made a special point of demonstrating its adherence to Marxist dogma and tried to be holier than the "Holy See" in Moscow. The secret police did its work thoroughly, though sometimes verging on the absurd, resorting to extravagant means like bugging Tito's and his wife's bed chambers. Nationality policy was based a the Yugoslav version of Soviet "friendship of peoples," in the form of numerous propaganda rituals and building the majestic "Brotherhood and Unity" Highway linking the capitals of the "fraternal nations" (and later used in the tank offensive on Ljubljana, Zagreb, and Sarajevo). Tito's baby, the Yugoslav People's Army, was one of the strongest in Europe, bracing itself against Soviet invasion (after Hungary and Czechoslovakia), but it was not destined to carry out the historic mission as defender of Tito's self-governing communism. Instead, in the early 1990s it was completely transformed into a punitive police body.

* * *

The war in Yugoslavia was from the outset the result of the agony of the communist regime, and putting an end to it is only a matter of time, or so it would have seemed. The Serbian democratic intelligentsia, raised in the years of resistance against Stalinist and Soviet totalitarianism, rallied round writer Vuko Draskovic in resisting Serbian Bolshevism. Their influence on society grew rapidly, but at the crucial time when Serbian youth were erecting barricades on Belgrade streets and the regime was shaking at its foundation, Milosevic (former Secretary of the YLC city organization) led the campaign to storm the Croatian city of Vukovar. Thus, collective instincts were contained, absorbing the social explosion's blast energy. The regime's collapse was slowed down, and it was evidence of the flexibility and foresight of the Serbian Bolsheviks in their attempt to reinforce their bastion of national communism in the Balkans.

Some one million Serbs inhabiting the Croatian Republic found themselves the captives of political strategists. A process of creating internal ethnic solidarity and confrontation with the other began, on the age-old "us-them" standard.

The "our" (as in "our troops") tribal identity makes the socium even more aggressive than ideology. Here the notion "them" has a purely negative meaning. It implies someone or something threatening the ethnos, a danger that must be eliminated. Usually, it starts with a verbal offensive. This rather archaic form of communication habitually includes open contempt for the Other. Expressions and actions, which under different circumstances would look utterly uncivilized, come to appear totally appropriate. In a primitive society mocking and tongue-lashing are a twisted form of relationships of dependence and exploitation between unequal social groups. It is precisely this archaic type of verbal gestures, which currently dominates mass ethnic consciousness in the Balkans.

Ukrainian-Russian Relations and Western Policy

Future historians, looking back at the former Soviet Union in the late twentieth-century, may well conclude that the fate of Ukraine dominated the quest for stability in the region. They may even speak of the "Ukrainian question" as the organizing problem of the period. By this they could mean one of two things: either Ukraine succeeded in establishing its independence and helped to reorganize Eurasia on the basis of viable nation-states, not empire; or Ukraine will have become the sick young man of Europe, absorbing the attention and efforts of Russia and the other powers to the detriment of reform and regional stability.

For contemporary statesmen the meaning of the Ukrainian question is less clear. Those witnessing the beginning of the Ukrainian question cannot be faulted for not recognizing its significance and for not pursuing policies that make stability more likely. Let us consider both potential aspects of the Ukrainian question and its relationship to the future of Russia.

§1. Power Combinations in The Former Soviet Union

The West is still unaccustomed to dealing with the territory of the former USSR as a region of international diplomacy. At least a partial reason for this reluctance lies in the West's reliance in a time of change on strategic continuities that would guide its policies, even as they delayed engagement with new realities. The two most important continuities are its continued support for reforms in Moscow and its focus on nuclear weapons, particularly the problem of a nuclear Ukraine.

It does not follow from this that these continuities were of little strategic importance or that Western policies reflected no understanding or change. Rather, one can assume only that the depth and breadth of the West's response to these two challenges had at least something to do with their familiarity. The West has been slower to see that this focus is unsustainable without addressing other potential sources of stability in the new "Eurasia." Chief among these sources is the appearance and viability of an independent Ukraine.

Ukrainian independence has two important and obvious geopolitical consequences. The first is as simple as the observation that strategically important territory and resources once under a single authority are now under two. This division of authority creates the possibility of new power combinations in the region. These power combinations might be more or less stable, but they do make less likely the reorganization of this region and its resources under an expansionist empire. In preventing the appearance of such an empire, Ukrainian independence is as important as Russian reform. The second observation is linked to the first: the contribution of Ukraine to the power of the Russian and Soviet empires means its independence affects not only the possibilities for organizing the region, but the possibilities for organizing Russia itself. Indeed, Ukraine could turn out to be the central external force shaping Russia.

§2. The Problem of Empire

It is important at the outset to understand what the problem of empire is and what it is not. For most of the past eight hundred years, "Eurasia" had been shaped either by imperial expansion or imperial collapse. Periods of the latter, such as the division and disappearance of the Mongol Empire and its successors, the great "Time of Troubles" in the beginning of the seventeenth, or the collapse of the

Russian Empire in our own, have given rise to new or even more totalitarian variations of the old. The only power at present capable over the next several decades of creating a Eurasian empire is Russia, and many in the West already see signs of an imperial strategy dominant in Moscow.

Three basic forces are at work in shaping Russian power in the region. The first is the intellectual horizon of Russia's leaders that is being drawn by the debate in Moscow over Russia's national interests. The second is Russia's actual involvement with the outside world, particularly with the new states on Russia's borders.

The debate in Moscow has steadily moved toward a more assertive definition of Russia's role in the world, particularly in its assertion of "special responsibility" for the territory of the former USSR. However, it is an error to see the debate in Moscow as already settled, with the imperial camp ascendant. The imperial habit of mind remains strong in Moscow, but the strongest foreign policy consensus in Moscow at present is that Russia should remain a great power. Not everyone believes such a power must be imperial, though this debate is being driven by domestic pressures toward a more assertive and imperial framework.

Beyond the debate itself, Russia's current troubles have radically affected its capabilities. Whatever the intentions of the leadership, these troubles limit its opinions and hinder any immediate implementation of a full blown imperial strategy in all but smallest and weakest states on Russia's border. Russia needs time to concentrate on what Yeltsin described earlier this year as "the grave illness of Russian statehood."[24] That illness is marked as Yeltsin himself describes by a serious pathologies— crime, economic hardship, regional disintegration, and ethnic tensions. One of its chief pathologies is the crisis in the military, which is struggling to increase cohesion and raise morale in the face of severe materiel shortages, a lack of training and equipment, and large-scale draft dodging. Imperial strategies require imperial armed forces, which at present do not exist. These pathologies compel Russia to seek a period of internal concentration reminiscent of Russian Foreign Minister Gorchakov's policy of *recueillement* after defeat in the Crimean War. This need for a breathing space creates incentives for moderation and deepens Moscow's understanding of its true capabilities, which do not always correspond to its rhetoric. It is within this breathing space that Russia's statesman and their foreign interlocutors must fashion incentives for post imperial patterns of behavior.

The pattern of Russia's involvement with its nearest neighbors, such as Ukraine, appears to undercut the analogy to Gorchakov's policy; for Russia, there is no real *status quo ante* into which it can retreat. The continued effect of Soviet integration in economics and security policy, plus the rise of new but weak states on its borders, compel Russia's interest in its new borderlands, sometimes even its intervention. Russia's engagement in this region will also be shaped by its confidence not only in its relative strength vis-a-vis these new states but in its absolute strength as well. The test will be whether that strength can establish stability while respecting the independence of its neighbors. The test will be made more difficult if, as a result of the West's own period of internal concentration, spheres of interest, if not influence, are created which drive Russia away from Europe and condemn Russia's neighbors to Neville Chamberlain's category of "far away countries of which we know nothing."

§3. Russian Policy Toward Ukraine

Even more than its relations with the West, Russian power is evolving through its encounter with these border states. It is here that the problem of empire arises, particularly where old legacies are strongest and stakes highest in Ukraine.

Russia's relationship with Ukraine is complicated by differing historical and psychological experiences on both sides. The most profound conflict between them is often at the level of conflicting national psychologies: Russians tend to view Ukrainians as part of an Orthodox Slavic civilization created in large measure by the union of the three East Slavic nations under Russian leadership; Ukrainians harbor a strong sense of themselves as a separate nation, with Russia playing only the role of the Other. At a time when Russia must define its national identity, Ukrainian independence is still a shock and, for some, a betrayal.

Russian nationalist opinion in particular is still stung by Ukrainian independence, though it is divided between those who advocate a policy of pressure designed to impose strategic and cultural affinity of Russia and "Orthodox Ukraine-Rus'" and those who seek the "return" of areas of concentrated Russian-speaking settlement in Ukraine.[25] The latter approach amounts to a grudging acceptance of an independent Ukraine, though within borders determined by Moscow.

The approach of Moscow's foreign policy establishment is culturally no friendlier toward Ukrainian independence. However, this establishment advocates policies that would create a relaxation of tensions between Kyiv and Moscow. Not long ago Andranik Migranian, a member of the Presidential Council, summed up this view, which he ascribed to a segment of Russian politicians and analysts opposed to strong-arm tactics and the exertion of pressure on Ukraine over Crimea. This view rests on the assumption that "Ukraine is a fragile, artificial, heterogeneous ethnopolitical formation lacking any real chance of the formation of its own statehood..."[26] However, Migranian describes the policy implications of this view largely in terms of Russia taking a "wait and see" approach with Kyiv on most questions, including nuclear weapons. Though such an approach sees its origins in the weakness of the Ukrainian state, it also reflects a candid assessment of Russia's own condition as well. For Kyiv, what is most important is that it receive a breathing space, not the sympathy and good will of Russian politicians and analysts.

Russia's Ukraine policy is a combination of conciliation and pressures "to keep the Ukrainian problem within certain limits and to prevent it from getting out of control."[27] Yeltsin and senior Russian officials have conspired with their Ukrainian counterparts in a regular pattern of resolving a host of complicated issues in principle, while letting their technical resolution lag or fall apart altogether. There are important exceptions. Russia has not surrendered what it sees as its vital interests in retaining the Black Sea Fleet in Crimea and other questions involving Ukraine's security orientation. It has also fought hard over issues where real financial gain was a stake, attempting to limit Ukraine's ability to claim its share of Soviet assets. At times, it appeared that the most difficult aspects of the negotiations over nuclear disarmament were precisely questions of financial compensation and the distribution of US technical and financial assistance.

Russia has attempted to exert economic pressure to shape Ukrainian policies, but it appears to have pursued this course half-heartedly. Russia has proposed to trade Ukrainian debt for controlling interest in important Ukrainian assets, such as the oil pipeline and refineries. It has regularly sought Ukrainian participation in various schemes that would bind it more closely to mechanisms of the Commonwealth of the Independent States. However, Russia has not made agreement to these mechanisms a genuine condition for economic cooperation or continued energy deliveries. In fact, Russia's approach to Ukraine's energy debt amounts to demands for Ukrainian acknowledgment of the debt and agreement to a repayment schedule yet a continuation of oil deliveries in the face of Ukraine's obvious inability to pay.

Russian strategy to date appears to be based on an understanding of Ukraine's weakness and Russia's inability to assume greater burdens than it already carries. The Russian government has focused instead on preserving its interests and influence over Ukraine, attempting to retain its political leverage while it addresses its own crisis. This current strategy does not mean that Russia has come to terms with Ukrainian independence or that it will surrender what it sees as its interests in Ukraine, only that Russia has not acted with regard to Ukraine in as reckless a manner as most outside observers have assumed. Russia's long range intentions will be clear only as Russia emerges from its crisis and regains its capabilities. It is crucial that in the next decade

Russian, Ukrainian, and Western statesmen use the current breathing space to consolidate Russia's reforms, Ukraine's independence, and the elements within current environment that support a stable Russo-Ukrainian relationship.

§4. Conflict or Cooperation

Though the pattern of relations described above seems an unlikely one to breed armed conflict, it is precisely the fear of Russo-Ukrainian war that has held the attention of the West. Evans and Novak provided one such scenario, in which Moscow inspires the Russian nationalist Crimean leadership to secession, thereby providing the pretext for Russian intervention and leaving the Ukrainian government the choice of capitulation or war. The columnists faulted the West for having no contingency plans for such an occurrence.[28]

For the next few years, however, the military crisis in Moscow precludes such an option. It is unlikely that despite having 1.5 million men under arms and more than hundred divisions worth of equipment, the Russian Army could field the multi-divisional force needed to attack or even pacify Ukraine. Even the most optimistic planner sees the rebuilding of the Russian armed forces as a task lasting well into the next decade. Ukrainian forces are in no better shape. This military situation radically reduces the risk of large scale Russo-Ukrainian conflict.

Western analysts would better spend their time in trying to understand and expand incentives for cooperation. On a host of issues, from cooperation in space (which the US should encourage) to conventional arms sales (which the US would dislike), Russia and Ukraine need each other. The glue of such cooperation is a basic stability in the Russo-Ukrainian relationship. This stability depends on Ukraine's confidence in its independence. It at present requires concerned effort from the US and the European Union to support Ukraine and create incentives for Russo-Ukrainian cooperation without a stable framework. Without such Western engagement, cooperation between a relatively strong Russia and an increasingly weak Ukraine will tend to erode Ukrainian stability and distort the relationship.

In providing support, the West distinguishes between steps that consolidate Ukrainian independence and those that encourage the geopolitical isolation of Moscow. The West must not create a *cordon sanitaire* between Russia and Europe. Such a policy would radically transform Russia's view of the emerging European security environment and its place in it. The West does not need another Versailles settlement, which founders as soon as a resentful power recovers enough strength to defy it.

Suspicions that the West is entertaining such a policy abound in Moscow, particularly in the nationalist camp. There is a strong tendency throughout the region to view the West's engagement as a zero-sum position, either supporting Moscow alone to the detriment of other states, or supporting those states to the detriment of Moscow. The political vocabulary of many Ukrainian politician suggests they see projects to create a "Eurasian Union" precisely in these stark terms, as a geopolitical state of nature in which presents a dilemma: either the West supports Russian domination or unites against it. Western statesmen must find a way of conducting a genuinely multipolar engagement in the former Soviet Union that links its recognition of Russian power in the region and support for its reform to abiding and steady support for the independence of Ukraine and other states of the region. The West must have a comprehensive well-balanced policy toward Russian, Ukrainian and nuclear problems.

The West has important tools for pursuing such a policy, if only it will fashion it. The G7 should create a package of incentives to encourage Ukrainian economic reform. It should examine how its support program for Russia affects Russia's neighbors and begin to design programs that support region-wide stability and reform. It should sponsor mutually beneficial Russo-Ukrainian cooperation on specific projects, such as civilian space exploration and modernization of the energy sector, while discouraging the creation of broad multilateral economic and political mechanisms that work against the consolidation of national independence.

The US, Russia, and Ukraine have established a trilateral framework for addressing nuclear and other security questions. This framework provides the US the opportunity to resolve bilateral differences early, before they escalate to crisis. The US should use this framework to help mediate outstanding Russo-Ukrainian differences over the division and basing the Black Sea Fleet. It should exercise its influence to keep Crimea from becoming an international crisis, encouraging continued restraint from Moscow and continued negotiations between Kyiv and Simferopil. The European Union and its individual members also have interests and resources which can be brought to bear to ensure a more stable Ukraine.

§5. The Sick Young Man of Europe

In the West, there is a pervasive sense of pessimism about Ukraine, even though it shares to a greater or lesser degree the same disintegrative forces common to all new states of the former USSR. Ukraine's economic troubles are serious. Its political divisions are real. But it is too early to sound to death knell for Ukraine. The explanation for western pessimism may be that, in the case of Ukraine, analysts tend to view these disintegrative forces and even the ordinary clash of interests common to all states through the lens of ethnicity. In this view, Ukraine is home to an intractable ethnic conflict, in which nearly 11,000,000 Russians in the East and the Ukrainian nationalists in the West are prepared to reenact Bosnia on an immense scale.

Ukraine is a divided nation, but the divisions are not simply ethnic nor are they reducible to two monolithic protagonists. Rather, the basic divisions are over power, as well as specific political and economic issues. At their core, they pit forces attracted to integrationist and state-dominated policies against national and reform-oriented forces. It is true that the first group is strongest in eastern Ukraine and among ethnic Russians. But it also includes multi-ethnic industrial, mining, and party interests that are maintained by socialist planning and subsidies. The second group's stronghold is in the West, the lands brought into the USSR only during the Second World War. Its main protagonists are ethnic Ukrainians but by no means is the independence of Ukraine an ethnic idea.

The actual patterns of interests and political forces in Ukraine are more complex. Between the East and West are the Center and South, regions that do not fall completely under either orientation, though their support of Leonid Kuchma in the July elections proved to be the difference.[29] The forces for integration are divided as well. Communists and Socialists won the largest declared block of seats in the March elections. They share a preference for etatist economics and cooperation with Russia, but differ profoundly over the value of Ukrainian statehood. By and large the Socialists want to preserve it; many Communists are at best indifferent. Both parties share an uneasy working relationship with the political force of the factory managers. In subsequent rounds of parliamentary elections, Eastern Ukraine produced greater numbers of independents and supporters of economic reform. On the opposite side, the nationalists are split over whether the first priority is reform or measures to strengthen the Ukrainian state. A strong party of economic reform is still missing from the scene, though the new parliament contains a reform party with ties to Kuchma and his advisors.

In the center, the government attempts to rule by forging uneasy compromises and striking balances among Ukraine's diverse political forces. Kravchuk tried to lean toward the integrationists on economic issues and the nationalists on foreign and security policy, except in the nuclear area. With the parliamentary elections and the victory of Leonid Kuchma, this uneasy balance is shifting perceptibly toward the integrationist forces, particularly as economic conditions worsen. However, even a triumph of these forces would not relieve the new leadership of the obligation to maintain this balancing act. Such a government cannot govern Ukraine without the support of Western and Central

Ukraine. And the economy simply does not permit more Kravchuk-style inaction.

The question is whether, in a time of political crisis, the political framework just described leads inevitably to collapse or whether analysts exaggerate the fragility of Ukrainian statehood. Though Ukraine faces serious challenges in the months ahead, there are also stabilizing factors at work, including apparently widespread popular support for the democratic process in Ukraine, the absence of a monolithic ethnic Russian political movement, and Russia's own lack of enthusiasm and capabilities for adventurism in Ukraine.

Despite economic hardship, this year's elections revealed a strong orientation toward the ballot box. Polls rather consistently showed throughout this period widespread disillusionment with Ukrainian leaders and their policies, but the Ukrainian electorate chose to address their disillusionment by voting, not through civil war. The Ukrainian political structure is stronger than many have realized. There is, of course, no comparison with Moscow, where many of the administrators, diplomats, and politicians simply changed allegiance from the USSR to the Russian Federation. Ukraine's progress must be measured from near absolute zero. It had no real experience of statehood, and thus no administrative cadre to support the basic activities of a state. The Ukrainian SSR was dominated by Moscow and supported by a local nomenklatura of dubious quality. The real shock should not be Ukraine's failures to date in state-building, but that it has gotten so far and been so successful on such a shaky foundation.

The elections also brought home the fact that ethnic Russians in Ukraine are not a fifth column. The Russians in Ukraine are a large minority; however, only in Crimea are they a majority of the population, and nowhere do they present a solid political bloc.[30] The high turnout in the Donbas for the March parliamentary elections demonstrated the region's strong orientation toward Kyiv.[31] Only in Crimea did we see enthusiasm for local institutions and separatist politics at the expense of the center. Elections and polls have shown that ethnic Russians in Ukraine want Russian as a second state language. They want close ties with Russia and reject attempts to define Ukrainian statehood over and against Russia. But they also do not want to be just another impoverished province of Russia. Since the election of Kuchma – whom the Crimean population overwhelmingly supported – there has been a palpable relaxation of tensions between Simferopil and Kyiv, followed by increased tensions between the Crimean executive and legislative branches. The long term danger is that cleavages in economic interests overlap with ethnic Russian concentrations, particularly in Donbas, and that conflicting economic and political interests will over time bring an ethnic dimension to the current internal crisis.

Though at present the integrationist orientations could dominate the government in Kyiv, there are inherent limits to the ability of the integrationists (even more the secessionists) to deliver on their promises. There is in fact a coming crisis of the left as it confronts the responsibility of governing. Russia itself is in no condition to take on new economic challenges of the size and magnitude anticipated by Ukraine's integrationist politicians. The Donbas leadership knows perfectly well what the Crimean leadership is also discovering: they can do better playing the regional card in Kyiv than by joining the long line for subsidies in Moscow. Integrationist schemes to restore the old prosperity through the restoration of old economic ties must confront the fact that Russia's industries are themselves engaged in furious competition for scarce resources. The current debate over the size of the Russian defense budget illustrates that, even if the Defense Ministry obtains what it considers the minimum it needs to sustain the military, there will be little to spread around to Ukrainian industries not absolutely vital to Russian interests. The rosy notion that integrationist policies can reverse basic trends in eastern Ukraine is likely to founder on reality.

Those most pessimistic about Ukraine's chances point to Ukraine's dismal economy, as if nothing more need to be said. Analysts must, however, reflect on the great disparity between the monthly statistics which chronicle Ukraine's ruinous conditions and the rather normal appearance of everyday life in Ukraine itself. This economic free-fall has gone on longer than can be explained by hidden stockpiles. Our economic and political models do not appear to capture all the forces at work that continue to keep Ukraine afloat. These forces are of mixed origins. Some are part of the old system (subsidies, housing benefits and access to special goods). Some reflect old ways of dealing with hardship (barter, black market). And some reflect commercial activity (legal and quasi-legal) that we have been unable to capture. These observations do not suggest that Ukrainian economic policy is anything but in ruins; only that we do not fully understand the dynamics of postcommunist societies.

The foregoing is not meant to predict smooth sailing ahead for Ukraine in the next year. Ukraine is likely to be battered by conditions that will further limit the government's freedom of action. This crisis deepens at precisely a time when the Ukrainian regime is in need of a second founding, oriented toward creating the fundamental legal, political, and economic structures that will sustain independence. However, these conditions should not be seen as inevitably bringing about the disappearance of the Ukrainian state. There may be in Ukraine's diversity and the government's tolerant approach to citizenship and minority rights a source of strength as well, particularly at a time when extreme nationalists throughout Europe proclaim the unnaturalness of multi-ethnic states and the liberal institutions that support them.

§6. Appanage, not Anschluss

Still, we must take the threat of Ukrainian disintegration seriously. This threat focuses the mind on the importance of a stable Ukraine. There are those in Moscow and in the West who believe that Ukraine's unraveling is both inevitable and cost free. One analyst has characterized this approach in the following terms: "All Russia has to do is to open its arms and in no time Ukraine can be integrated into

Russia again."[32] This "Anschluss scenario" avoids thinking through what is truly destabilizing about the disintegration of the central government in Kyiv.

More sober voices in Russia and elsewhere point to the costs and problems of managing Ukraine's collapse. An *Anschluss* would require a massive military operation to keep or restore order, something beyond the capabilities of the Russian military today. Even an operation focused on nuclear and other crucial sites would require a force beyond Russia's current capacity. Such a scenario also presupposes the support or at least the passivity of the local population, something that could not be counted on throughout Ukraine. For Russia, the main problem is that intervention in Ukraine under any scenario would require the assumption of economic responsibility for a nation the size of France, with an economy in collapse. Russia's own economic and political reforms could not bear up under such a burden. All this leads to the conclusion that "the disintegration of Ukraine does not bring any benefits at all to Russia."[33] By the same token, this would also be highly undesirable for Western and East Central Europe from the standpoints both of geopolitics and that of political and economics stability.

No better illustration of the value of Ukrainian independence exists than thinking through its unraveling. However, the resolution of the Ukrainian question in favor of Kyiv's independence does not end history. It merely helps to consolidate the anti-imperialist organization of the former Soviet Union and Russia's own reform efforts. It creates a geopolitical theater of nation-states, with Russia remaining preeminent but no longer a state that Henry Kissinger described as "either too weak or too strong for the peace of Europe."[34] These nation-states will be weak for some time to come, susceptible to disintegrative pressures within and conflicts without. This configuration of the region brings problems of its own with which the West must deal. To do so, the West must first understand them.

Statesmen at present must attempt to understand the new situation and to act on this imperfect understanding so as to make stability more likely. The main factor of this stability will be the consolidation of Russia and Ukraine as democratic states and the creation of stable relations between them.

Ultimately, western policy must exploit those elements within the current situation that support the overall objective of regional stability. The relative lack of violence in the aftermath of the collapse or the USSR testifies to those elements and to good fortune. This fortune may not endure. That is the nature of breathing space.

References

Chapter 1

1. "I will use the term modern to designate any science that legitimizes itself with reference to a metadiscourse of this kind making an explicit appeal to some grand narrative, such as the dialectics of spirit, the hermeneutics of meaning, the emancipation of the rational or working subject, or the creation of wealth." — Jean- François Lyotard, *The Post-Modern Condition: A Report on Knowledge* (Minneapolis, 1991), p. xxiii.
2. See: David Held, "Editor's Introduction," *Political Theory Today,* ed. D. Held (Stanford, 1991), pp. 1-2.
3. See: Ottfried Höffe, *Politische Gerechtigkeit: Grundlegung einer kritischen Philosophie von Recht und Staat* (Frankfurt am Main, 1987), (1.4).
4. We use the term "coherence" instead of such traditional ones as unity, integrity, or commonality in order to, first of all, avoid the possible connotations and assumptions connected with their traditional usage in contexts which express a uniquely *Modern* approach to solving problems that are included in the terms themselves (the possibility of obtaining a "complete," "total," "full," or "final" social quality). Secondly, because as a concept, "coherence" expresses only a certain set of elements of society in their mutual relationships, and designates the main undecided problem of the postcommunist transformation of society, the problem of sociopolitical organization.
5. J.-F. Lyotard, *op. cit.,* pp. 37-39.
6. See: Jacques Derridas, *Otobiographies* (Paris, 1984), p. 29.
7. See: *The Union Could Have Been Saved: A White Book of Documents and Facts on M. S. Gorbachev's Policy to Reform and Preserve the Multinational State* (Moscow, 1995), pp. 94-256, published by the Gorbachev Fund in Russian.
8. B. A. Hayevsky, F. M. Kyrylyuk, and M. I. Obushny, *Conceptual Foundations of Ukrai*

nian Political Science (Kyiv, 1993), pp. 1, 5 (in Ukrainian). The authors of these "conceptual foundations" are Kyiv Shevchenko University Professors.

9. *Ibid.*, p. 7.
10. D. Tkachuk, *Ukrainian Nationalism* (Prague, 1940), p. 10 (in Ukrainian).
11. Ivan Lysiak-Rudnytzkyj, *Sketches on the History of Modern Ukraine* (Lviv, 1991), p. 62 (in Ukrainian).
12. D. Tkachuk, *op. cit.*, p. 5.
13. *Ibid.*, p. 8.
14. "Political rule is the self-government of free and equal people."— Jürgen Habermas, *Demokratia. Razum. Nravstvennost': Lektsii i Interviu* (Moscow, 1992), pp. 31, 66 (in Russian).
15. See: Jürgen Habermas, *"Legitimation Problems in the Modern State,"* Jürgen Habermas, *Communication and the Evolution of Society* (London, 1976), p. 178.
16. Immanuel Kant, "The Idea of General History in the Universal-Civic Perspective," in Kant, *Collected Works in Six Volumes* (Moscow, 1969), vol. VI, p. 21. For the universalist —general civilizational — foundation of the idea of democracy as it is advocated for by theoreticians of the seventeenth and eighteenth centuries, see: I. Yu. Solovev, and I. Kant, *Vzaimodopolnitelnost Morali i Prava,* (Moscow, 1962), pp. 19-27.
17. The standard work on this issue is Jürgen Habermas, "The Problem of Legitimization in the Modern State," in: Habermas, *op. cit.*, pp. 178-206. In this connection it should be noted that the notion of consensus in its exact definition as a special procedure of reaching general agreement in the process of public discussion is not consistent with the one referred to above as "proto-consensus" — *the silent* ethnocultural unity of people.
18. Nikolai Berdyaev, *On Human Slavery and Freedom* (Paris, 1936, in Russian). The concept of the unofficial group-censor was suggested by Anna Makolkin in her article "The Absent-Present Biographer in V.Veresaev's *Pushkin v Zhiznie,*" *Canadian Slavonic Papers,* XXXI/1, March 1989, pp. 43-56.
19. Maurice Pechman, *Triumph of Romanticism* (Columbia, SC, 1970).
20. *Ibid.*
21. Northrop Frye, Study of English Romanticism (New York, 1968); *idem.*, "Myth, Fiction and Displacement," *Fables of Identity* (New York, 1963), pp. 21-39.
22. Bill Butler, *The Myth of the Hero* (London: Rider & Co., 1979).
23. Anna Makolkin, *Name, Hero, Icon* (Berlin - New York, 1992), pp. 21-39.
24. *Literaturna Ukraina*, July 14, August 17, September 12, September 26, 1991.
25. The motif of "indigenous population" is becoming an alarmingly prominent theme in the current socio-economic and political discourse in general, but it is not limited to Ukraine nor to the newly independent states of the former Soviet Union and

other parts of Eastern Europe. It reminds one of the eternally present fear of "the Other" and the dormant virus of intolerance.

26. Allusion to John Steinbeck's, *The Winter of Our Discontent* (1961), which won him a Nobel Prize the following year.
27. Arthur de Gobineau, *Selected Political Writings* (London, 1970). His attempt to establish the original state of the "ingenuous population" and fear of contact with "the Other" would be replayed by the ideologues of fascism and later by ideologues of Marxism-Leninism.
28. *Ukraina,* No. 18 (September), 1991.

CHAPTER 2.

1. See, for example, the US General Accounting Office Report, *Poland and Hungary — Economic Transition and US Assistance,* May 1992, pp. 18-26, 30.
2. Duration of the phases above are influenced by the nature of the gestation prior to the final collapse of communism. The four basic types of positive/negative gestations which impact the pace of transformation are: (1) both political and economic changes are positive; (2) political changes are positive, but the economic are negative; (3) political changes are negative, but the economic are positive; and (4) both the political and economic changes are negative. (Hungary and Poland fall generally into the first category, Russia into the second category, China reflects the third group, and Romania is an example of the fourth category.)
3. See Michael Prowse, "Miracles Beyond the Free Market," *Financial Times,* April 26, 1993.
4. A useful compendium of Saburo Okita's writings on this subject is contained in "Steps to the 21st Century," *The Japan Times,* 1993. In addition to Saburo Okita's numerous writings, see also D. W. Nam (former Korean Prime Minister), "Korea's Economic Take-off in Retrospect," paper presented at the Second Washington Conference of the Korean-American Association, Washington, DC, September 28-29, 1992; and N. Yonemura and H. Tsukamoto (both of MITI), "Japan's Postwar Experience: Its Meaning and Implications for the Economic Transformation of the former Soviet Republics," March 1992.
5. As reported by KYODO, May 24, 1993. Further shocking details regarding the diversion of Western aid for illicit purposes are contained in Grigory Yavlinsky's op-ed article "Western Aid is No Help," *New York Times,* July 28, 1993.
6. Based on the *CIA World Fact Book of 1991,* with the per capita GNP for Germany being $14,600, for Austria $14,500, for CSFR $7,700, for Hungary $5,800, and for Poland $4,200.
7. See also "Measuring Russia's Emerging Private Sector," *Intelligence Research Paper* (CIA: Washington, DC),

November 1992.

8. We refer the reader to the classic work, Max Weber, *The Protestant Ethic and the Spirit of Capitalism.*
9. For more details on this paradox see: "Verkhovna Rada Ukrainy: Paradigmy i Paradoksy," *Eksklusiv Ukrainskoi Perspektyvy,* No. 1, 1995 (in Ukrainian).
10. Andrew Wilson, Valentyn Yakushyk, "Political Organizations in Ukraine," *Suchasnist',* No. 5, 1992, p.165 (in Ukrainian).
11. George Orwell, *1984 and Essays of Various Years,* (Moscow, 1989), pp. 142-146 (in Russian).
12. Yevhen Holovakha, "The Peculiarities of Political Awareness: the Ambivalence of Society and Personality," *Politolohichni chytannia,* 1992, No. 1, p. 28 (in Ukrainian).
13. Moshe Lewin, "Society, State, and Ideology During the First Five Year Plan" *Cultural Revolution in Russia,* 1928-1931, ed. S. Fitzpatrick (Bloomington, 1978), p. 41.
14. A. Motyl, *Dilemmas of Independence: Ukraine After Totalitarianism* (New York, 1993), pp. 54, 65.
15. *Demos,* No. 1, October 19, 1994 (in Ukrainian and English).

CHAPTER 3.

1. Put forward by T. Bauer, "Building Capitalism in Hungary," lecture given at the IRSES (Paris, 1991) and taken up by E. Hankiss, *East European Alternatives,* (Oxford, 1990). See also J. Staniszkis, "Nowa karta konfliktow," *Tygodnik Solidarnosc,* December 15, 1989, pp. 1, 7.
2. See: *Gazeta wyborcza,* December 27, 1991.
3. "Law VI 1988 on companies of an economic vocation" (passed in August 1988 and therefore before the change in regime) and "Law XIII of 1989 on the transformation of public companies, cooperatives, *etc.* into private companies."
4. For a company to convert itself into a private concern it needed to expand its capital, finding external shareholders, by at least 20%. Two examples illustrate the implementation of these rules: (1) the state holds 20% of company shares. The other 80% can be sold by the company. If not sold within three years the state will take back the 80%. If the company is sold, 80% of the value of the company returns to the State, 20% to the company (the State retaining the original 20% of shares). The law authorizes managers to sell with the agreement of the company board. (2) In the case of companies in debt, the company may convert its debts into shares by establishing the lending bank as shareholder. This enables possible national and international strategies. The 80% of shares are, in this case, shared between the company and the bank, according to the level of debt (the bank may, in addition, buy new shares). Here there is even more reason to sell, as the company and the lenders share 80% of the

company's worth (20% remaining in the state's hands) and the state reaps no profit from its holding.

5. The framework of this paper requires us to produce a summary of the actual sociological research undertaken. This will be published in exhaustive detail elsewhere.
6. S. Szelenyi, *Socialist Entrepreneurs: Embourgeoisement in Hungary* (Madison, 1988); I. and S. Szelenyi, *Classes and Parties in the Transition to Postcommunism: The Case of Hungary, 1989-1990* (Stanford, 1990).
7. "How to Steal a Billion and Preserve Mind, Honor, and Conscience," *Komsomolskaya Pravda,* November 19, 1991.
8. *Gazeta wyborcza*, November 12, 1991.
9. Bohdan Tsymbalisty, "The Political Culture of the Ukrainian People," *Suchasnist'*, 1994, No. 3, pp. 94-105; No. 4, pp. 77-90. (in Ukrainian).
10. M. V. Popovych, *World View of the Ancient Slavs* (Kyiv, 1985), pp. 55-62.
11. John Armstrong, "Nationalism in the Former Soviet Empire," *Problems of Communism,* XLI:1, January-April 1992, pp.121-133.
12. *The Social Image of Youth* (Kyiv, 1990), pp. 25-33 (in Russian). See also: "Political Portrait of Ukraine," *Bulletin of the Democratic Initiatives Research and Educational Center,* December 1993, No. 5 (in Ukrainian).
13. A. Wilson, A. Bilous, "Political Parties in Ukraine," *Europe-Asia Studies,* XLV:4, 1993, pp. 693-703.
14. Yevhen Holovakha, "Political Involving of Population: Level of Information, Activity, Competence," *Politolohichni chytannia,* 1992, No. 2, pp. 18-27 (in Ukrainian).
15. N. Panina, "Popular Readiness to Social Protest," *Politolohichni chytannia,* 1992, No. 2, pp. 28-38 (in Ukrainian).
16. G. Bremmer, "The Politics of Ethnicity: Russians in the New Ukraine," *Europe-Asia Studies,* XLVI:2, pp. 261-283.
17. S. Oksamytna, S. Makeev, "Sociological Aspects of the Political Geography in Ukraine: A Political Map of Ukraine," *Bulletin of the Democratic Initiatives Research & Educational Center,* 1995, No. 5.
18. Claude Levi-Strauss, *Structural Anthropology* (Moscow, 1983), pp. 245-257 (in Russian).
19. A. Giddens, "Agency, Institution and Time-Space Analysis," *Toward an Integration of Micro- and Macrosociologies,* ed. K. Knorr-Cetina and A.V. Cicourel (London, 1981), pp. 168-171.
20. K. Davis, and W. Moore, "Some Principles of Stratification," *Readings on Social Stratification,* ed. M. Tumin (New Jersey, 1970), pp. 368-377.
21. M. Weber. "Class, Status, Party," *Readings on Social Stratification,* pp. 29-39.
22. *Social Structures: A Network Approach,* ed. B. Wellman and S. D. Berkowitz (New York, 1988), pp. 19-61.
23. W. Thomas, *The Unadjusted*

Girl (Boston, 1931), p. 41.

24. P. Bourdieu, *The Sociology of Politics* (Moscow, 1993), p. 72 (in Russian).
25. *Ibid.*, pp. 76-77.
26. V. Polokhalo and A. Slyusarenko, "Political Process and Political Elite," *Political Thought,* No. 1, 1993, p. 12.
27. V. Volovych and S. Makeyev, "Social Stratification and Politics," *Political Thought,* No. 1, 1993, pp. 15-16.
28. Cornelius Tacitus, *Selected Works in Two Volumes* (Moscow, 1993), Vol. II, p. 34 (In Russian).
29. Leo the Deacon, *History* (Moscow, 1988), p. 62. (in Russian).
30. Ivan Bunin, *The Accursed Days* (Krasnodar, 1991), p. 57 (in Russian).
31. Mykhailo Hrushevsky, *On the Threshold of a New Ukraine* (Kyiv, 1991), p. 12 (In Ukrainian).
32. Yevhen Holovakha, "The Peculiarities of Political Awareness: the Ambivalence of Society and Personality," *Politolohichni chytannia,* 1992, No. 1, pp. 24-29 (in Ukrainian); Yevhen Holovakha, and N. Panina, "The Development of a Democratic Political Identity in Contemporary Ukrainian Political Culture," *Nationalism, Ethnicity, and Identity: Cross-National and Comparative Perspectives,* ed., R. Farnen (New Brunswick, NJ, 1994), pp. 403-425.
33. P.-J.-G. Cabanis, and L. Nass, *The Revolutionary Neurosis* (St. Petersburg, 1906) (in Russian).
34. Karl Gustav Jung, *On Modern Myths* (Moscow, 1994), pp. 228, 229, 241 (in Russian).
35. Erich Fromm, *The Anatomy of Human Destructiveness* (Moscow, 1994), pp. 307, 318 (in Russian).
36. Johan Huizinga, *Homo Ludens. In the Shadow of Tomorrow* (Moscow, 1992), p. 266 (in Russian).
37. "Capitalism and Schizophrenia: An Interview of Catherine Clement with Giles Deleuze and Felix Guattari," *Ad Marginem '93: Yezhegodnik*, 1994, p. 405 (in Russian).
38. Yevhen Holovakha, and N. Panina, "The Pathology of Post-Totalitarian Society: from Psychiatric Self-Diagnosis to the Analysis of Specific Social Pathologies," *Filosofskaya i sotsiologicheskaya mysl'*, 1993, No. 5; pp. 19-39; Y. I. Holovakha, and N. V. Panina, Social Insanity: History, Theory and Contemporary Practice (Kyiv, 1994). (in Russian).
39. Yu. A. Alexandrovsky et al., *Psychogenics in Extreme Conditions* (Moscow, 1991) (in Russian). N. V. Panina, "The Legend of Radiophobia," *Filosofskaya i sotsiologicheskaya mysl'*, 1990, No. 1, pp. 30-37 (in Russian).
40. G. D. Berdyshev, "Radiophobia and Genocide of the Ukrainian Population," *Chornobyl and the Press* (Kyiv, 1992), p. 66 (in Russian).
41. Robert Merton, "Social Structure and Anomie," *Sotsioligiya prestupnosti,* 1966, pp. 299-313 (in Russian).

42. Y. I. Holovakha, and N. V. Panina, "Kyiv: Democracy with a Totalitarian Subconsciousness: The Results of Sociological Studies," *Vestnik informatsionnogo agenstva Postfactum,* 1990, No. 13, pp. 9-13 (in Russian).

CHAPTER 4.

1. See: "The Art of Conflict Prevention," *Brassey's Atlantic Commentaries,* 1994, No. 7, pp. 1-2; James Brusstar, "Russian Vital Interests and Western Security," *Orbis,* XXXVIII:4, 1994, pp. 611-613.
2. See: V. I. Yevintov, *Mizhnarodne spivtovarystvo i pravoporiadok (teoretychno-pravovyi analiz)* (Kyiv, 1993), pp. 11-13, 19-28 (in Ukrainian).
3. *NATO Review,* June 1994, Supplement in Russian, p. 20.
4. "The Russian Approach to Peacekeeping Operations," *UNDIR Research Papers,* 1994, No. 28, pp. 17-18.
5. *Rossiya: drama peremen* (Moscow, IMEPI RAN 1994), p. 160 (in Russian).
6. Zbigniew Brzezinski, "A Plan for Europe," *Foreign Affairs,* January-February 1995, LXXV:1, p. 39.
7. See: *Izvestiya,* August 6, 1994.
8. See: *Transition Events and Issues in the Former Soviet Union and East, Central and South-Eastern Europe,* 1994, part 1.
9. A detailed study is: Dimitry Simes, "The Return of Russian History," *Foreign Affairs,* January-February 1994, LXXV:1, pp. 67-82.
10. *Izvestiya,* January 13, 1995.
11. See in particular: Paul Gobble, "Russian Break-Up," *NEFTE Compass,* January 15, 1993, II:2; Jessica Eve Stern, "Moscow Meltdown: Can Russia Survive?" International Security, Spring 1994, XVIII:4, pp. 40-65.
12. James Shenn, "Russia: Geopolitics and Crime," *The World Today,* February 1995, LI:2, p. 33.
13. P. Baev, "Russian Military Thinking and the 'Near Abroad'," *Jane's Intelligence Review,* December 1994, VI:12., pp. 531-533; S. Clark, "The Russian Military in the Former Soviet Union: Actions and Motivations," *ibid.,* p. 541-542.
14. V. Budkin, "Politics and Ideology in the External Economic Strategy of the New Independent States," *Political Thought,* 1994, No. 2; S. Valentey, "The Post-Soviet Economic Space," *Rossiiskii ekonomicheskii zhurnal,* 1993, No 7; V. Kirichenko, "CIS: The Dialectic of Unity and Disunity," *Rossiiskii ekonomicheskii zhurnal,* 1993, No 10; A. Schuller. "Nationale Reformen und internationale Ordnung: Zur aussenwirtschaftlichen Neuorientirung der RGW-Länder," *Jahrbuch für neue politische Ökonomie,* 1991 (Tübingen).
15. P. Bofinger, "A Multilateral Payments Union for Eastern Europe," *Banka Nazionale del Lavoro Quarterly Review,* 1991, No 176, pp. 69-88; J. A. Brabant, *Central European Payments Union* (New York, 1991); *Trade, Payments and*

Adjustment in Central and Eastern Europe, ed. J. Flemming, J. M. C. Rollo (London, 1991); Oleh Havrylyshyn, and J. Williamson, *From Soviet Disunion to Eastern European Community?* (Washington, 1991); "Proceedings of a Conference on 'A Payments Union for Eastern Europe', Rome, .June 28-29, 1990," *CEPR Bulletin,* (London, 1990).

16. *Economic Survey of Europe in 1993-1994* (New York, Geneva, 1993), pp. 116, 118.
17. *Ibid.*
18. Hannah Arendt, *The Origins of Totalitarianism* (New York, 1973), pp. 222-266.
19. B. V. Chirko, "Stalinism and the Fate of National Minorities in Ukraine," *Pamiataty zarady zhyttya* (Kyiv, 1993), p.92 (in Russian).
20. V. I. Kozlov, *Natsional'nosti v SSSR: Etnodemograficheskii obzor* (Moscow, 1982), pp. 241-242 (in Russian).
21. See: Martha Brill Olcott, "The Collectivization Drive in Kazakhstan," *Russian Review*, 1981, No 2, pp. 136-137.
22. Valeriya Novodvorskaya, *"Zhovta Gvardia, Synii Baron,"* Toloka, 1994, No. 1, p. 43 (in Ukrainian).
23. See, for example, P. Rudyakov, "Dismembering Yugoslavia — a New Partition of Europe," *Political Thought*, No. 3, 1994, pp. 219-223. (Editors' note: this article was reprinted, unfortunately under a different heading and without editors' knowledge and consent, by the newspaper *Holos Ukrainy*).
24. Ostankino Television, February 24, 1994.
25. Cf. Natalya Narochnitskaya, "Russia—Neither East nor West," *Mezhdunarodnaia zhizn'*, 1993, No. 9, pp. 44-45; Aleksandr Solzhenitsyn has championed the idea of a unified "Rus'," including Russia, Ukraine, Belarus and parts of Kazakhstan. He has also proposed that, in the event of a separation, "only the local population [should] determine the fate of a particular locality" [*Rebuilding Russia* (New York, 1991), pp. 8-9, 18]. See also his exchange of letters on this topic with Vladimir Lukin (*Literaturnaya gazeta,* April 1, 1992).
26. *Nezavisimaya gazeta,* January 18, 1994.
27. See the report written by Sergey Karaganov on Russo-Ukrainian relations, leaked to *Vechirniy Kyiv,* June 18, 1992, p. 2.
28. See the column by Rowland Evans and Robert Novak in *The Washington Post,* June 9, 1994.
29. See Dominique Arel and Andrew Wilson, "The Ukrainian Parliamentary Elections," *RFE-RL Research Report,* III:26, July 1, 1994, pp. 6-17 and "Ukraine under Kuchma: Back to 'Eurasia'," *RFL-RL Research Report,* III:32, August 19, 1994, pp. 1-12.
30. On Russians in Ukraine and the potential challenges they pose to Kyiv, see Ian Bremmer, "The Politics of Ethnicity: Russians in the New Ukraine," Europe-Asia Studies, 1994, No. 2 (46), pp. 261-283; and Roman Solchanyk, "The Politics of State Building in Post-Soviet Ukraine,"

Europe-Asia Studies, 1994, No. 1 (46), pp. 47-68.

31. Roman Szporluk, "Reflections on Ukraine After 1991: The Dilemmas of Nationhood," *The Harriman Review,* 7 (7-9) March-May 1994, pp. 1-10, especially 1-2.
32. *Nezavisimaya gazeta,* March 19, 1994.
33. Arkady Moshes, *Nezavisimaya gazeta,* March 19, 1994.
34. Henry Kissinger, "Russian and American Interests After the Cold War," in *Rethinking Russia's National Interest,* ed. Stephen Shestanovich, (Washington, 1994), p. 3.

Index of Names

About the Authors

Oleh BILYI – Doctor of Philology, Supervisory Research Fellow, Institute of Philosophy, Ukrainian National Academy of Sciences, Editor for History, Ethnopolitics and Culture Studies, *Political Thought.*

Markian BILYNSKY (Great Britain) – Director, Pylyp Orlyk Institute for Democracy (Kyiv), Member, International Consultative Council, *Political Thought.*

Jan BRZEZINSKI – Director, Program for National Security, Consultative-Advisory Council, Verkhovna Rada (Parliament) of Ukraine.

Zbigniew BRZEZINSKI – Political scientist, Professor, former US National Security Adviser to the Carter Administration (1977-1981).

Ihor BURAKOVSKY – Candidate of Economics, Associate Professor, Ukrainian Institute of International Relations, Editor for Economic Analysis and Forecasting, *Political Thought.*

Yevhen BYSTRYTSKY – Doctor of Philosophy, Department Chair, Institute of Philosophy, Ukrainian National Academy of Sciences; Chairman, Department of Culture, Ukrainian Academy of Arts; President, Ukrainian Philosophical Foundation, Editor for the Politics of Culture and Philosophy of Politics, *Political Thought.*

Oleksandr DERGACHOV – Candidate of History, Chairman, Department of Political Science, Kyiv-Mohyla Academy University; Editor for International and National Security and Geopolitics, *Political Thought.*

Andriy FEDOROV – Candidate of Philology, Research Fellow, Institute of Literature, Ukrainian National Academy of Sciences.

Sherman W. GARNETT – Senior Associate, The Carnegie Endowment for International Peace (USA)

Yevhen HOLOVAKHA – Doctor of Sociology, Department Chair for Social Psychology, Institute of Sociology, Ukrainian National Academy of Sciences.

Andriy KLEPIKOV – Research Fellow, Institute of Philosophy, Ukrainian

National Academy of Sciences and the Perspektyva Center for Scientific Analysis.

Nataliya KOSTENKO – Doctor of Sociology, Supervisory Research Fellow, Institute of Sociology, Ukrainian National Academy of Sciences.

Oleksandr KRYVENKO – former Editor in Chief, *Post-Postup* (Lviv); Editor, *Internews Inc.*, Kyiv.

Mykola KULYNYCH – Doctor of History, Department Chair at the Ukrainian Institute of International Relations.

Vadym LEVANDOVSKY – Candidate of Sciences in Philosophy, Research Fellow, Institute of Philosophy, Ukrainian Academy of Sciences.

James E. MACE (USA), Ph.D. in History, Director, Ukrainian Peoples Institute of Genocide Studies; Supervisory Research Associate, Institute of Political and Ethnic Studies, Ukrainian National Academy of Sciences; Deputy Editor-in-Chief, *Political Thought*.

Serhiy MAKEYEV – Doctor of Sociology, Department Chair, Institute of Sociology, National Academy of Sciences of Ukraine.

Anna MAKOLKIN – Ph.D., Professor, University of Toronto, Canada.

Viktor MALAKHOV – Doctor of Philosophy, Department Chair, Institute of Philosophy, Ukrainian National Academy of Sciences.

Kostantyn MALEYEV – Research Associate, Institute of Philosophy, Ukrainian National Academy of Sciences.

Georges MINK – Director, Center for the Study on Postcommunist Societies, Nation Center for Scholarly Research (CNRS, France).

Svitlana OKSAMYTNA – Research Fellow, Institute of Sociology, Ukrainian National Academy of Sciences.

Yevhen PASHCHENKO – Candidate of Philology, First Secretary, Ukrainian Embassy in Croatia.

Yuri PAVLENKO – Senior Research Fellow, Institute of World Economy and International Relations, Ukrainian National Academy of Sciences.

Volodymyr POLOKHALO – Candidate of History; Docent, Department of History, Taras Shevchenko National University;Editor-in-Chief, *Political Thought.*

Mykola RYABCHUK – Literary Critic, Political Scientist, Deputy Editor-in-Chief, Vsesvit.

Leonid SHKLYAR – Senior Research Fellow, Institute of Philosophy, National Academy of Sciences of Ukraine.

Volodymyr SIDENKO – Candidate of Economics; Department Chair, Institute of World Economics and International Relations, Ukrainian National Academy of Sciences.

Jean-Charles SZUREK – Research Fellow, Center for the Study on Postcommunist Societies, CNRS, Paris.

Mykola TOMENKO – Candidate of History; Chairman, Department of Political Science, Institute of Public Administration and Local Government, Cabinet of Ministers of Ukraine.

Volodymyr VOLOVYCH – Doctor of Philosophy; Professor and Chair, Department of Sociology and Psychology, Taras Shevchenko National University, Kyiv.

Vira VOVK – Candidate of Philology; Senior Research Fellow, Institute of Sociology, Ukrainian National Academy of Sciences.

Valentyn YAKUSHYK – Doctor of Political Science; Professor, National University of Kyiv University Academy, Kyiv.

Aleksandr ZINOVIEV – Professor, Doctor of Philosophy, writer (Munich, Germany).

Eastern European Studies
Texas A&M University Press

Cigar, Norman. *Genocide in Bosnia: The Policy of "Ethnic Cleansing,"* 1995.

Cohen, Philip J. *Serbia's Secret War: Propaganda and the Deceit of History,* 1996.

Gachechiladze, Revaz. *The New Georgia: Space, Society, Politics,* 1996.

Meštrović, Stjepan G. *The Conceit of Innocence: Losing the Conscience of the West in the War against Bosnia,* 1997.

Quinn, Frederick. *Democracy at Dawn: Notes from Poland and Points East,* 1998.